ACTION RESEARCH IN IRELAND

Edited by

Jean McNiff
Gerry McNamara
Diarmuid Leonard

Proceedings of the Conference

Action Research
and the Politics of Educational Knowledge

The Educational Studies Association of Ireland
in association with
The School of Education, Trinity College Dublin
November 1998

September Books
Dorset and Dublin

First published 2000
by September Books
3 Wills Road, Branksome, Poole,
Dorset BH12 1NQ. UK

Typeset in Graramond
Printed by A and J Print Dunshaughlin Ltd.,
Co. Meath

British Library Cataloguing in Publication Data
A catalogue record for this book is available from the British Library.

ISBN 1-902047-01-X

CONTENTS

Acknowledgements — vi

Contributors — vii

Preface
Sheelagh Drudy — xi

Overview
Diarmuid Leonard — 1

Introduction
Jean McNiff — 13

PART ONE   KEYNOTE PRESENTATIONS: ISSUES

1   Developing research-based professionalism through living educational theories
Jack Whitehead — 25

2   Equality Studies, the Academy and the role of research in emancipatory social change
Kathleen Lynch — 55

3   Towards a new architecture of learning
Michael Schratz — 91

4   Response to keynote presentations
Bernadette Ní Áingléis — 105

PART TWO   CASE STORIES

5   Rethinking nursing knowledge through action research
Siobhán O'Halloran — 113

iv

6   Action research: a means of changing and improving
     the clinical learning environment
     Agnes Higgins   129

7   Action research, multiple intelligences, and the
     politics of educational knowledge
     Ann FitzGibbon and Anne Fleishmann   145

8   External constraints, internal resistances: changing
     cultures, mindsets and practices: A response to
     Ann FitzGibbon and Anne Fleischmann
     Joan Hanafin   161

9   Introducing multi-skilling training programmes
     for time-served craft persons in a pharmaceutical
     manufacturing company
     David Taylor   167

10   Action research in an industrial setting
     Senan Cooke   189

11   Using action research as a means of exploring
     organisational culture
     Miriam Judge   201

12   Using Information and Communications Technology
     (ICT) to support action research and distance education
     Margaret Farren and Edward Tweedy   217

13   Reclaiming school as a caring place
     Carmel Lillis   227

14   Education for Mutual Understanding
     Seamus Farrell   243

15   An exploration of the education and training needs
of educationally disadvantaged participants on a
VTOS programme
Anne O'Keeffe   255

16   The Mol an Óige Project
Dan Condren   273

17   Action research in Initial Teacher Education
Diarmuid Leonard and Teresa O'Doherty   291

PART THREE   POTENTIALS

18   Action research for organisational change
Gerry McNamara and Joe O'Hara   305

Acknowledgements

We wish to thank the *Economic and Social Review* for permission to reproduce the article by Kathleen Lynch which appears as chapter 2, 'Equality Studies, the Academy and the role of research in emancipatory social change'. The work first appeared in the *Economic and Social Review*, Vol. 30, No. 1, January 1999, pp. 41–69.

Contributors

Dan Condren was Manager of the Mol an Óige Project. His research interests include examining ways in which schools can become centres of learning for all.

Senan Cooke is Manager of Training and Communications, Waterford Crystal. He specialises in action research approaches to the facilitation of communication within organisational settings.

Seamus Farrell worked with the Education for Mutual Understanding Promoting School Project before joining the School of Education University of Ulster on its 'Education and Social Cohesion Project', Bosnia Herzegovina.

Margaret Farren lectures in the School of Computer Applications at Dublin City University. Her particular research interest is Computers in Education.

Ann FitzGibbon is Senior Lecturer in the Education Department at Trinity College, Dublin, and currently co-ordinates the Division of In-Service Education.

Anne Fleischmann is a Secondary teacher and was for five years Director of the Nagle-Rice Project. Multiple Intelligences and action research became the frame for the work of the Project.

Joan Hanafin lectures in education at the National University of Ireland, Cork. Her research interests include equality in education, research methodologies and professional development.

Agnes Higgins is a nurse tutor currently employed as the Director of Education and Development at St Francis Hospice, Raheny, Dublin. She has many years' experience of teaching nurses at undergraduate and postgraduate level and is interested in what constitutes a quality clinical learning environment for nurses.

Miriam Judge is a doctoral research fellow in educational technology at Dublin City University. Her research interests include the use of information and communications technology to support collaborative and online learning environments.

Diarmuid Leonard is Professor and a teacher educator at the University of Limerick. He has worked in various roles in Irish and European initiatives aimed at teacher professional development and school improvement.

Carmel Lillis worked as a learning support teacher and Home/School/Community Co-ordinator in Dublin Inner City, before becoming Principal of an Infant School in Dublin. She is currently studying for her PhD in education.

Kathleen Lynch is Professor and Co-ordinator of the Equality Studies Centre, University College Dublin. She has published internationally in the areas of equality, education and sociology, and her work is acknowledged to inform policy on education and equality in Ireland.

Gerry McNamara is Head of the School of Education studies, Dublin City University. His major research interests include practitioner-led school-based research, organisational change and improvement and curriculum development and evaluation. He has published internationally and has acted as programme evaluator on a number of transnational programmes.

Jean McNiff is an independent researcher working in Ireland, and internationally. She support educators from a variety of professions for their Masters and Doctoral degrees. She has published internationally on action research and professional education.

Bernadette Ní Áingléis is a member of the Inspectorate and works in the Evaluation Support and Research Unit in the Department of Education and Science, Dublin.

Teresa O'Doherty lectures in Education at the University of Limerick.

Siobhán O'Halloran is a nurse advisor to the Department of Health and Children on education and intellectual disability.

Joe O'Hara is a lecturer at the School of Education, Dublin City University. His areas of interest include investigation into the role of evaluation as a catalyst for organisational change and the changing role of the evaluator in collaborative organisational settings. He has worked as an evaluator on a number of national programmes.

Anne O'Keeffe is Director of the Further Education Centre, Abbeyleix, with responsibility for the co-ordination of Co. Laois VEC VTOS programme.

Michael Schratz is Associate Professor of Education at the University of Innsbruck. He has published internationally in the fields of educational innovation and change with a particular focus on qualitative research methodology.

David Taylor currently works as Employee Relations and Development Manager in a large pharmaceutical manufacturing company in Dublin. He is responsible for HR, personnel policies and procedures, and training and development. He has considerable experience of working in industry in a variety of contexts.

Edward Tweedy is Assistant Professor at Rockingham Community College, North Carolina. He is interested in videoconferencing and distance learning.

Jack Whitehead works as a lecturer in Education at the University of Bath. His contributions to educational research and theorising can be accessed in the Writings and Living Theory Sections of the homepage http://www.actionresearch.net. He is a former President of the British Educational Research Association, a Distinguished Scholar in Residence at Westminster College, Utah, and a Visiting Professor at Brock University in Ontario.

PREFACE

Action research is becoming an increasingly important element in educational change and professional development. It is an area of research where teachers and other practitioners make a vital contribution to reflective practice. Action research may be conducted by individuals or organisations. It involves them in a process of constructing understanding about their practice in order that they might improve it. Action research can therefore give participants a greatly increased confidence in their practice as well as enhanced quality. It can also be a route to developing or improving democratic practices in schools, colleges or other workplaces.

This form of research has been under way in many classrooms, schools, universities, colleges and other education and training situations in Ireland for some years. In this context, and in the light of policy developments which place an emphasis on self-evaluation and quality assurance in all educational sectors, it seemed both timely and appropriate to hold a conference on this theme. Therefore, in November 1998, the Educational Studies Association of Ireland held a conference on the theme 'Action Research and the Politics of Educational Knowledge', in association with the School of Education, Trinity College, and the collaboration of the three editors of this book.

The Educational Studies Association of Ireland is a voluntary, non-political, non-sectarian body, dedicated to the advancement of educational research in Ireland. Through its activities, the Association seeks to ensure that public educational discourse in Ireland remains acquainted with educational research activities and enlightened by research perspectives. It provides a forum for a wide diversity of perspectives on educational questions. The ESAI was thus very pleased to provide a forum wherein action researchers from Ireland, England and Austria could debate issues relating to research, and present the findings of their research in a variety of different contexts and settings.

While the research reported here does not purport to be exhaustive of the many and varied types of action research in Irish education, it nevertheless gives numerous examples of the variety of themes and cases, and the exciting potential of action research to enhance professional practice in diverse situations. The research reported was conducted not only in education and training programmes in schools and third level institutions, but also in industrial and vocational training settings. The papers in this volume reflect both the theoretical issues explored, as well as the results of practitioners' research. The views are, of course, the authors' own, and do not necessarily represent the ideas of the Educational Studies Association of Ireland.

Apart from this volume, one of the outcomes of the conference was the establishment of a network of action researchers. This network should provide a source of advice, support and linkage for those interested in action research. This will help to ensure further development in this important area of research. The authors and editors in this volume are to be congratulated for the commitment to education and to democratic professional practice evidenced by the critique and case studies in action research presented here.

Dr Sheelagh Drudy
President of the Educational Studies Association of Ireland
April 2000

Action Research in Ireland

Overview

Diarmuid Leonard

Ireland is not known for its rapid acceptance of innovative practices in education. However, educational historians of the future will no doubt trace with interest the fast spread of action research in Ireland in recent years. This collection of papers from the ESAI conference on action research, held at Trinity College in November 1998, goes some way to explain the appeal of action research for a variety of contexts. It raises some interesting questions which also appear in wider contemporary debates. The three parts of the book are now considered.

Part one

Jean McNiff's initial chapter underlines the transformative potential of action research. She poses a real and highly personal challenge to practitioners when she invites us to view our practice as a moment to moment project of bringing our lives into harmony with our values. Action research offers a route to realising personal values which is based on an improved understanding of personal practice and its context. It is a form of enquiry that enables practitioners to engage with ill-defined and uncertain issues of practice. It is not simply a methodology of investigation but a process through which, as practitioners enquire into their own efforts to improve practice, they may assert their responsibilities and values. In the 'swampy lowlands' of practice (Schön, 1983), where problems are amorphous, unpredictable and messy, solutions to the problems of everyday living cannot be read off from abstract theory. Practitioners' practical knowledge becomes an essential element of their work.

Action research is attractive too for those who wish to turn a vision of life-enhancing workplace practice into reality. This applies to most work settings, for example, universities, schools, hospitals, factories. Action research, McNiff suggests, gives hope to practitioners who operate in organisations that may not provide much scope for individual autonomy. She notes too that attempts to define and categorise action research are increasingly proving to be fruitless; its broad appeal rests on its versatility in many areas of practice and in disparate settings.

A recurrent theme in this book is that issues of power and the politics of knowledge inevitably surface when something so potentially subversive as new knowledge in an area of practice emerges. Traditionally researchers have not been regarded as practitioners, and practitioners have their reasons for being wary of researchers. The growth of practitioner research is therefore something of a challenge to those who feel they are authorised to prescribe the practice of others. Action research questions our perceptions of our identities as researchers or practitioners, as well as the perception and definition of what a problem might be, and even the purposes and values of the context in which practice is conducted. Possibly it is this element of scepticism that accounts for the attractiveness of action research in occupations and settings where professionalism in practice is itself problematic.

These themes are also addressed in the widely different perspectives of the keynote speakers, themes to do with the generation, production, validity and uses of research-based knowledge. Problems raised include power relations between researcher and researched, the split between researcher and participant, the involvement of practitioners in planning and participation, the ethics and uses of research-based knowledge, and the ecology of conditions surrounding research and action.

Kathleen Lynch, writing from a social scientific perspective, shows the huge potential for inequity in the unequal power relationships between researchers and those they are researching. She poses a central question of ethics for responsible social research: how to safeguard the rights of the researched? Lynch points out the possible abuses of research when it portrays people as objects of research, and its arrogance in carefully explaining to people the meanings of their own lives. Research knowledge can be used for manipulation and control as much as for emancipation: marginalised groups may become further marginalised, not less. This chapter makes the case for distributing power more democratically in the conduct of research.

For practitioners who are researching their own practice and culture, a set of issues surrounds them: What counts as valid data? Whose data become knowledge? How do data become knowledge? Michael Schratz helps us to see how improvement in methodology can blur the demarcation described by Lynch. For example, photography by students can open up deeper understandings of a school's multiple realities. Viewed from a student's rather than a teacher's perspective, school life becomes open to scrutiny in ways unfamiliar to adult practitioner-researchers. Schratz's argument is that teachers may arrive at a distorted picture of the reality they wish to understand or change if they do not allow their students to participate in the process of data collection. Teacher-researchers' understanding could be improved if they regarded those who are traditionally seen as objects of research instead as collaborators.

However, as Jack Whitehead reminds us, a powerful state may wish to contest and even control teacher thinking. Against the backdrop of what is happening in the United Kingdom he enthusiastically shows the confidence and purposefulness of teacher action research. He tells of teachers' successes in recent years in constructing a research base for the development of research-based professionalism through the generation of their own living educational theories. His position is not unduly rosy. He makes a point of particular relevance to Ireland when he warns of the experience of the Teacher Training Agency in England and Wales: namely that teacher professionalism has become not solely a matter of debate on how to develop a research-based professionalism, but also an arena for issues of power and control. His warning is a challenge to the Teaching Council of Ireland to safeguard the rights of teachers to a research-based rather than a regulatory professionalism.

Bernadette Ní Áingléis in her response to the keynotes highlights the potential of action research for constructing a knowledge base which has intimate relevance to school development and teacher professionalism, and which democratises research inasmuch as it helps promote 'learning webs', networks of educative relationships between schools and other education communities. To work at nurturing educative partnerships and realising democratic values in research requires researchers to be sensitive to issues of power and control, issues which must be recognised within the complexities of relationships within learning communities, and which are played out through the production of research-based knowledge. She challenges researchers to reconcile values of partnership with the realities of responsibility within organisational life.

Part two

The accounts in this part show how the uses of action research vary, sometimes sharply. Researchers in school, hospital, industrial and company settings inquire into the meanings and problems of improving social processes and environments. Highly personal aims may include personal and professional development, resolution of problems of personal practice, and the aim of bringing personal action into harmony with personal values. At a broader level, some researchers try to understand problematic workplace cultures, to improve problematic situations, to facilitate learning, to improve organisational settings, to enhance learning environments. The stories all demonstrate how conceptual divisions of purpose and approach collapse in the face of responding to real emerging needs.

Together, Ann FitzGibbon and Anne Fleischmann, and also Joan Hanafin, consider their work in two action research projects on teaching through a multiple intelligences (MI) approach. Action research and multiple intelligences approaches share the same kind of visionary and sustaining ideals: they value individuals' learning and make possible the democratisation of knowledge. FitzGibbon and Fleischmann illustrate how difficult it is for MI theory-in-use (the nature of MI classrooms) to emerge from classroom experimentation. As the two papers make clear, the external constraints of classroom life consistently frustrate experimentation on MI teaching. Hanafin draws attention also to a subtle but no less powerful source of constraint: while rarely questioned, the power of the linguistic-numerical paradigm has shaped our thinking and indeed the education system in ways that militate heavily against the claims of an MI approach. While these papers bring to light the tacit, pervasive mediation of power through the language, structures and practices of education, they also illustrate the potential of practitioner action research to drive the search for alternatives to dominant teaching modes.

From rather different starting points, Carmel Lillis and Seamus Farrell share a concern to improve aspects of school life. Carmel Lillis addresses her own role as a new principal of an infant school. To bring her practice into harmony with her personal values, she focuses her action on communications across the school, as well as staff development and nurturing a climate of care. Her account exemplifies the close connections between her focus on living her personal theories of educational leadership and her resolve to improve the work environment of her colleagues. Seamus Farrell writes as a university-based researcher promoting new practice in the area of Education for Mutual Understanding in Northern Ireland. Describing his project in civics education, he makes clear the commonality of values that animate democracy, reflective practice and a culture of collaborative enquiry. Democracy, he argues, is antithetical to much of what we take for granted in school life: many school practices are centred on control of students. Action research he finds is particularly appropriate to the transition from the rhetoric to the practice of democracy: it models values and practices which could lead to sustainable school democracy.

Anne O'Keeffe writes about her reconnaissance of the training needs of participants in a Foundation course within a VTOS centre. She finds that in their efforts to secure an education, this group suffered individually from numerous disadvantages. Making an appropriate response to the special needs of marginalised students is deeply problematic. Using an action research approach to promote school self-renewal, Dan Condren addresses the concerns of teachers in schools. He finds that in successful school-focused action research no one should underestimate the needs for supporting teacher learning or the extent of action required to do so. Condren's project regards as problematic not only its task of promoting new school and teacher practice but also its own self-definition. Several valuable pointers for successful school change emerge, including the key point that school-focused action research is more likely to be successful when there is an integrated focus on teachers' learning, students' learning and continuous school improvement.

The reports by Siobhán O'Halloran and Agnes Higgins each illustrate values that animate much practitioner-based research. Siobhán O'Halloran's account of how she introduces her students to self-direction in a nursing course explores the inherent open-endedness of action research. Triggered by the practical question of how to use a six-week period of 'unspecified' study time, her initiative becomes a collaborative critical enquiry that changes her students' notions of education. Agnes Higgins studies the difficulties that nursing staff meet in supporting the education of students as practitioners. She acknowledges conflicts in perspectives and priorities between outsiders' research knowledge and insiders' research practice. Researchers' efforts to enter into dialogue with their participants are grounded in respect for participants' perspectives and experience: they share data with the participants, establish safe environments for critical reflection, and take care to move the research along at a pace comfortable to people new to action research. In these studies, self-awareness, openness to change and improvement, and the emergence of theories are linked, in that all are facilitated by the values of collaboration.

These kinds of collaborative values help foster the sensitivity required to democratise research. However, action researchers cannot afford to ignore technological advances either. Indeed one of the lessons in Michael Schratz's chapter demonstrate how useful research techniques such as child-friendly photography can widen perspectives and methodologies in research. Margaret Farren and Ed Tweedy develop this theme by describing ways in which newly available technology can help researchers improve their efforts to communicate through real-time interaction and efficient editing and presentation of text.

Reflecting some of the ways in which corporate life in Ireland finds itself coming to terms with rapid change, three research reports address problems that in their different ways need to give attention to the socio-psychological needs of employees in modern companies. As a training manager in a manufacturing company, David Taylor reports on his project to improve a training programme. He addresses the difficulties experienced in a multi-departmental company in introducing novel approaches to training in an area unaccustomed to such change. His project rests on democratic principles, aimed to achieve greater levels of participation, consultation, ownership and transparency. Taylor's remarks on doing his project are chastening for anyone who might suppose that action research is an infallible, easy or stand-alone method of resolving difficult organisational problems while carrying through an innovation. Nonetheless he finds his action research methodologies invaluable to him in ways also acknowledged by Senan Cooke. Cooke writes from the perspective of a manager of training and communications in a large-scale manufacturing company where, against a history of divisiveness and suspicion, competitive need calls for rapid change towards a flexible team-oriented work ethos. Team briefing is introduced to facilitate information flow throughout the company, in order to promote among a previously sceptical workforce confidence, commitment and team building in support of change. Both Taylor and Cooke find action research helps maintain a clear focus on key issues while working in the midst of live emerging situations. Taking seriously the views, insights, and feelings of the participants through a highly participative methodology of action research at every stage of their new programmes represents a move towards democratising their projects by building ownership among participants. Miriam Judge bases her action research on her intuition that the apparently successful corporate culture of a high-tech multinational company may be at some deep level experienced by Irish employees as a source of dissatisfaction. Her investigation discovers a much less favourable (more power-oriented, less caring, less open, less supportive, more impersonal) perception of the organisation than the image vigorously projected by the company to its employees. By uncovering at some depth the thinking of her participants she gives voice to a silent problem in an assertive power-oriented culture. However, her account illustrates a difficulty in much organisation-based action research: a lone researcher may help to identify and understand a serious problem, but to take action to resolve that problem may lie outside an internal researcher's scope.

In the final chapter, Diarmuid Leonard and Teresa O'Doherty explore the potential of action research as a learning experience for student teachers. Most opted to focus their action inquiry on aspects of teacher control and discipline. A positive if unexpected finding is that the students felt they gained in self-reliance and self-confidence. However, contradictions between institutional power and personal autonomy and also issues of continuity and coherence in degree programmes set up tensions that require further exploration and action.

The chapters in Part Two illustrate themes raised in Part One. Though circumstances, approaches and responsibilities vary enormously, problems of power, control and the use to which research knowledge is put raise serious issues for practitioner-researchers. If action research is a dialectical process that aims at truth, values and understanding as well as generating action, the process is likely to trigger unpredictable questions and actions, but in this process key questions remain: Whose data? Whose questioning? Which decisions? Which choices for action are important for which ends and values? At what point does collaboration between researchers and practitioners become a sharing of control and decision-making with practitioners?

Issues of power and relationship

Key issues arise about how power may be seen to reside in the relationships between researchers and practitioners, and whether, if practitioners were to be regarded as researchers and researchers came to be regarded as practitioners, their relationships might generate positive power-laden practices which would contribute to the educational development of all participants.

In the fluidity of an action research process, means and ends merge. A feature of several chapters is that action aimed at individual improvement can generate social improvement, and vice versa. Carmel Lillis for example finds that her effort to develop her personal professionalism as a school principal shapes her staff's social environment, while Dan Condren finds that school improvement is intimately linked with teacher development.

Aware of their power as researchers, some authors show how they took considerable care to respect the integrity of the participants in their research. They show how they became aware of power differentials and aimed to reduce inequalities by using participative methodologies, building collaborative and empowering relationships (Lillis and Condren) and by taking seriously participants' opinions and feelings (O'Halloran, Higgins and Judge).

Paradoxically, while action research might challenge outmoded inequitable structures and practices, organisational structures exist which potentially frustrate action and inquiry. FitzGibbon and Fleischmann find that teacher experimentation in multiple intelligences projects is constrained by the structures of time, knowledge, and the organisation of activity and assessment practices that shape learning and teaching in schools. Seamus Farrell concludes that school structures are organised for control, not democracy.

The dominant institutional culture is one of power and control. In numerous settings, action research becomes contra-cultural in its modelling of reflective practice, democratic values and inquiry, and in its striving for an improved social order. Seamus Farrell notes the contradictions inherent in school systems which espouse democracy yet aim to exert control over pupils. Carmel Lillis chooses to act in ways that oppose the traditional cultural expectations that a principal will act autocratically. Dan Condren's project evolves largely into an effort to transform school culture. Siobhán O'Halloran's inquiry moves towards a culturally innovative conception of the student nurse-as-learner.

Deep assumptions about institutional orthodoxies and received wisdoms are exposed to critical reflection. Examples of this are to be found in O'Halloran's work on nursing education, in the work of FitzGibbon and Fleischmann, and Hanafin on the meaning of multiple intelligences in the classroom, and Miriam Judge's insights that the company rhetoric of support in the workplace can conceal the promotion of self-image and company values, while Leonard and O'Doherty critically question the assumption that modularised higher education provides for student teacher action research.

Some researchers focus on their own area of concern to find that constraints exist within organisational or institutional settings and are too powerful to be ignored in subsequent action research processes. Examples of this include the chapters by O'Halloran, and Leonard and O'Doherty, all of whom were working in highly structured institutional settings.

Organisational change might seem to be a straightforward implementation of insights and solutions suggested by earlier phases of action research which deepen personal understanding of problematic situations and then move from knowing to effecting change in organisations. This view is naive. As Higgins, for example, demonstrates, multiple realities and conflicts in perspectives have to be acknowledged and investigated. Yet pursuing ambiguities and potential meanings (as in Taylor's account of a training programme, or in Judge's study of a corporate culture, or in FitzGibbon and Fleischmann's account of potentially problematic classroom innovations) may help clarify issues and build ownership, but may not always yield well-defined lines of possible action nor engage organisational capacity to adopt them.

Moving from reconnaissance to action becomes especially tricky when action is enmeshed in power relations or involves the interests of others who are inevitably involved in, but not necessarily committed to, the action. Action research can be unsettling in the still largely unreflective atmospheres of traditional organisation cultures. Its emphasis on values, its messy unpredictability, and the value it places on researchers' search for understanding and improvement place it at odds with the rational assumptions and culture that drive management in many traditional institutions. Managing change is invariably problematic for organisations, and some features of action research contribute to the destabilisation. Its open-endedness and unpredictability is not welcoming to an ideology of management that values predictability, control and decisive action towards predetermined goals. Neither may research-driven questioning of accepted cultures and practices be welcome to workers in a predominantly unreflective culture. By 'rocking the boat', action research poses a threat to the stability of power hierarchies and balances in the complex social relations of organisations. Recognising that action research is often in itself an innovative element in the lives of participants, many researchers make clear their commitment to respect, understand and appreciate the perspectives of their research participants. No single methodology however emerges in the accounts presented here as being readily successful in most contexts for the purpose of moving from individual research to organisational change. This problem emerged as the central theme at the 1998 conference, and came to be acknowledged as an area fraught with difficulty that needed opening up for further study and research. The issue is synthesised in the final chapter, which also suggests ways of addressing this problematic task as a future agenda for action research to realise its potential for organisational and wider social change.

Part three

Gerry McNamara and Joe O'Hara address the major problem of how to integrate individual action research with institutional change and improvement. Insights from several research perspectives (for example, Argyris, 1995; Fullan, 1991; Jarvis, 1992) indicate that inhibitors of organisational action for change include factors of several kinds, including the very real differences within organisations in terms of individuals' and groups' roles; the perspectives and interests of different groups; organisational preference for routine rather than reflective inquiry; the limitation of most organisational learning to single-loop learning (that is, the ability to learn changes in procedures and means as against the capacity to reflect on organisational aims and values); and not least, the complex, unpredictable and irrational nature of organisational change processes. The assumptions of some of the literature of action research are therefore unduly optimistic when they regard organisational change as almost an automatic outcome of collaborative planning. McNamara and O'Hara's argument is that the improvement of the organisation is likely to follow from the action research of its members only when organisations become learning organisations. The subtlety of what they propose is seen in their account of such an integrated approach in a school project where concerns over authority, responsibility, risk and ownership are played out in emancipatory processes of critical collaboration. They suggest as key requisites for organisational change a degree of collegiality; a willingness to engage in critical self-reflection and to challenge the cultural presuppositions of the institution; confidence to take risks; and commitment to change. To achieve readiness for change, they conclude, organisations need to move towards becoming learning organisations as well as to engage in action research. They support therefore the efforts of current researchers who would integrate theories of organisational change with action research.

Conclusion

A conclusion from this collection is that individuals' personal action inquiries help persons in key roles in their organisations to fashion new personal visions and practices that can improve certain social situations, such as in workplaces and in learning environments. It is also clear that for various reasons, influencing the process of change through action research meets all kinds of powerful resistance. McNamara and O'Hara's contribution helps clarify the linkage between the task of mobilising internal organisational change and the evolution of a learning organisation. If in an era of continuing knowledge revolution the organisations of the twenty-first century have to become learning organisations, then possibly practitioners may find that their organisations and institutions should see benefit in supporting the efforts of action researchers in developing a research-based professionalism. Conceivably the scope to develop such professionalism may one day be considered a necessary part of every organisation's planning and development. Of course, another strand of thought, pungently expressed by Jack Whitehead, warns that as management distances itself from the professionalism of practice, research may become further embroiled in issues of politics and power. Perhaps, as Jean McNiff warns, action researchers should not look forward to an easy life.

References

Argyris, C. (1995) *On Organisational Learning.* Cambridge, MA., Blackwell.

Fullan, M.. with Susan Stiegelbauer (1991) *The New Meaning of Educational Change.* London, Cassell.

Jarvis, P. (1992) *Paradoxes of Learning: On Becoming an Individual in Society.* San Francisco, Jossey-Bass.

Schön, D. (1983) *The Reflective Practitioner: How Professionals Think in Action.* New York, Basic Books.

Introduction

'Fundamentally important educational arenas for investigation ...'

Jean McNiff

Former president of the American Educational Research Association (AERA), Alan H. Schoenfeld, reflects on the question, 'How might one characterise fundamentally important educational arenas for investigation, in which theoretical and practical progress can be made over the century to come?' (1999: 4). He suggests a series of arenas, including the need to find new theories of education which integrate conceptual and practical ways of knowing.

The question was originally posed as part of Schoenfeld's presidential address at the 1999 AERA annual meeting in Montreal, Canada. The AERA is probably the world's largest and most influential educational research association, and certainly its annual meetings are unparalleled for their exuberance, intensity and sheer size. The question however was addressed and, I believe, partially answered at the more modestly scaled yet no less exuberant meeting of practitioner action researchers in Dublin, November 1998.

At this conference the issue arose consistently that a fundamentally important educational arena for investigation was how educators could demonstrate whether their action enquiries had improved the quality of educational experience in their workplaces. Practitioners from a wide range of professional contexts gave accounts of their action enquiries which showed how they addressed, in a variety of ways, the question, 'How do I improve my work?' (Whitehead, 1989), and aimed to produce evidence to show that they had done so. This they did not by trying to define their work in terms of the conceptual categories of traditional scholarship but by demonstrating, in a lived sense, how they had investigated their practice in order to improve it.

I think such an approach is essential if we are to make theoretical and practical progress. Too much time and energy is currently spent splitting conceptual hairs in debates about what action research is or is not. There is, in any case, an elusive quality about action research that defies its rigid definition, a quality that reflects the transient and vulnerable nature of life itself. Definitions exist everywhere in contemporary work. Have a look at the analyses of researchers such as Marilyn Cochran-Smith and Susan Lytle (1999). Some definitions are a replay of others; some a reconceptualisation of what action research is (or should be) about. Most are offered in a conceptual sense. While linguistic analyses are important and useful, they are limited. A dog may be an animal with four legs according to a dictionary; many people's dogs are far more to them than that. Meanings lie not so much in words, Wittgenstein tells us, as in the way we live our lives. Definitions of action research are less important than the values we bring to the process of studying our work, how we try to live those values in our practices, and how we use our knowledge of practice for wider social betterment.

It was refreshingly clear at our conference that practitioners wanted to tell their stories of professional learning, to talk about their work in a practical way with other practitioners who share the same professional commitments. The whole conference in this sense became a sharing of knowledge, and the generation of new knowledge, a 'crucible of action', as Grimmett says (1988). I am reminded of how Clandinin and Connelly (2000: xiii) explain their theoretical framework for narrative inquiry: 'Our approach is not so much to tell you what narrative inquiry is by defining it but rather to show you what it is by creating a definition contextually by recounting what narrative inquirers do.' The same commitment animated our conference: it was not so much an attempt to say what action research is but rather to show its nature and its potential by recounting what action researchers do. Consequently, what emerged at the conference was a joyous celebration of good practice, and more; it was a unanimous commitment to the potential of personal professional knowledge for sustainable social orders.

The variety of theoretical approaches in the literature is evident in the methodological approaches adopted for the research accounts as they now appear in our book. Some demonstrate an interpretive approach, some a critical theoretic approach, some a living educational theory approach. All are underpinned by the same unifying commitment to social improvement through personal enquiry. This, I believe, constitutes a fundamentally important arena for investigation: how we can show our commitment to developing social improvement and sustainable social orders through our personal enquiries. The key issue, it seems to me, is how to find ways to make theoretical and practical progress in terms of theorising professional knowledge, or, in practical terms, how to find ways to capture the spirit of the exuberant commitment of our conference and use it purposefully to transform our wider social contexts.

I want to explore this issue in terms of what Schön (1995) calls the new scholarship (see also Boyer, 1990).

Schön says that in the topology of professional knowledge there is a high ground and a swampy lowlands. On the high ground, people work with clean abstract issues. These issues lend themselves to clear-cut analysis to produce neat conclusions. In the swampy lowlands, however, people work with the messy, unarticulated problems of real life. These problems do not lend themselves to clear analysis, because often the problems are not well defined, and tend to change. Life in the lowlands is often a case of inspired guesswork and best options.

Schön maintains that traditional forms of scholarship, the ones we live with in our institutional contexts, value technical rationality, a form of high-ground knowledge which deals with facts and information, over practical theorising. Technical rational knowledge is abstract, generated using traditional forms of research categories such as controlled experimentation and the statistical analysis of manipulated variables, and aims at producing generalisable conclusions. Technical rationality is easily recognised as the favoured epistemology in most institutional contexts, yet, says Schön, often lacks significant use value in the lives of practitioners who are trying to understand their work. Real-life practice, in Schön's words, is often messy, unpredictable and uncontrollable, and far removed from the clean sanitised world of abstract theory. The situation arises that people's lives are at risk of distortion as they try to live up to the standard theory; and the idea of knowledge itself is potentially distorted, presenting as a body of facts rather than lived experience.

Technical rationality, he continues, is the dominant epistemology at the traditional university, a context for the generation of abstract theory. In principle, abstract theory is passed on to consumers who then apply it to their practice, using the traditional propositional form of logic of 'if x then y'. This kind of logic, however, and the knowledge it generates, is not appropriate for addressing questions of the kind, 'How do I try to understand this situation here?' or 'What do I do now?' While the disciplines of psychology, sociology, philosophy and history are useful and important, they do not help us to address dilemmas such as how to comfort a troubled child, or how to evaluate whether we are in fact improving the quality of education in schools and workplaces. For this we also need a form of practical knowledge. While abstract theory is important for helping us to conceptualise how things might be, it needs to be balanced by practical theory which helps us to understand how to realise the vision in practice. Both kinds of knowledge are important and need to be integrated in practice.

Practical knowledge is a form of knowing-in-action. When we act, we often cannot say explicitly what we are doing or why. We act in a way that seems right; we trust our intuition and our sense of right response, built up over years of experience, existing as a reservoir of tacit knowing which guides action. A cook, for example, will know when the soufflé is ready without a timer; a manager develops a sense of what people's feelings are about a particular issue. Sensitive teachers anticipate questions before they arise; good doctors base their treatment of a specific ailment on how they perceive the whole person. These are all instances of knowing-in-action. To check that our knowing-in-action is appropriate, however, as part of good professional practice, we need to ensure that we are acting in a way that is right for the other person, and this we do by watching ourselves and evaluating our practice. Did I do this right? Could I have done it better? This reflection on knowing-in-action is often not a conscious process; it is what thoughtful practitioners do all the time. We often reflect on practice informally, such as when we drive home or watch the television, and sometimes we do it consciously – when we deliberately reflect on action (not easy in the hurly-burly of real practice), or in conversation with a colleague. In some work contexts, reflective practice is institutionalised, and built into procedures such as appraisal processes, or systematic professional evaluations, not in a traditional 'inspectorial' sense, but in a sense of professional dialogue in which practitioners exchange ideas about practice for personal professional accountability.

Practical knowing, however, is not widely accepted by the traditional university, where abstract categories tend to be prioritised over real lives. It is hardly surprising that this results in epistemological disputes. Occupants of the high ground tend to dismiss low-ground problems on the basis that these are part of everyday living and not really worthy of serious theorising; while swamplands practitioners claim that the problems of everyday living are precisely those issues that are most deserving of sustained investigation. The current situation is that the traditional high ground occupants maintain their privileged position. Conventions take a long time to be replaced by others, and interesting systems of control exist that prevent people from upsetting systems, created and held in place by powerful interest groups whose purposes it serves not to question or change established norms. Dyrberg (1997) comments on the circular nature of power; this is nowhere more evident than in the protectionist strategies developed by traditional forces in the academy to persuade practitioners that officially received forms of knowledge should be maintained, and that practitioners should collude in their own subjugation by agreeing that the current situation is as it should be. There are no more powerful chains than the ones we forge ourselves, observed Gramsci (1971) from within Mussolini's prisons. If we are prepared to believe that systems are axiomatic, we create our own psychic prisons (Morgan, 1997). Who needs a jailer when we can successfully monitor ourselves?

A new kind of knowledge base is needed, a new way of theorising, which values practical knowledge as much as conceptual knowledge, and integrates theory and practice in real lives; as well as a new kind of political action that will enable practitioners to claim validity for their personal professional knowing. As they reflect on practice, practitioners generate personal theories of practice which are rooted in their tacit knowing. Often, professional settings require us to act out of experience rather than cognitive rationalising: our actions are still informed by theory, but the issue now becomes the kind of theory that is most appropriate for the job.

The important arena for investigation adopts a Janus-like quality. The university is still the highest legitimating body in debates about what counts as valid knowledge. The dominant epistemology within university and other education settings is technical rationality. This denies the values base of professional practice, as well as relegating those who regard themselves as occupants of the swamplands to lesser status. A situation arises of potential social injustice and a denial of the Enlightenment values of rational thinking and unprejudiced forms of understanding which underpin the university as a site for the negotiation of educational and social purposes (Newman, 1915; MacIntyre, 1990). It is not only a matter of challenging the epistemological base, but also a matter of challenging the politics of the settings in which the epistemological base enjoys its uncontested monopoly. One cannot happen without the other.

Our conference embodied such a challenge, not always overtly stated, but implicit by the fact that the conference took place at all. This was the first time in the history of the State that a group of practitioner researchers had come together in such force to show their commitment to improving the quality of education through reflective practice. As such, it represented a momentous occasion. A group of some 250 participants gathered to declare their commitment to their own professional theorising. This group constituted a community of reflective practitioners, all engaged in producing their own personal theories of practice, and as such epitomising a mighty commitment to generating theories of practice, as lived out in their own lives, for the benefit of others. The group, located in Trinity College, represented a commitment to practical theory, rooted in a personal epistemological base, to show a desire for active social renewal through creative conversation. Here was the beginning of a concerted form of radical knowing, a challenge to the dominant epistemology to acknowledge and make room for other personal forms of knowing that have the potential for educational renewal in Irish society.

I have to say that the challenge should not be seen in conflictual terms. While it is a challenge for recognition, it is not a challenge for domination. Action research is not about colonising hearts and minds to the extent of excluding other forms of knowing. Traditional scholarship and its categories of analysis are as important as personal theorising. Different forms of theory represent different ways of coming to understand our present realities and create new ones. The issue is one of the democratisation of educational ideas, and the extent to which all participants in the discourse are prepared to recognise one another's truth claims as valid and worthwhile. As Bernstein (1983) comments, what matters is how we respond to one another, whether we are prepared to respect other truth claims as potentially legitimate, or whether we resort to our own prejudicial standpoints and refuse to entertain the idea that other ways of knowing might be as legitimate as our own. Developing tolerance for pluralistic forms of knowing requires humility and personal restraint, but this is what is required to nurture communities of good practice:

> ... the pragmatic legacy is especially relevant, in particular the call to nurture the type of community and solidarity where there is an engaged fallibilistic pluralism – one that is based upon mutual respect, where we are willing to risk our own prejudgments, are open to listening and learning from others, and we respond to others with responsiveness and responsibility (Bernstein, 1983: 339).

I believe that it is the responsibility of action researchers to demonstrate their responsiveness and responsibility by engaging with others from rival traditions to show the benefit of action research for others' lives. This means building solid bodies of case evidence, to show that claims to improved practice and improved lives are not empty claims or supposition, but are supported by empirical evidence, sometimes spoken in the voices of other research participants, to show how the quality of their education was enhanced. We can claim to have contributed to an improved quality of other people's lives when those other people state that this is so, in a spirit of non-coercion and free association. Further, if we can and are prepared to make such claims, it is then our responsibility to use our knowledge deliberately for social renewal. This means producing accounts of practice that demonstrate our accountability to others, that show how we live our values in our practice, and how we intend to use our knowledge for further social benefit.

This all sounds quite grand and visionary. I think in fact it is entirely ordinary and practical. I write not from a naive or romantic perspective, but from a view of social renewal as perfectly actionable, indeed, something we all ought to be doing as part of our commitment to sharing our humanity. It is very easy to see significant change in the grand epiphanies of our lives; it is not so easy to see significant change in moment-to-moment living. Yet this is what we need to do. In our moment-to-moment living lies our future. We create the kind of future we want through the quality of our response to one another. If there is for me any one fundamentally important educational arena for investigation, it is how we can ensure that our quality of response is such that we enable ourselves to come together in free association and on an equal footing, as communities of practitioners whose values include independence of mind and spirit, in the pursuit of commonly agreed educational goals (see also Chomsky, 1996).

So where does my own action research feature in all of this? I said above that we should aim to show the meanings of our lives in a contextualised way, and not only through linguistic definitions. I therefore need to show how the process of my own understanding has improved through my participation in this conference.

I joined the Executive Committee of the Educational Studies Association of Ireland with the specific intent of sharing ideas about practitioner action research. This included a commitment to organising with others a conference which would show the popularity of the approach, to disseminate ideas, as well as show its potential for wider educational renewal. I have been fascinated by the central position of politics and power in actually making the conference a reality, and I recognise this as part of the wider epistemological debates as discussed in this collection. I have become increasingly aware of how one's epistemological stance is inextricably related to personal identity, and how, when new ideas emerge, they are often perceived as a threat to personal status and identity, even though those ideas hold promise for substantial social renewal (this applies as much to myself as to anyone else). I have undertaken, to all intents and purposes, an action enquiry into how I could work with others to make the conference a reality, in order to live out the values of commitment to shared dialogue and the generation of new forms of knowledge within an ethic of tolerance for new forms of discourse. The tacking and re-tacking in negotiating the process has been a real enquiry: how to persuade others of its viability, and how to develop a conference that would communicate through its form the values it espouses. I have learnt how important it is for people of similar commitments to work together in solidarity, especially in the face of the real anxieties expressed by people working in alternative traditions; and how important it is not to be defensive of a new idea but to share it with joy and good humour, to submit it to the critical scrutiny of others, and to be glad when it is accepted, possibly not even as really valuable knowledge, but at least as worth considering. I love Iris Murdoch's observation, that Jesus's commandment, 'Be ye therefore perfect,' could be interpreted as, 'Be ye therefore slightly improved' (Murdoch, 1985: 62). This gives me hope, stuck as I am with my great tendency for making mistakes. Working towards slight improvement is enough for today.

I believe that our conference marked the beginning of a new enquiry for many participants which constitutes for them a fundamentally important arena for investigation, in which they can make theoretical and practical progress over the century to come. To take steps in this direction, however, does require considerable energy and personal exposure to risk. Making our claims to personal educational knowledge invites critique on a whole range of fronts; and we had better make sure that we have the empirical evidence to support those claims if we wish our professional lives to be taken seriously. However, while the challenge for personal change is significant, it is entirely actionable. Chomsky (1996: 131) says of the process of progressing freedom and human rights, 'The first step is to penetrate the clouds of deceit and distortion and learn the truth about the world, and then to organise and act to change it. That's never been impossible, and never been easy. It's not impossible now, and not easy either.' I think the same sentiments apply to the process of contributing to educational and social change: it has never been impossible, and it has never been easy. Those of us who position ourselves as action researchers know this; but perhaps we never wanted a quiet life anyhow.

References

Bernstein, R .J. (1983) *The New Constellation: The Ethical-Political Horizons of Modernity/Postmodernity.* Cambridge, Polity Press.

Boyer, E. (1990) *Scholarship Revisited: Priorities of the Professoriate.* New Jersey, The Carnegie Foundation for the Advancement of Teaching.

Chomsky, N. (1996) *Powers and Prospects: Reflections on Human Nature and the Social Order.* London, Pluto Press.

Clandinin, D.J. and Connelly, M.F. (2000) *Narrative Inquiry: Experience and Story in Qualitative Research.* San Francisco, Jossey-Bass.

Cochran-Smith, M. and Lytle, S.L. (1999) 'The Teacher Research Movement: A Decade Later' in *Educational Researcher*, Vol. 28, No. 7, pp. 15–25.

Dyrberg, T.B. (1997) *The Circular Structure of Power.* London, Verso.

Gramsci, A. (1971) *Selections from the Prison Notebooks* (trans.) Q. Hoare, and G. Nowell-Smith (eds). New York, International Publishers.

Grimmett, P. (1988) 'The nature of reflection and Schön's conception in perspective' in P. Grimmett and G. Erikson (eds) *Reflection in Teacher Education.* New York, Teachers College Press.

MacIntyre, A. (1990) *Three Rival Versions of Moral Enquiry: Encyclopaedia, Genealogy, Tradition.* Guildford, Duckworth.

Morgan, G. (1997) (2nd Edition) *Images of Organization.* California, Sage.

Murdoch, I. (1985) *The Sovereignty of Good.* London, Ark Paperbacks.

Newman, Cardinal J.H. (1915) *On the Scope and Nature of University Education.* London, J.M. Dent & Sons.

Schoenfeld, A.H. (1999) 'Looking Toward the 21st Century: Challenges of Educational Theory and Practice' in *Educational Researcher*, Vol. 28, No. 7, pp. 4–14.

Schön, D. (1995) 'Knowing-in-Action: The New Scholarship Requires a New Epistemology' in *Change,* November/December, pp. 27–34.

Whitehead, J. (1989) 'Creating a Living Educational Theory from Questions of the Kind, "How do I Improve my Practice?"' in *Cambridge Journal of Education*, Vol. 19, No. 1, pp. 41–52.

Part 1

KEYNOTE PRESENTATIONS ISSUES

Chapter 1

Developing research-based professionalism through living educational theories

Jack Whitehead

I want to thank the organisers of this Conference of the Educational Studies Association of Ireland for inviting me to give this address. Such opportunities have played a fundamental part in my productive life in education. The discipline of writing for an audience and to a deadline has always helped to take my enquiries forward. However, I feel I should warn you of my history of disasters in my lectures and workshops on action research. In 1985 I felt elated when a large local authority asked me to tutor more than 70 advisory teachers to support action research approaches to professional development in schools around Bath. I began a session to a roomful of gloomy faces. They had all received their termination notices that morning. This highlights the form of rational educational policy-making favoured by English politicians. You spend money on policy formation and then sack the people you need to implement the policy. Last February, I began a similar action research workshop with principals and administrators in the Grand Erie Board in Ontario. In contrast to the previous session I was welcomed by a roomful of delighted and happy individuals. It is difficult to describe the euphoria. Initially, in my conceit, I put it down to the idea that I was such a popular international figure that they were simply looking forward to hearing my talk. Then they explained to me that they had just heard that morning the good news that if their age and length of service came to 85 they could retire without penalties to their pension because the government wanted to take some 15,000 teachers out of service. The moral of these stories is that there appears to be a connection between my talks on action research and teachers leaving the profession. I hope to reverse this trend today.

In particular I want to share with you my learnings over the ten years 1988-1998. In 1988 I presented my Presidential Address to the British Educational Research Association on *Research-Based Professionalism* (Whitehead, 1989a) and wrote my paper on *Creating a Living Educational Theory from Questions of the Kind, 'How do I improve my Practice?'* (Whitehead, 1989b).

For those of you who are not familiar with the ideas of research-based professionalism and of living educational theories it may be helpful if I say that, for me, research-based professionalism refers to the process of enhancing teacher professionalism through constructing our professional knowledge-base from our self-studies of our own professional practice. Living educational theories are, for me, the descriptions and explanations which individuals offer for their own professional learning as they ask, answer and research questions of the kind, 'How do I improve what I am doing?'. Living theories are different from the traditional kind of theory in which the explanations are presented in terms of general concepts. Living theories are part of the way individuals create their own form of life. They are living because of the way they explain a present practice in terms of an evaluation of the past and in terms of an intention to create something better in the future in one's own practice. The fundamental explanatory principles are not presented in abstract, linguistic concepts. They are presented as values, embodied in one's practice and embedded in a particular social context. Their meanings emerge through practice, and require for their communication both ostensive and linguistic definition. In other words we both 'show' and 'tell' when we try to communicate the meanings of the values which constitute our relationships as 'educative'.

I want to bring the two ideas together in a new synthesis on 'Developing Research-Based Professionalism through Living Educational Theories' in the context of:

1 Creating a Teaching Council in Ireland: Learning from the Work of the Teacher Training Agency in England and Wales and the Ontario College of Teachers in Canada.

2 Legitimating teachers' professional knowledge in partnerships between Universities, Professional Development Centres and a Teachers' Council.

3 Demonstrating the potential of the Internet for professional learning.

I now want to develop these ideas in more detail.

1 Creating a Teaching Council in Ireland: Learning from the work of the Teacher Training Agency in the UK and the Ontario College of Teachers in Canada.

The 1995 White Paper on *Charting our Education Future* acknowledged:

> ... a unanimous acceptance of the need for a cohesive policy on, and a comprehensive programme of, in-career professional development of teachers, related to the long-term development of the teaching profession and the education system generally (Government of Ireland, 1995: 126).

The concept of the teaching career and career-long professional learning is seen as the key to improving education. The 1998 report of the Department of Education and Science's Steering Committee on the Establishment of a Teaching Council contains a commitment to:

> accredit and review national inservice initiatives designed to support new policies and programmes (Government of Ireland, 1998: 27).

I want to focus on the importance of accrediting the knowledge of professional educators.

I imagine that many members of the Educational Studies Association of Ireland have supervised students for initial teacher awards and the awards of Master of Education, Master of Arts, Master of Science, Doctor of Philosophy or for the newer Ed.D. degrees. The presentations for such degrees in Education are often text-based dissertations and theses, bound for display and placed on library shelves. I imagine that some of you, like me, have been awarded advanced qualifications in Education *without having to provide any evidence that we have influenced the education of anyone.*

Learning from the Teacher Training Agency

In England and Wales the Teacher Training Agency has produced a framework for the professional development of teachers. At the present time it includes some 63 standards of practice which novice teachers must meet for them to be awarded their credentials of Qualified Teacher Status. It also includes the national standards for Subject Leaders, for Special Educational Needs Co-ordinators and for Headteachers. A General Teaching Council is in the process of being established and a College of Teachers has recently been created from the College of Preceptors and The Education Council. These developments give some indication of the importance being given to the professional development of teachers in England and Wales. This concern is accompanied by a major recruitment crisis. The professional status of teaching (and I include pay within this) is not high enough in England and Wales to attract sufficient numbers of good quality entrants into the profession and to retain the numbers we need. It will require a major cultural shift to change the public perception of teaching as a profession. Quotations from Ted Wragg (1998) highlight the problem when he talks of:

> .. the zombie method of training heads or teachers, whereby complex human behaviour is atomised into discrete particulars, or 'competencies'. This mechanical approach, much favoured by the hapless Teacher Training Agency, is an unmitigated disaster … The tyranny of brain-corroding

bureaucracy must end ... Most important of all is to support creativity and imagination, collegiality and trust, not just foster the mechanical implementation of dreary, externally driven missives (p. 22).

I hope that, in Ireland, you will avoid some of the problems associated with the way the TTA has set out its standards in its professional framework. Jim Graham (1998) in an excellent article on teacher professionalism has added his voice to the growing criticism of the negative influences of the TTA when he says:

> For teacher professionalism, the over-prescribed, centralist regulation by the TTA established a technicist model of teaching at variance with the autonomy, flexibility, collegiality necessary to create the learning organisations required to socialise the new generation of knowledge workers (Graham, 1998: 17).

In contrast to the errors of the TTA I want to recommend the work of the Ontario College of Teachers (OCT) as it develops its standards of practice. Explicitly influenced by action research approaches (Squire, 1998), OCT appears much more aware of the need to view standards of professional practice in terms of the living values which teachers use to give meaning and purpose to their productive lives in education.

Fran Squire works with Linda Grant of the Ontario College of Teachers on the development of standards of practice. Her enquiries are focused on the questions,

> **What implications arise when standards of practice are linked to action research endeavours?**

> **How do we keep the spontaneity and individualism inherent in action research as we establish criteria for its recognition in the educational community?**

The reason I think that the work of Fran Squire, Linda Grant and the OCT is so important is that they are developing, to use Jean McNiff's phrase, a 'generative' form of action research (see McNiff, 1988, 2000). Unlike the Teacher Training Agency, they appear to understand that the standards of professional practice are the living values used by teachers in their educative relationships with their pupils. OCT is a learning organisation which is enquiring into the process of relating standards and professional learning to the creation of a professional learning community which is concerned with the development of required professional knowledge.

In some ways the development of the research-based professionalism I have in mind is more developed in Ireland than in other parts of the world and in some ways it is less developed. As Hyland and Hanafin (1997: 162) have said:

> Action research has gained considerable ground as a model of teacher professional development internationally, although it has made relatively little impact in Ireland apart from its introduction into some accredited university/college courses and various curriculum projects (Leonard, 1995). One example of action research used for incareer development in Ireland is the Marino Institute of Education Action Research Pilot Project which comprised nineteen case studies (McNiff and Collins, 1994).

Action research is well developed in the work of Jean McNiff and the teacher-researchers she has been supporting. In her 1994 book, edited with Úna Collins on *A New Approach to In-Career Development for Teachers in Ireland*, Jean describes the initial phases of the work of teacher-researchers as their enquiries begin and are supported over time. In July 1998 I attended a celebration in Bristol, following the graduation ceremony of the University of the West of England. Some 15 Irish teachers were awarded their Masters Degrees for their action research programmes in which many had embraced a living theory approach to their professional development. The Irish teachers, with Jean as their main tutor, found it necessary to move outside Ireland for the accreditation of their academic self-studies of their professional learning. In gaining this accreditation I believe these Irish teachers are contributing to the construction of a knowledge-base for professional educators. Gaining this recognition through an English university highlights a difficulty in the Irish context of a lack of support for legitimating action research studies in some Irish Universities; and I now want to focus on the issue of legitimating teachers' professional knowledge

2 Legitimating teachers' professional knowledge in a partnership between Universities, Professional Development Centres and a Teachers' Council

At the same time as the degrees were being conferred on Irish practitioners at the University of the West of England, a colleague in another university had sent me an action research dissertation which had been given a very low mark by an internal examiner. He asked for my advice because his own judgement on the dissertation was much more favourable. The internal examiner's judgements were, to me, clearly being made from within a different paradigm of the kind which has been analysed in the December 1998 issue of *Educational Action Research* (Hughes, Denley and Whitehead, 1998). I advised my colleague to seek the judgements of other experts in the field of action research to see if it might be in the student's interest to question his colleague's judgement. Before he did this the external examiner's report had arrived, full of praise for the action research study, and the dissertation received the high mark it deserved. For those interested in the way a view of 'education as text' and a 'cleverness' in manipulating linguistic concepts can blind examiners to the educational knowledge of professional educators in action research accounts, I recommend the afterword to Kevin Eames' PhD. This is on the Action Research Homepage at http://www.bath.uk.ac./~edsajw

To give some further indication of the problems which can surround action research enquiries I recall a letter received by a student at a UK University from its research committee. This University had a good track record of successfully completed MA action research studies. The research committee had written to the research student, who had submitted a proposal for an MPhil/PhD programme, to ask that the personal pronoun 'I' be removed from the title of the enquiry! For those who understand the importance of 'I' appearing in action research enquiries of the kind, 'How do I improve my practice?', the request revealed the bias, prejudice or inadequate assessment of members of this research committee.

I was delighted to see one action research study reported by Dublin City University in their Conference Proceedings of the Third European Conference on 'Integrating Information and Communications Technology in the Curriculum'. I know Maggie Farren at Dublin City University is providing much needed help for practitioner researchers who wish to gain accreditation from an Irish University for their action research studies. The one action research study, however, was within some 30 quantitative studies.

What I now want to do is to draw your attention to the kind of educational action enquiries which have already led to the awards of MPhil or PhD degrees. The teachers have created their own living educational theories in which they describe and explain their own professional learning as they ask, answer and research the following kinds of question:

'How **can I help my pupils** to improve their learning?'
Dr Moira Laidlaw

'How **can I help** to establish action research approaches to professional development **in my** school?'
Dr Kevin Eames
Dr Moyra Evans

'How **can I support teachers** in establishing action research approaches to professional development **in their school** in a way which can help to improve the quality of pupils' learning?'
Professor Pam Lomax
Dr Jean McNiff

'How **can I fulfil my system's responsibility** for staff appraisal, staff and/or curriculum development?'
Jackie Delong and Dr Ron Wideman
Erica Holley

These questions have been asked in local, regional, national and international contexts and supported by centres of professional development. Your Professional Development Centres are ideally placed to support such enquiries and I know such programmes have been developed for teachers of Drama in Cork. The teachers' accounts below show what has been learnt in answering these questions. I have no intention of 'speaking for' the individuals below. They have all done this for themselves. My purpose in presenting these accounts and saying why I value the work so highly, is to see if I can captivate your imagination in a way which will motivate you to access their work.

'How can I help my pupils to improve their learning?'

Dr Moira Laidlaw
(1996) 'How can I create my own living educational theory through accounting to you for my own educational development?'
PhD Thesis, University of Bath.
Examiners: Professors Morwenna Griffiths and Richard Winter.

1998 'In Loco Parentis with Sally: A matter of fairness and love'. Discussion paper for the Chat Room on http://www.bath.ac.uk/~edsajw

Moira Laidlaw is an English teacher in a Bath comprehensive school. The general prologue to her doctoral thesis is a most inspiring piece of reflective writing on her experience of being a teacher. Moira uses Coleridge's *Poem of The Ancient Mariner* to help to communicate the spiritual and moral values she brings into her educative relationships with her pupils. In creating her living educational theory she demonstrates how educational standards of judgement are themselves living and changing within the educative relationships themselves as she works at helping her pupils to improve their learning.

'How can I help to establish action research approaches to professional development in my school?'

Dr Kevin Eames
(1995) 'How do I, as a teacher and an educational action-researcher, describe and explain the nature of my professional knowledge?'
PhD Thesis, University of Bath.
Examiners: Professors Chris Day and David Sims.
The afterword is a particularly powerful expression of how a teacher-researcher can contribute to transcending the truth of power in the Academy.

I don't often refer to researchers' work as heroic but I do think Kevin's work is worthy of particular mention. In 1987 Kevin gained his MPhil degree from the University of Bath. He had not been permitted to register for a Doctoral programme until he had been awarded his MPhil degree on the sole ground that he was doing his research through action research! Kevin obtained his MPhil then registered for his Doctorate which he was awarded in 1996. His PhD Thesis is a remarkable achievement and shows how a teacher-researcher can contribute to the legitimation of a new discipline of educational enquiry. His publications are also significant for the way in which they show how school-based teacher-researcher groups can be sustained over several years. Kevin's work has been influential in the development of action research approaches to teachers' professional development in Ontario.

Kevin's publications include:
1987 'The Growth of a Teacher-Researcher's Attempt to Understand Writing, Redrafting, Learning and Autonomy in the Examination Years'; MPhil, University of Bath.

1988 'Evaluating a Teacher-Researcher's Choice of Action Research' in *Assessment and Evaluation in Higher Education*, Vol. 13, No. 3, pp. 312-318.

1990 'Growing Your Own: The Development of Action Researchers Within An Action-Research Approach to Whole-School Development' in *British Journal of In-Service Education*, Vol. 16, No. 2.

1993a 'Action research in schools: Into practice' in *British Journal of Curriculum and Assessment*, Vol. 3, No. 3, pp. 29-33.

1993b 'A dialectical form of action research-based educational knowledge: A Teacher-Researcher's view', in T. Ghaye and P. Wakefield (eds) (1993) *CARN Critical Conversations: A Trilogy, Book One, The Role of Self in Action Research*; Bournemouth, Hyde Publications.

Dr Moyra Evans
1996 'An action research inquiry into reflection in action as part of my role as a deputy headteacher' (See Chapter 8 – Creating my own living educational theory). PhD Thesis, University of Kingston. Examiners: Professors Jean Rudduck and Michael Bassey.

Moyra Evans is a Deputy Headteacher at Denbigh School in Milton Keynes.

The reason I believe that Moyra's contributions are so valuable in legitimating the knowledge base of professional educators is not only because of the originality of her contribution to educational knowledge in her PhD Thesis. It is also because of her work as a deputy head and supervisor of the Diplomas and Masters Degrees of her staff in association with Kingston University. The latest group of teacher-researchers include the following enquiries:

How can I work with members of the English team in order to improve exam results at KS3? *Sheila Baldwin*

How can I develop effective learning strategies with my Year 11 GCSE French group? *Clayton Hughes*

How can I work with the Deputy Head of Year and Year Team in order to become a more empowering teacher? *David Sulley*

How can I make a personal career development plan and prepare myself for the next stage of my career? *Diane Lewis*

Moyra's publications include:

1997 'Shifting the Leadership focus from Control to Empowerment – a case study' in *School Leadership and Management*, Vol. 17, No. 2, 1997, pp. 273-283.

1998 'Using Story to Promote Continuing Professional Development for Teachers' in *Journal of In-Service Education*, Vol. 24, No. 1, 1998, pp. 47-55.

'How can I support teachers in establishing action research approaches to professional development in their school in a way which can help to improve the quality of pupils' learning?'

Dr Jean McNiff
1989 'An Explanation for an Individual's Educational Development Through the Dialectic of Action Research'
PhD Thesis, University of Bath
Examiner: Professor John Elliott

Jean has been particularly influential in a range of local and international contexts in developing action research approaches to teachers' professional development and the processes of improving the quality of pupils' learning. Without Jean's enthusiasm and commitment to generative forms of action research and the creation of living educational theories, the ideas would not have spread through a range of national and international contexts. Her spirit has been an inspiration and I want to acknowledge a huge debt of gratitude. The Symposium on 'Education for Mutual Understanding', to which she contributed at the British Educational Research Association in Belfast in August 1998, with colleagues from Queen's University and elsewhere, was a highlight of the conference.

Jean's publications include:

1988/1992 *Action Research: Principles and Practice*. London, Routledge.

1993 *Teaching as Learning: an action research approach*. London, Routledge.

1994 (edited with Úna Collins) *A New Approach to In-Career Development for Teachers in Ireland*. Bournemouth, Hyde.

1996 (with P. Lomax and J. Whitehead) *You and Your Action Research Project*. London, Routledge.

2000 *Action Research in Organisations*. London, Routledge.

Professor Pam Lomax

Pam is Professor of Educational Research at Kingston University and this year's (1998) President of the British Educational Research Association. Her Presidential Address to the British Educational Research Association on *Working Together to Create Community Through Research*, contains an excellent bibliography of her writings and a description of the support developed by Pam and her colleagues in creating the Kingston Hill Action Research Group. Pam and Moyra Evans developed the award winning partnership between Denbigh School and Kingston University as they worked together to support the creation of a teacher-researcher group at Denbigh School. Pam's proposal on *Creating Educative Communities through Educational Research* has been accepted as the BERA Symposium at the American Educational Research Association in Montreal in April 1999 and the papers will be available on the Action Research Homepage in April.

Working with Pam has been a great sustaining force and some of the results of our collaboration have recently been published in the paper:

(1998) 'The process of improving learning in schools and universities through developing research-based professionalism and a dialectic of collaboration in teaching and teacher education, 1977-1997', in *British Journal of In-Service Education*, Vol. 23, No. 3.

'How can I/we fulfil my/our "system" responsibility for teacher development, standards of practice, staff appraisal or curriculum development?'

Jackie Delong and Ron Wideman

Jackie and Ron, working in the context of Ontario, show what can be achieved in a partnership between staff working in a School Board (Grand Erie) and a University (Nipissing). Their publications include: Delong, J. and Wideman, R. (eds) (1997) *Action Research: School Improvement through Research-Based Professionalism*. This Action Research Kit, which includes a video and introductory text by Jean McNiff, highlights the experiences of educators participating in the process of action research in Ontario classrooms, schools, and boards of education. The approaches being developed by Jackie and Ron view action research as learning in action; as an on-going cycle of acting, reflecting and revising which is focused on improving practice; as working best when a teacher has a critical friend or a staff group with whom to share; as a way in which teachers can take charge of their own professional growth which is committed to improving the quality of student learning.

The Grand Erie Board in which Jackie works as a Superintendent of Schools and Peter Moffatt is the Director of Education will be trialling the new standards of practice being developed by the Ontario College of Teachers.

Jackie's and Peter's publications include:

Delong, J. and Moffatt, P. (1996) 'Building a Culture of Involvement' in *ORBIT*, Vol. 27, No. 4. pp. 33-36.

Erica Holley

(1997) 'How do I, as a teacher researcher, contribute to the development of living educational theory through an exploration of my values in my professional practice?'
MPhil Thesis, University of Bath.
Examiners: Dr Paul Denley and Dr Tony Ghaye.

Erica Holley is Head of Upper School of Greendown Community School, in Swindon, UK.

In one section of her thesis Erica shows how she responded to 'managerial demands' that she 'appraise' staff in relation to linguistic lists, through a collaborative form of peer appraisal which was focused on a mutual concern to help one another to improve the quality of pupils' learning.

Erica's achievement is all the more noteworthy as she sustained her commitment to her enquiry through the time when the economic rationalist policies of a Conservative Government were creating enormous pressures on teachers through the cutbacks in the support services of our local authorities.

Legitimating living educational theories

Having focused on the practitioner researchers whose work I am commending to you I now want to concentrate on the processes of legitimating the living educational theories which have been created and embodied in most of their work and which help to guide them. In particular I want to focus on the nature of the living values or standards of judgement which the teacher-researchers have used to validate their claims to professional knowledge. I also want to explore the implications of legitimating living educational theories as teachers' professional knowledge in partnerships between the Academy, Professional Development Centres and a Teachers' Council.

Because of the ferment in academic life, related to what has become known as the postmodern condition, I feel the need to locate my ideas on reconstructing educational knowledge in relation to this condition and in relation to the nature of the values used by teacher-researchers in creating and testing their professional knowledge.

In his important report for the University of Quebec in 1979 on *The Postmodern Condition: A Report on Knowledge*, Lyotard (1984) describes this condition as a 'scepticism towards Grand Narrative'. In advocating that each individual creates their own living educational theories in their autobiographies of their learning, I do locate myself in a postmodern context. Yet, I also want to hold on to some of the values of a Grand Narrative. For example, the world is gripped by the globalisation of capital movements. The Chicago academics who founded the Fund for Long Term Capital Management have played the 'free market' and lost billions of dollars as they moved them around the world in search of the maximisation of profits with no concern for the effects of such large global movements of cash on the economies of the countries concerned. The Grand Narrative of Capitalism does provide me with some valuable understandings of some of the economic and political forces which are influencing what I am able to do in education. I see no difficulty in holding on to both a sense of the postmodern in the creation of living educational theories and the integration, within these living theories, of insights from Grand Narratives in the form of conceptual abstractions in propositional theories.

Indeed, I find analyses, such as those offered by Jim Graham (1998), both helpful and disturbing. I find it helpful to be able to understand how teacher professionalism has been one of the key arenas in which the contradictions of economic and social change have been played out in a series of crises of control for the state (p.11). I find the analysis offered by my colleague Hugh Lauder (Brown and Lauder, 1996: 6) on Fordism, Neo-Fordism and Post-Fordism most persuasive as it helps me to understand my present disquiet with the policies being pursued by our New Labour Government, a government I voted for and fought hard to see elected. I share Graham's concern that far from being a radical transformation to recognise the importance of teachers as professionals in the premier division of international economic and social activity, the current policies are 'locked in the Tory legacy of blinkered bureaucratic myopia essentially committed to maintaining traditional patterns of power and control at the expense of precisely the social and economic objectives they propose to achieve' (p. 12).

Whilst I find such Grand Narratives provide me with helpful insights, I often find myself disturbed by the way some of their totalising conclusions appear, within their powerful rhetoric, to embrace a concern with the local and living, yet manage to obliterate any evidence of this concern within the totalising structures of their language. This characteristic they share with traditional forms of theory.

It may be helpful at this point if I share some of the ideas which led me to reconstruct my view of educational theory.

A focus for my own learning about the nature of the knowledges and theories created by different educational researchers occurred in 1971, whilst doing some classroom research for my masters degree. I was trying to understand how to answer and research my classroom questions of the kind, 'How do I help you to improve your learning?', in relation to my pupils. At the beginning of my enquiry, largely through the influence of my physical science degree programme, the cognitive psychologists and the linguistic philosophers tutoring me, I held the view that educational theories were constituted by general forms of conceptual, abstract explanation. From the general form of explanation I believed a theory could produce a valid explanation for the actions of individuals or groups. I believed that educational theory was constituted by such general forms of explanation in the philosophy, psychology, sociology and history of education (Peters, 1966; Hirst and Peters, 1970). I also believed that statements of fact and statements of value formed independent realms of discourse and that contradictions must be eliminated from correct thought.

As I was conducting my classroom enquiries with my pupils I came to question these fundamental assumptions in my view of educational theory. Through focusing on my enquiry, 'How do I improve my practice?', and being open to the influence of Michael Polanyi's (1958) ideas in *Personal Knowledge*, I came to see, with the aid of video-tapes of my practice, that 'I' existed as a living contradiction in my claim to know what I was doing as I worked at my classroom enquiries of the kind, 'How do I improve my practice?'. I also understood that I created matters of fact, in moving my classroom resources to support enquiry learning, from matters of value, as I worked at enabling my pupils to form their own questions and at providing the resources which would enable them to answer them.

These insights helped me to see that my living educational theories were not constructed in the form of the conceptual or propositional frameworks of the traditional disciplines of education, but were living forms of explanation. By this I mean that the explanations were embodied in my present practice in terms of an evaluation of my past and in terms of an intention to create something better in the future.

The explanatory principles which constituted my explanations as 'theory' were the values I used to give my life its meaning and purpose and whose meanings emerged through action. The communication of these values to others needed both ostensive definitions, related to practice, and value-words such as loving care, freedom, justice and democracy. One of the problems with text-based theses which are bound on library shelves is that our written language cannot carry our non-verbal communications. Yet I imagine that we would all acknowledge the importance of non-verbal communication. I do support Elliott Eisner's (1993) call for us to extend the forms of representation we use in communicating our educational research and claims to educational knowledge. Michael Schratz and Ulrike Steiner-Löffler (1998), and Rob Walker and Ron Lewis (1998) have shown the potential of such extensions through their use of photographs and the use of the world wide web. I will come back to this point when I look at the potential of the Internet for communicating to one another our educational research and standards of judgement.

In 1989 the publication of Richard Winter's *Learning from Experience* helped to take my ideas forward on the ways in which the 'rigour' of action research accounts could be enhanced through the use of dialectical and reflective critiques, the use of multiple resources and a plural structure, highlighting risk and emphasising the processes of theory practice transformations. Richard also helped to take my ideas forward in his keynote address to the Collaborative Action Research Network (CARN) Conference in November 1997 where he developed the idea that theories in action research could be seen as forms of 'improvisatory self-realisation'. This idea fitted well with my commitment to supporting action researchers in the creation of their own living theories. You can access Richard's keynote address from my homepage link to the CARN Homepage.

I also want to thank John Schostak of the University of East Anglia, whose enthusiasm for the work of Seyla Benhabib (1992: 6) stimulated my reading of her work on situating the self and helped me to see more clearly the importance of discourse in establishing the validity of my truth claims and the importance of narrative in constituting my identity and values base through self-study.

In making these points about different kinds of educational knowledge and theory I agree with David Bridges (1998) that, as an educational researcher, I am also engaged in the articulation of propositions, in relation to my questions, which assert the truth of falsity of what I have to say and that I am operating with identifiable theories of truth. Where I need to extend my understanding is in relation to the appropriate forms of representation of the spiritual, aesthetic and ethical values which help to constitute my educational enquiries, my educative relationships and my truth claims. I also need to deepen my understanding of how knowledge-claims which contain such values can be tested for validity and legitimated.

The importance of such research can be seen in the problems of establishing appropriate standards of judgement for examining teachers' professional learning.

Throughout my academic life I have met colleagues who simply accept that they have the competence to make these judgements. Until 1991, in my University, their academic judgements were protected by the regulations, against being questioned under any circumstances. Thankfully, this no longer applies and questions are permitted on the grounds of bias, prejudice and inadequate assessment. Kevin Eames is a teacher-researcher who included correspondence on this issue as an afterword to his PhD Thesis on the professional knowledge-base of teaching. I have already recommended his work to you.

John Elliott (1998) who has been doing much to support action research in Ireland, draws on the work of the Ford Teaching Project to show how a professional knowledge-base can be constructed through action research, as teachers engage in standards-setting. I accept his recommendation that teachers engage in a form of 'creative compliance' in relation to external standards setting. He advocates that the teaching profession responds to external requirements by developing the capacity to accommodate and creatively reinterpret the external standards as part of the profession's well articulated and publicly defensible standards framework.

I view each of the 'living theory' accounts on the Web, at the above address, as a contribution to the creative re-interpretation of such professional standards of practice and judgement for the teaching profession.

Recognising and dealing with power

In making these points about legitimation and values as standards of judgement, I do not want to ignore the importance of researching the influence of power relations on the processes of legitimation and validation. Morwenna Griffiths (1998) has focused on helping researchers who want justice to argue among themselves in such a way that they are united. I agree with Morwenna's analysis about the importance of attempts to draw on theory and philosophy to help members of the research community to gain in reflexivity and clarity about the possibilities of empowerment and voice, and about the different assumptions about power which underlie them.

In the creation and testing of living educational theories I accept the gains in such reflexivity and clarity as part of an individual's education. If you do adopt your own living theory approach to professional development I would urge you to integrate insights from Griffiths' philosophical analyses of education within your enquiries of the form, 'How do I live my values more fully in my practice?' and 'How do I help you to improve your learning?'. I am thinking of forms of integration which show our practical engagements, as educators, with the power relations associated with legitimising and validating our knowledge in the Universities in the process of asking, answering and researching such questions.

I will emphasise this by focusing on the action research thesis of Jacqui Hughes and the circumstances surrounding its examination.

Hughes, J. (1996) 'Action Planning and Assessment in Guidance Contexts: How can I understand and support these processes?'
PhD Thesis, University of Bath.
Examiners: Professors Ian Jamieson and Michael Bassey.

The analyses of her learning and the learning of her supervisor and tutor as they developed their understanding of some of the power relationships surrounding the legitimation of this educational knowledge appears as:

Hughes, J., Denley, P. and Whitehead, J. (1998) 'How do we make sense of the process of legitimising an educational action research thesis for the award of a Ph.D. degree? – a contribution to educational theory', in the *Educational Action Research Journal*, Vol. 6, No. 3, pp 427–452.).

This paper stresses the importance of engaging with the power relations within one's own workplace when such relations appear to support the truth of power rather than the power of truth. The paper also raises the issue of the 'unconscious incompetence' of academics in the context of supervision and examination.

I have developed this analysis in more detail in the two papers to BERA 1998. The first (Whitehead 1998a) was presented as a 'victory' narrative to the Symposium 'Philosophy and Educational Research', convened by David Bridges. The second (Whitehead 1998b) was presented as research as 'ruin' to the Symposium 'Educational Change in Higher Education', convened by Roger Murphy. Both of these papers can be downloaded from my Action Research Homepage in the menu section on Writings related to my Work/BERA and AERA presentations.

I will conclude this section with an emphasis on the importance of Professional Development Centres for providing appropriate opportunities for teachers to extend their professional learning. Here are some details from a Portfolio Assessment programme for teachers' professional development I have been involved in with Professional Development Centres in England.

Learning Outcomes

1 The participants will learn how to gather evidence of their professional development as they work at questions related to improving the quality of pupils' learning.

The evidence in the portfolios will be drawn from data such as:

- prior professional development;
- pupils' test scores;
- pupils' work which shows their learning;
- contributions to departmental or school policy;
- autobiographical accounts which reveal professional values and commitments;
- action plans;
- data from classroom, school and other activities used as evidence in a description and explanation for your professional learning;
- an annotated bibliography of your professional reading;
- critical familiarity with relevant research;
- application of research evidence in your school based project;
- video-tapes and other visual and audio records of classrooms and other professional practices;
- evaluations of actions in terms of values, skills and understanding;
- new action plans which show a modification of concerns, action plans and actions in the light of evaluations;
- evaluations from colleagues which show how you have validated your claims to understand your professional learning as you influence/improve/understand your pupils' learning;
- evidence from another colleague's portfolio which shows how you are influencing their professional development in the process of helping pupils to improve their learning;
- creative use of a variety of media for analysis and sharing of work in progress e.g. hypertext.

2 The participants will learn how to construct a portfolio in a form which shows and explains the relationships between the professional learning and the processes of improving the quality of pupils' learning.

Participants in this process have been given information on how to access the above teacher-researcher accounts from the Internet and I now want to consider the potential of this medium for teachers' professional learning.

3 Demonstrating the potential of the Internet for:

- Constructing, communicating and testing teachers' professional knowledge.

- Defining and communicating the values used by teachers for evaluating the validity of their living educational theories. I am thinking particularly of the different meanings of the spiritual, aesthetic and moral values which can be communicated through multi-media presentations.

The power of the Internet is part of a global transformation in communications. I am thinking both of its help in communicating teachers' narratives and its potential, with the expanding band widths, to carry video-images as well as words, pictures and sound.

The dramatic increase in users of the Internet is a phenomenon of our time. Let me just see how many of you have browsed the Internet or downloaded material from the Internet. When I asked this question of my novice teacher groups two years ago, only 2 out of 30 had this experience.

This year all 50 had used the Internet in these ways. When my son Jonathan created my action research web-page in March 1995 there were almost 1000 logins during the first year and some 2000 in the second year. So far this year it is over 5000. The Web is full of innovation. If you look at David Geelan's PhD Thesis from Curtin University you will see how the Internet can be used to assist in the construction of theses and dissertations as well as to take educational enquiries forward. If you look at the Pepsi Cola homepage you will see how the multi-media technology could be used to extend our understanding of how to integrate film, sound, graphics and text within the narratives of our educational journeys.

My own interest in the Internet is now focused on its capacity to communicate the spiritual, aesthetic and moral qualities in educative relationships. I have been helped in this growing awareness by Helen Hallissey, an Irish drama teacher who has been exploring the value of drama in developing pedagogy across the curriculum. Helen has been working with a Professional Development Centre in Cork and has been most influential in showing me the power of images for communicating feelings in educative relationships.

Let me just give you an example of the new power of communication provided by CD-Roms and the Web. These CD-Roms contain the contents of my action research homepage and Tom Russell's homepage at Queen's University in Kingston Ontario. Just by dropping the main file onto a netscape icon you have access to all the information on my web page. The growth of on-line journals is also a great support for teacher-researchers. From my action research homepage you can go to other sites of interest including such on-line journals.

Just imagine the different meanings we will be able to communicate with the aid of video-images. If you access the picture of Jane Verburg, a teacher at Oldfield Girls School in Bath in my paper to BERA '98 (Whitehead 1998a) I wonder what you will see and feel is being communicated to her pupil at this moment? The spiritual energy I feel in my educative relationships is communicated to me through Jane's being as she shows her delight in being with her pupil.

Loving care, the values of freedom and justice, as they are embodied in teachers' lives, do not shine through the linguistic checklists of standards of practice of the TTA. They do however shine through the general prologue of Moira Laidlaw's PhD which was viewed by her external examiners as amongst the best pieces of reflective writings they had read. As The Teachers' Council in Ireland works on the procedures for accrediting teachers' professional learning I am suggesting that it will enhance professionalism and morale in teaching by awarding professional recognition to these values as fundamentally important in the lives and professional learning of teachers and educators.

What the Internet is enabling us to do is to build up our case studies and studies of singularities as we describe and explain our professional learning as we ask, answer and research questions of the kind, 'How do I live my values more fully in my practice?'. It is enabling us to create valid explanations for the educative influences of teachers with their pupils (Holley, 1997) in ways which can embrace the qualities more usually communicated through the expressive arts. I fear, however, that the possibilities of the technology in helping to create new forms of educational knowledge and theory is running ahead of our capacity to accredit and legitimate teachers' knowledge in the Academy as we remain bound to our text-based cultures.

In conclusion, in sharing my learning over the past decade and some of my hopes for the next decade, I would say: learn from the partnerships created by Jean McNiff with the University of the West of England and between Moyra Evans at Denbigh School and Pam Lomax at Kingston University. These kinds of partnership are the bedrock of professional development because they focus on the generative capacities of teachers to improve the quality of pupils' learning and the professional status of teaching. They rest on the enthusiasm, commitment and care of teachers for their pupils and their education, and the sustained commitment of providers of in-service support for professional learning in Professional Development Centres.

Then comes the need for sustained support for professional and academic recognition through accredited programmes of Education which also lead to the recognition of professional educators. I have suggested that the Irish Education System has much to learn from the Teaching Training Agency and the Ontario College of Teachers.

I am thinking of learning from what Ted Wragg has referred to as an 'Unmitigated Disaster' in approaches used by the TTA. I am thinking of learning from what I have referred to as the creative and generative capacities of the Ontario College of Teachers. I am sure you will find a uniquely Irish way of creating and sustaining partnerships between your Universities, Professional Development Centres and Teachers' Council for the professional development of teachers in a way which will have wider significance in our international contexts. It may be that the Teachers' Council will be the first such body to recognise the professional learning of teachers in terms of initial accreditation as a Teacher, followed by opportunities to develop as Teacher-Educators, Master-Educators and Doctor-Educators. Whatever arrangement you come to for enhancing professionalism in teaching, I feel sure that you will create a network of support for teachers' professional learning which will be focused on what I imagine is the shared concern of helping pupils to improve the quality of their learning.

I want to acknowledge the importance of the following organisations in providing forums for the public presentations of my papers. Without these forums I doubt if I would have had the motivations to gather my ideas together and to take my enquiries forward. I also know the importance for my productive life and enquiries of my colleagues in our Monday evening teacher-researcher group and of the company of Sarah Fletcher, Jen Russ, John Fisher and Carmel Smith in our Department of Education.

TAKING CHARGE OF EDUCATIONAL CHANGE WITH ACTION RESEARCH

A keynote address to the Annual Conference of the National Association for Pastoral Care at Warwick University, UK, on 11 October, 1998.

THE EDUCATIONAL THEORIES OF AN EDUCATOR AND SOME PHILOSOPHIES OF EDUCATION

A revised paper following a presentation to the Symposium convened by David Bridges on 'Philosophy of Education and Educational Research' at the Annual Conference of the British Educational Research Association in Belfast, 27–30 August, 1998.

EDUCATIONAL THEORIES OF EDUCATIONAL CHANGE WITHIN HIGHER EDUCATION: ROBUSTNESS IN THE ROMAN RUINS

A paper presented at the Annual Conference of the British Educational Research Association in Belfast, 27–30 August 1998, to the Symposium on 'Educational Change Within Higher Education' convened by Roger Murphy.

ACTION RESEARCHERS CREATING THEIR OWN LIVING EDUCATIONAL THEORIES

A paper presented to the Action Research SIG session 9.45 of the American Educational Research Association Conference in San Diego on 14th March 1998.

References

Benhabib, S. (1992) *Situating the Self: Gender, Community and Postmodernism in Contemporary Ethics*. Cambridge, Polity.

Bridges, D. (1998) 'Educational research: pursuit of truth or flight into fancy?'; a paper to the Symposium on 'Philosophy and Educational Research' convened by David Bridges at the Annual Conference of the British Educational Research Association, Belfast, August.

Brown, P. and Lauder, H. (1996) 'Education, globalization and economic development' in *Journal of Educational Policy*, Vol. 1, pp. 1–25.

Delong, J. and Moffatt, P. (1996) 'Building a Culture of Involvement' in *ORBIT*, Vol. 27, No. 4, pp. 33–36.

Delong, J. and Wideman, R. (eds) (1997) *Action Research: School Improvement through Research-Based Professionalism*. Toronto: Ontario Public School Teachers' Federation.

Eames, K. (1987) 'The Growth of a Teacher-Researcher's Attempt to Understand Writing, Redrafting, Learning and Autonomy in the Examination Years.' Unpublished MPhil Thesis, University of Bath.

Eames, K. (1988) 'Evaluating a Teacher-Researcher's Choice of Action Research' in *Assessment and Evaluation in Higher Education*, Vol. 13, No. 3, pp. 312–318.

Eames, K. (1990) 'Growing Your Own: The Development of Action Researchers Within An Action-Research Approach to Whole-School Development' in *British Journal of In-Service Education*, Vol. 16, No. 2.

Eames, K. (1993a) 'Action research in schools: Into practice' in *British Journal of Curriculum and Assessment*, Vol. 3, No. 3, pp. 29–33.

Eames, K. (1993b) 'A dialectical form of action research-based educational knowledge: A Teacher-Researcher's view' in T. Ghaye and P. Wakefield (eds) *CARN Critical Conversations: A Trilogy, Book One, The Role of Self in Action Research*. Bournemouth, Hyde.

Eames, K. (1995) 'How do I, as a teacher and an educational action-researcher, describe and explain the nature of my professional knowledge?' Unpublished PhD thesis, University of Bath.

Eisner, E. (1993) 'Forms of Understanding and the Future of Educational Research' in *Educational Researcher*, Vol. 22, No. 7, pp. 5–11.

Elliott, J. (1998) 'Evidence-based Practice. Action Research and the Professional Development of Teachers'. A paper to the Symposium on 'Philosophy and Educational Research' convened by David Bridges at the Annual Conference of the British Educational Research Association, Belfast, August.

Evans, M,. (1996) 'An action research inquiry into reflection in action as part of my role as a deputy headteacher' (see Chapter 8 – Creating my own living educational theory). Unpublished PhD thesis, University of Kingston.

Evans, M. (1997) 'Shifting the Leadership Focus from Control to Empowerment – a case study' in *School Leadership and Management*, Vol. 17, No. 2, pp 273–283.

Evans, M. (1998) 'Using Story to Promote Continuing Professional Development for Teachers' in *Journal of In-Service Education*, Vol. 24, No. 1, pp. 47–55.

Farren, M. (1998) 'Using the Internet for Professional Development' in *Proceedings of the Third European Conference on Integrating Information and Communications Technology in the Curriculum*. Dublin, Dublin City University.

Government of Ireland (1995) *Charting Our Educational Future: White Paper on Education*. Dublin, Stationery Office.

Government of Ireland (1998) *The Teaching Council: Report of the Steering Committee on the Establishment of a Teaching Council*. Dublin, Stationery Office.

Graham, J. (1998) 'From New Right to New Deal: nationalism, globalisation and the regulation of teacher professionalism' in *Journal of In-Service Education*, Vol. 29, No. 1, pp. 9–29.

Griffiths, M. (1998) 'Research for Social Justice: Empowerment and Voice'. A paper to the Symposium on 'Philosophy and Educational Research' Convened by David Bridges at the Annual Conference of the British Educational Research Association, Belfast, August.

Hirst, P. and Peters, R. (1970) *The Logic of Education*. London, Routledge and Kegan Paul.

Holley, E. (1997) 'How do I, as a teacher researcher, contribute to the development of living educational theory through an exploration of my values in my professional practice?' Unpublished MPhil thesis, University of Bath.

Hughes, J. (1996) 'Action Planning and Assessment in Guidance Contexts: How can I understand and support these processes?' Unpublished PhD thesis, University of Bath.

Hughes, J., Denley, P. and Whitehead, J. (1998) 'How do we make sense of the process of legitimising an educational action research thesis for the award of a PhD degree? – a contribution to educational theory' in *Educational Action Research*, Vol. 6, No. 3, pp. 427–452.

Hyland, Á. and Hanafin, J. (1997) 'Models of Incareer Development in the Republic of Ireland: An Analysis' in *Irish Educational Studies*, Vol. 16, pp. 144–172.

Laidlaw, M. (1996) 'How can I create my own living educational theory through accounting to you for my own educational development?' Unpublished PhD thesis, University of Bath.

Laidlaw, M. (1998) 'In Loco Parentis with Sally: A matter of fairness and love'. Discussion paper for the Chat Room on http://www.bath.ac.uk/~edsajw

Leonard, D. (1995) 'Quality in Education and Teacher Development' in *Irish Educational Studies*, Vol. 15, pp. 56–67.

Lomax, P. (1998) 'Working Together to Create Community Through Research': Presidential Address to the British Educational Research Association, Belfast, August.

Lomax, P. and Whitehead, J. (1998) 'The process of improving learning in schools and universities through developing research-based professionalism and a dialectic of collaboration in teaching and teacher education, 1977–1997' in *British Journal of In-Service Education*, Vol. 23, No. 3.

Lyotard, J.F. (1984) *The Postmodern Condition: A Report on Knowledge*. Manchester, Manchester University Press.

McNiff, J. (1989) 'An Explanation for an Individual's Educational Development Through the Dialectic of Action Research.' Unpublished PhD thesis, University of Bath.

McNiff, J. (1988) *Action Research: Principles and Practice*. London, Routledge.

McNiff, J. (1993) *Teaching as Learning: an action research approach*. London, Routledge.

McNiff, J. (2000) *Action Research in Organisations*. London, Routledge.

McNiff, J. and Collins, Ú. (eds) (1994) *A New Approach to In-Career Development for Teachers in Ireland*. Bournemouth, Hyde.

McNiff, J., Lomax, P. and Whitehead, J. (1996) *You and Your Action Research Project*. London, Routledge.

Parker, Z. (1998) 'PhD students and the Auto/Biographies of Their Learning' in M. Erben (ed.) *Biography and Education: A Reader*. London, Falmer.

Peters, R. (1966) *Ethics and Education*. London, Allen and Unwin.

Polanyi, M. (1958) *Personal Knowledge*. London, Routledge and Kegan Paul.

Schratz, M. and Steiner-Löffler, U. (1998) 'Pupils Using Photographs in Self-evaluation' in J. Prosser (ed.) *Image-Based Research*. London, Falmer.

Shobbrook, H. (1997) 'My Living Educational Theory Grounded In My Life: How can I enable my communication through correspondence to be seen as educational and worthy of presentation in its original form?' MA dissertation, University of Bath.

Squire, F. (1998) 'Action Research and Standards of Practice: Creating Connections within the Ontario Context.' A paper presented at the Self-Study of Teacher Education Practices, Second International Conference on 'Conversations in Community', Herstmonceaux Castle, August.

Usher, R. (1998) 'The Story of the Self: Education, Experience and Autobiography' in M. Erben (ed.) *Biography and Education: A Reader.* London, Falmer.

Walker, R. and Lewis, R. (1998) 'Media Convergence and Social Research: The Hathaway Project' in J. Prosser (ed.) *Image-based Research.* London, Falmer.

Whitehead, J. (1989a) 'How do we improve research-based professionalism in education? – A question which includes action research, educational theory and the politics of educational knowledge' in *British Educational Research Journal*, Vol. 15, No. 1, pp. 3–17.

Whitehead, J. (1989b) 'Creating a Living Educational Theory from Questions of the Kind, "How do I Improve my Practice?"' in *Cambridge Journal of Education*, Vol. 19, No. 1, pp. 41–52.

Whitehead, J. (1998a) 'The philosophies of a professional educator and some philosophies of education'. A revised paper following presentations to the Symposium on 'Philosophy and Educational Research' convened by David Bridges at the Annual Conference of the British Educational Research Association, Belfast, August. Available from http://www.bath.ac.uk/~edsajw menu section Writings related to my Work.

Whitehead, J. (1998b) 'Educational Theories of Educational Change in Higher Education: Robustness in the Roman Ruins'. A paper presented to the Symposium on 'Educational Change Within Higher Education', convened by Roger Murphy at the Annual Conference of the British Educational Research Association, Belfast, August. Available from http://www.bath.ac.uk/~edsajw menu section Writings related to my Work.

Winter, R. (1989) *Learning from Experience.* London, Falmer.

Winter, R. (1997) 'Managers, spectators and citizens: where does theory come from in action research?' Keynote address to the 1997 International Conference of the Collaborative Action Research Network. Available from http://www.bath.ac.uk/~edsajw/Carn/

Wragg, T. (1998) *Times Educational Supplement*, 16.1.98.

Chapter 2

Equality Studies, the Academy and the role of research in emancipatory social change[1]

Kathleen Lynch

1 Introduction

Origins of Equality Studies

As both the academic origins and historical development of Equality Studies has been analysed elsewhere (Lynch, 1995; Baker, 1997) these matters will not be discussed here. However, some key factors facilitating the development of Equality Studies will be presented to help contextualise the debates presented in the paper.

Equality Studies began in response to a series of research practices, political changes and institutional initiatives which had developed in Irish intellectual and political life in the late 1980s (Lynch, 1995). It resonated with similar developments in other countries including the development of Women's Studies; Disability Studies; Peace Studies; Racial and Ethnic Studies; and Gay and Lesbian Studies. In academic terms, it was first an attempt to develop both an inter-disciplinary and a pluri-disciplinary project around the study of equality issues. There was a widely shared view among many of us working within different disciplines in the University, that no single discipline provided a comprehensive view of the complex subject of equality, or indeed an adequate analysis of how to address inequalities and injustices as they arose. A co-operative, interdisciplinary and pluri-disciplinary mode of inquiry was deemed essential. Equality Studies brought together sociologists, political theorists, lawyers, economists, feminists and policy analysts, each with a unique contribution to make to the understanding of equality and social justice.

Another generative force in the development of Equality Studies was the visible failure of liberal public policies to promote radical social change in society in the post-war era. A large body of research on equality issues, both nationally and internationally, particularly on questions such as social-class related inequality, gender inequality, and poverty indicated that liberal policies were not effective in eliminating major social inequalities within our own society, or indeed internationally (Arnot, 1991; Arnot and Barton, 1992; Baker, 1987; Breen *et al.*, 1990; Callan, Nolan *et al.*, 1989; Clancy, 1988; Cobalti, 1990; Fischer *et al.*, 1996; Nolan, 1991; Shavit and Blossfeld, 1993). In addition, it was increasingly evident with the growing emergence of 'the politics of difference' that social justice was not purely about economic justice in a simple distributive sense; it was also about cultural and political justice (Fraser, 1995). While economic equality remained central to any egalitarian project, it was increasingly evident that the boundaries of class had been increasingly altered by gender, race, age, ethnic and dis/ability-related differences (Young, 1990); cultural and political institutions reproduced inequalities outside the economic realm.

There were therefore, a series of generative forces which led to the development of Equality Studies, including intellectual, institutional and political developments. All of these factors presented a challenge to all those interested in egalitarian theory and policy, to develop a deeper understanding of what constituted an egalitarian society, and an improved analysis as to how to develop it.

The intellectual focus

Equality Studies is focused on the analysis of significant equalities and inequalities in human life, both as it has been and as it might be (Baker, 1997: 62). It involves the research of at least five key issues, including: (1) the analysis of patterns of equality/inequality and their interrelationships; (2) the development of explanatory frameworks for the understanding of equality/inequality; (3) the identification of core principles or equality objectives which egalitarians are trying to achieve; (4) the identification of institutional and policy frameworks for achieving equality; and (5) the articulation of political strategies for egalitarian-based change. While the identification of patterns of inequality and the development of explanatory models for understanding them (issues (1) and (2)) is part of the work of several major disciplines within the social sciences, Equality Studies tries to go beyond this. It attempts to anchor explanatory frameworks to normative egalitarian theory, thereby breaking the traditional dichotomy which has developed between normatively and positively-oriented disciplines within the social sciences. It tries to articulate a vision of an egalitarian society and global order which is grounded in the analysis of institutional, policy and political frameworks which facilitate or inhibit egalitarian change (Lynch, 1995: 101–102).

Equality Studies works within an epistemological tradition which supposes that the purpose of academic discourse is not only to describe and explain the world, but also to change it. It shares its intellectual and epistemological origins with critical theory (as developed by Habermas particularly), Marxism, Feminist theory, and other inter-disciplinary fields of investigation focused on transformative action including Disability Studies and Women's Studies. The basic questions it asks are not only descriptive or explanatory therefore, they are also visionary and utopian. It tries to focus on potentiality as well as on actuality, on what is possible as much as on what is; it attempts to develop a concept of the alternative rather than simply accepting the given.

Like other cognate disciplines and fields of enquiry, Equality Studies also recognises that research is inevitably politically engaged, be it by default, by design, or by simple recognition. No matter how deep the epistemological commitment to value neutrality, decisions regarding choice of subject, paradigmatic frameworks, and even methodological tools, inevitably involve political choices, not only within the terms of the discipline, but even in terms of wider political purposes and goals, the academy itself, and academic knowledge in particular is deeply implicated in the business of power.

One of the purposes of this chapter is to examine the structural conditions under which Equality Studies (and other cognate disciplines focused on the study of inequality or injustice) operates within the academy. These are conditions of work which it shares with many other researchers in the human rights and social scientific fields, conditions which impinge directly on the outcomes of research. For it is the case, that many of those who study issues such as human rights, race, gender, social class, poverty or disability are not simply detached scholars with no interest in policy or change. Most work on such issues because of the apparently unjust and evil outcomes which blatant racism, sexism, homophobia, classism, and/or disabilism visit upon society (Siraj-Blatchford, 1995: 209). Their work has its origin in the Enlightenment vision of education and research as tools for the development and improvement of society, even though such a vision may not always be explicitly articulated. The question which has to be addressed first however, is whether the academy, which is so deeply implicated in the cultural reproduction of elites, can facilitate emancipatory change *via* research and education.

Given the embeddedness of the academic world in the business of cultural production and reproduction, it is not at all self evident how a given discipline or academic discourse can contribute to radical social change. Universities *qua* institutions are engaged in elite forms of cultural production. Moreover, they are heavily engaged in the practice of cultural monopoly, not only through their selection procedures for students and staff, but also through their rigorous boundary maintenance procedures within and between disciplines, and between what is defined as academic knowledge and what is not (Bourdieu, 1978, 1984). Yet, within all institutions there is scope for resistance; there are contradictions which can be exploited and utilised at all levels of education, including higher education (Giroux, 1983).

2 Research on equality and the limitations of traditional positivist[2] methodologies

There has been very little independent research funding available to the social sciences in Ireland since the foundation of the State. Although State aid for social science research was substantially increased in 1998, the research fund of the Irish Social Science Research Council (SSRC) was only in the region of £100,000 per annum as recently as the mid-

1990s. While some of the international research foundations did offer grants to Irish researchers, there was no major Foundation within Ireland sponsoring social scientific research. Up to the end of the millennium, therefore, the bulk of the money available for social science research was available for commissioned studies for State-sponsored projects. Such funding provided the core funding for the work of the Economic and Social Research Institution (ESRI) and the Educational Research Centre (ERC) (Drumcondra). The absence of either a well-funded SSRC, or well established research foundations, has meant that Irish researchers have had two options in relation to research funding: either they undertook government-funded research (if and when they were invited to tender for it), or they sought out some of the minor funding offered by a host of voluntary, statutory and other agencies.

The lack of funding for basic research meant that much of the work undertaken was of an applied nature, frequently designed to answer a specific policy query for the funder. Such a system was, and is, heavily biased in favour of empirical (especially quantitative) research in the positivist tradition. The published work of the ESRI and the ERC exemplifies the strong hold which positivism has had in the social sciences in Ireland. Although there have been moves away from this tradition in recent years (as is evident from the nature of the material published increasingly in the *Irish Journal of Sociology* or in *Irish Educational Studies*), positivism still maintains a strong hold on social scientific practice. In view of its strong position, it is important to identify its strengths and limitations, especially in relation to such a morally loaded subject as equality.

Much of the policy debate about poverty and inequality in society generally (especially in terms of social class/socio-economic groups) has been framed within the language-of-analysis of positivism. In the education area in particular, work within the positivist tradition has played an important role in the policy arena. The work of what are sometime called the 'equality empiricists' has been especially effective in holding the State to public account regarding the implementation of its stated policies on equality. In Ireland, for example, the work of Breen *et al.* (1990); Clancy (1988, 1995); Callan, Nolan *et al.* (1996); Cormack and Osborne (1995); Dowling (1991); and Hannan, Smyth *et al.*, (1996) has played an important role in challenging the State on the effectiveness of various policies for the promotion of social justice in education and society generally. In certain respects, this type of 'political arithmetic' is crucially important for holding the State publicly accountable. It is a vital tool of democracy in a world where inegalitarian ideologies are gaining hold:

> At a time of increasing social inequalities and injustice, when the 'self-regulating' market threatens to undermine the foundations of social solidarity; ... and when the dominant ideology of meritocracy in liberal democratic societies has been seriously weakened at the same time that right wing politicians proclaim the 'classless society', a new political arithmetic must be asserted as a vital tool of democracy as well as of sociology (Brown *et al.*, 1997: 37).

When positivist research is sufficiently critical and independent, it also has the potential to facilitate social and individual reflexivity; it informs the general body politic, giving them access to knowledge which is detached from the powerful interests of government and media (Halsey, 1994).

In the international arena the merits of traditional positivist methodologies for the understanding of social phenomena generally, and inequality in particular, have been debated intensely in recent years. Positivism has not been without its defendants; Hammersley (1992, 1995) although not subscribing to a crudely positivist view, has been among the more vocal of these. Postmodernists, critical theorists and feminist scholars have been, however, among the most ardent critics of positivist epistemologies and methodologies (Bernstein, 1976, 1983; Harding, 1987, 1991; Harré, 1981; Humphries, 1997; Lentin, 1993; Reay, 1996; Smith, 1987; Stanley and Wise, 1983). Their work demonstrates how, despite its visible benefit as a tool of political arithmetic, mainstream positivism has severe limitations from both a philosophical and a moral standpoint (Reason and Rowan, 1981; Reason, 1988).

The model of the person employed is one which regards people as 'units of analysis'; it treats them as 'variables' whose attributes can be neatly reified into dependent and independent types. People are not defined therefore in a holistic way; understanding of their subjectivity and their relational conditions of structured inequality often become invisible. What Bourdieu (1973) once referred to as 'the substantialist atomism' of the social sciences, conceals the structural and relational conditions which generate inequality, injustice and marginalisation. The person is treated as a detached atom (undoubtedly with attributes of gender, class, race, ethnicity, etc.); the language-of-analysis does not identify the sets of relations through which particular attributes are translated into particular inequalities. The research focuses on how particular characteristics, such as colour, class or religion, are associated or correlated with particular outcomes, such as occupational status, education or legal provision. There is a tendency to locate the causative factors contributing to particular inequalities, therefore, in the attributes of those experiencing inequality, in their gender, poverty, or race, rather than in the structured relations, the planned and unplanned exclusionary systems, which transform individual attributes into generative forces for inequality.

Moreover, once the research has identified correlations and associations between individual attributes and inequality outcomes, this is generally regarded as sufficient for promoting an understanding of the underlying causes of inequality. This methodological individualism creates a silence around the social, economic, political, legal and cultural relations of inequality. There is no space in which to debate or frame radical structural critiques or alternative visions based on relational understanding.

While it could be argued that the failure to examine the relational character of inequality is a universal problem within the social sciences, rather than one which is tied to positivist methods, the fact that the issue has received so little attention is undoubtedly related to the culture of assumed objectivity which dominates positivist discourse. The role of the researcher is defined as that of 'disinterested' observer and analyst; one is expected to discover 'truth' *via* the use of reliable research instruments and rational discussion; the goal is to represent reality accurately, no matter how limited that particular reality may be. The researcher is defined as beyond politics, their knowledge is 'innocent', untainted by political agendas. Thus, a culture of objectivism prevails which precludes a debate about the politics of research production. It allows methodological individualism to persist as long as it operates according to the scientific canon of objectivity. There is no framework for analysing the epistemological and ethical limitations of one's own position; questions regarding the purposes and outcomes of research are defined as being the work of policy-makers rather than researchers.

The methodological individualism underpinning positivism also focuses attention on the powerless rather than the powerful, while failing to explore relations between the two. While there are studies of inequality which focus on the impact and influence of the powerful and wealthy in society (studies on white collar crime by McCullagh (1995) and Tomlinson *et al.* (1988) being cases in point), there are proportionately many more studies on the vulnerable and subordinate (Chambers, 1983). The lack of a substantial body of empirical data in Ireland on the egalitarian/social justice implications of the operation of the money markets or the ownership structures of equities and other forms of corporate and productive wealth [3] indicates how biased the focus of analysis has been. We are often presented with a detailed analysis of the life style of those who are subordinate or poor, while little attention is devoted to the analysis of the generative forces and processes which maintain others in positions of dominance and/or affluence.

The relative social scientific silence which exists around the relational systems governing the interface between the powerful and powerless, is no doubt related to the ability (including legal protections) of particular groups to hide from the research gaze, and to refuse access to sensitive information; the poor are studied as they are on open access; the rich are not. Whatever the reason, the focus of research attention on the attributes of those experiencing inequality means that the causes of injustice are often sought in the lifestyle of the marginalised themselves, the most visible and measurable group. Poor people or ethnic minorities thus become associated with, or even 'blamed' for crime, not the poverty-inducing and degrading structures which induced and facilitated crime in the first place.

The dichotomy which is drawn between fact and value in the positivist tradition also discourages analysis of the impact of funding bodies on the nature of the questions asked. When research on equality is funded by the state, for example, it is frequently undertaken for the purposes of controlling or containing the 'problem of inequality'. Big research studies based on national data sets are big business. The research is designed to answer the questions of those who pay for it; it is undertaken in a managerial context.

Furthermore, large-scale studies of poverty, such as those currently being undertaken across several countries in the EU, are prime examples of state-funded, top-down surveys[4]. They are designed and planned by 'experts' generally without systematic dialogue and collaboration with the subjects of the research. Such research often 'studies those at the bottom while holding up its hands for money to those at the top' (Reason and Rowan, 1981: xv). The methodologies and interpretations employed are based on models and paradigms which have been derived from a conception of poverty developed by academics, and approved by senior policy analysts and policy-makers, without the consent of those who are the subjects of the research.

Without intent, this type of research can and does operate as a form of colonisation. It creates public images about groups and contexts of inequality (in both the academic and the policy world) over which most people participating in the pain and marginalisation of injustice and inequality have little or no control. Poor people, Travellers, asylum seekers, disabled people, and increasingly, women, become the subjects of books and papers in which their lives are recorded by professional middle class experts who are frequently removed from their culture and lifestyle. This creates a context in which professional researchers know and own (as do the policy institutions and state departments which pay them) part of people's worlds about which people themselves know very little. By owning data about oppressed peoples, the 'experts' own part of them. The very owning and controlling of the stories of oppression adds further to the oppression as it means that there are now people who can claim to know and understand you better than you understand yourself; there are experts there to interpret your world and to speak on your behalf. They take away your voice by speaking about you and for you. This is sometimes regarded as the 'hit and run model of research' wherein the career advancement of the researchers is built on their use of alienating and exploitative methods of inquiry.

Colonisation by experts is especially acute for low income working class communities and for ethnic minorities and other groups, such as Travellers, whose cultural traditions are strongly oral (Lynch and O'Neill, 1994)[5]. For 'Classes exist twice over, once objectively, and a second time in the more or less explicit social representation that agents form of them' (Bourdieu, 1993: 37). While there are women, albeit upper middle class women, who can challenge, mediate and redefine the images of women in the policy and academic arena, and while the same holds true for many other groups such as disabled persons, religious or ethnic minorities, this cannot happen for working class people; by designation, working class people are not part of the defining classes in society.

Within traditional positivist research, reflexivity is not a requirement of the research task. The fact that the perspective of the expert is only one viewpoint, and one which is generally at least one step removed from the oppression, is rarely discussed. Researchers present what is a select viewpoint as one which is more comprehensive and epistemologically powerful than others; it is often presented as being superior to that of other researchers (especially ethnographic researchers), and to that of people living out inequality. The net effect of interpreting the world from the perspective of the 'expert' is that the viewpoint of the outsider is privileged over that of the insider who has experienced the inequality. The privileging of the expert produces perspectives on inequality and injustice, therefore, which are politically and emotionally detached from the experiences which generated their articulation in the first place.

While academic understanding involves abstractions, the abstractions need not revisit the research subjects as 'expert opinions' which are superior to their own understanding[6]. It is possible to create knowledge and understanding through partnership between the researcher and the research subject, while recognising the differences between the two positions. Knowledge created in this manner is owned by the research subject in a way that non-partnership-knowledge is not. The fact that the subject is co-creator of the knowledge means that they can exercise control over definitions and interpretations of their lifeworld. They are also in a position to be introduced to research practice through their ongoing involvement in the research process.

3 The normative and transformative tradition in critical and feminist research

Both critical theory (in the Habermasian tradition) and feminist theory have played a central role in generating a critique of positivist discourse; in this sense, they have formed the intellectual backdrop to debates about emancipatory research. Given this, it is important to comment on the development of emancipatory research and theory to date.

Critical theory

One of the important contributions which critical theory has made is to highlight the importance of the emancipatory potential of research. Research within the critical paradigm has had an 'emancipatory interest' which seeks to free people not only from the domination of others, but also from their domination by forces which they themselves do not understand (Habermas, 1971). Although critical theory shared Durkheim's commitment to the scientific analysis of society, critical analysis was also oriented to the emancipatory transformation of society. The scientific analysis of the world was not seen as an end in itself. It was regarded as a necessary step towards understanding which would guide transformative action, and would help create a world which would satisfy the needs and powers of women and men. What distinguished critical theories therefore from the positivist disciplines was their emphatic *normative* and *transformative* orientation. They were theories with a 'practical intent' (Benhabib, 1986: 253) working on the assumption that we live in a world of pain but that 'much can be done to alleviate that pain, and that theory has a crucial role to play in that process' (Poster, 1989: 3).

Research within the critical tradition also tries to highlight the contexts and spaces where resistance is possible. In *Communicative Action*, Habermas notes that the 'seams between system and lifeworld' offer special scope for resistance in the contemporary era. He regarded conflicts and contradictions emerging in areas of cultural reproduction, social integration and socialisation (rather than distribution) as offering special scope for transformative action.

Both critical and feminist theory have also presented an enormous counter-point to positivist hegemony and the values it endorsed. They have challenged the epistemological foundations of positivism, in particular the naive understanding of value freedom and objectivity. The work of critical theorists shifted interest from the almost exclusive concern with 'how biased is the data?' (a concern most often expressed when the academic and policy interrogator did not like the findings) to concern about whose interests are served by the bias (Lather, 1991: 14). It has highlighted the interests of the 'disinterested' researcher and her funders.

Overall critical theory encourages self-reflection on behalf of the researcher and the research subject. It promotes a deeper understanding, both on the part of those being researched and of the researcher herself, and of the issues being examined. The goal is not just to generate empirically grounded theoretical knowledge but to ensure that people know and understand their own oppressions more clearly so that they can work to change them. Dialectical theory building replaces theoretical impositions by experts. Research subjects are therefore actively involved in the construction and validation of understandings created about themselves. The relationship between researcher and researched is reciprocal rather than hierarchical (Fay, 1987); it is ultimately concerned with eliminating inequalities.

How effective critical theory has been overall in producing knowledge which has transformative outcomes is the subject of considerable debate. Some regard critical theory as having become estranged from its audience (Fay, 1987; Cocks, 1989) while others regard much of the research on women undertaken in the name of critical theory as being a new form of imperialism operated by western women on women in majority world countries (Lugones and Spelman, 1985). Apple (1991: ix) holds that critical theorists need to shift from being 'universalizing spokespersons' *on behalf of* oppressed groups to 'acting as cultural workers whose task is to take away the barriers that prevent people from *speaking for themselves*'. Lather (1991) has called for the development of research approaches which empower those involved to change the world as well as understanding it. She has suggested that the methodological implications of critical theory have remained relatively unexplored.

Feminist theory

Feminist scholars have been especially effective in challenging the core epistemological and methodological assumptions of mainstream social scientific practice. They have challenged patterns of bias in research design, including the absence of research on questions of central importance to women; the focus on elitist research topics; the naive understanding of objectivity; the improper interpretation and overgeneralisation of findings; and inadequate data dissemination (Jayaratne and Stewart, 1995: 218).

Not only have feminist theorists been to the fore in the critique of positivism, they have also been leaders in developing a theory of emancipatory action through education and research (Harding, 1987; Humphries and Truman, 1994; Lather, 1991; Lentin, 1993; Mies, 1984; Smith, 1987; Stanley and Wise, 1983; Weiler, 1988). They have encouraged women to engage in action both in and through education, and through research; they have also attempted to document the type of the procedures which must be followed in order to create an emancipatory research approach. Lather claims that:

> ... the development of emancipatory social theory requires an empirical stance which is open-ended, dialogically reciprocal, grounded in respect for human capacity, and yet profoundly sceptical of appearances and 'common sense'. Such an empirical stance is, furthermore, rooted in a commitment to the long-term, broad-based ideological struggle to transform structural inequalities (Lather, 1986: 269).

The challenge posed by critical and feminist theories for research in terms of reflexivity, dialogue and co-operation with marginalised people, are considerable. An even greater challenge is how to establish collaborative practices between theorist/researcher and marginalised peoples which will ensure that the understandings arrived at can work towards a transformative outcome. To confront the latter challenge is to confront the forces of interest within the academy itself.

4 Challenges and issues to be addressed in developing an emancipatory research model

While several feminist theorists have engaged with the contradictions of their class position in relation to emancipatory research, critical theorists often tend to ignore the logic of the sets of cultural relations within which academic knowledge is produced. Critical theorists, no more than other intellectuals 'tend to leave out of play their own game and their own stakes' ... Yet, 'the production of representations of the social world, which is a fundamental dimension of political struggles, is the virtual monopoly of intellectuals ...' (Bourdieu, 1993: 37). Even academics who are themselves critical of the failure of critical theory to problematise its own fundamental assumptions, do not address themselves to the problem of the academically embodied context in which theory is constructed (Sayer's 1995 critique of critical theory is a case in point). Academics create virtual realities, textual realities, ethnographic and statistical realities. These overhang and frame the lived existence of those who cannot name their own world; it is frequently in the context of these detached and remoter realities that public policy is often enacted. The frame becomes the picture in the public eye. Yet theoretical knowledge has serious limitations imposed upon it by the conditions of its own performance.

The relations of cultural production within which critical theory, feminist theory, and egalitarian theory are produced are generally no different to those that operate for the study of nuclear physics, corporate law or business and finance. Although some academics may view themselves as radical, reforming, feminist or emancipatory, they occupy a particular location within the class system (Bourdieu, 1993: 36–48). They are part of the cultural elite of society. It is the designation of cultural elitism which provides them with the structural conditions to write; it gives them credibility over other voices and reinforces the perception of superiority which maintains the salary differentials between themselves and other workers. Being granted the freedom from necessity to write and discuss is a privilege which academics (be they liberal, radical or conservative) in well-funded universities are rarely asked to reflect upon, however.

Yet, academics are also subordinate to powerful corporate interest groups in the business and industrial sector. In a sense, therefore, they occupy a contradictory class location (Davies, 1995), being at once an elite in the cultural sphere and relatively subordinate in the industrial or financial sphere. Thus, while the concept of the 'free-floating, disinterested intellectual' may be part of the ideology of academia it is not grounded in any sociological reality; even radical intellectuals are culturally, and relatively financially, privileged.

Operating within a contradictory state, of being personally radical and publicly privileged, makes it difficult for many politically left-wing academics to be progressive in cultural or university politics. It is much simpler to be progressive in general politics that do not touch the core values of one's own work. Bourdieu (1993: 45) suggests that there is no easy resolution to this dilemma for radical intellectuals. He proposes a radical, ongoing reflexivity wherein one prepares 'the conditions for a critical knowledge of the limits of knowledge which is the precondition for true knowledge' as the principal protection available. In this way, researchers know where they themselves stand in the classification system.

Even if academics do engage in ongoing reflexivity, this does not alter the structural conditions under which they work. The dilemma posed by unequal power between researcher and research subject is not rapidly resolved, even when the researcher works with emancipatory intent (Lentin, 1993: 128; Martin, 1996). It is generally the researchers who produce the final text, the written record of the research event. This gives them a power of definition which cannot be abrogated at will. Moreover, the very efforts of those interested in transforming the relations of research production (from those of dominance to those of partnership or emancipation) are deeply implicated in the exercise of power. One cannot escape the reality of power relations even within the language of emancipation.

In addition, intellectuals work in institutions which lay down working conditions based on the dominant meritocratic principles of our time – ostensibly at least, promotion is based on merit. The way in which merit is measured is in terms of conformity to the dominant norms of intellectual and academic discourse. This includes not only writing within the dominant paradigm (Kuhn, 1961) but writing about what is currently intellectually fashionable. Without at least a nodding recognition of the importance of the dominant discourses, then one's work is not likely to be published⁻. And it is through their publications that intellectuals in universities are generally assessed. While 'there is something desperate in the docility with which "free intellectuals" rush to hand in their essays on the required subject of the moment' (Bourdieu, 1993: 43) the fact remains that academics' jobs and incomes are often dependent on such conformity.

Not only does the academy generally only recognise those who conform to the intellectual norms of the day, it penalises those who attempt to redefine the purpose of the academy. Lectures, consultations and involvements with non-academic bodies do not count in terms of the enumerations of one's work or achievements[8]. This acts as a very effective control on academic work limiting and containing interests within the safe confines of the university. It also works effectively to preclude intellectuals from involving themselves, and the university, in radicalising initiatives. While 'established or tenured' academics can afford to indulge in such developments, sanctioning *via* limited promotional opportunities continues to exercise control even over these.

Yet, public lectures and involvements with voluntary, statutory, community and other organisations is essential if research findings are to be circulated outside the narrow confines of the academy. Given that the production of scientific knowledge generally is often legitimated on the grounds that it will contribute to progress, and to the ultimate general good of humanity, it is difficult to see how this can happen without the dissemination of the findings outside the academy in accessible contexts and language.

What is interesting about the boundary maintenance which goes on in universities is that it is not confined to any one field (Bernstein, 1971). It occurs within and between disciplines, and between the university itself and the 'outside community'. Academic knowledge is defined as 'superior' knowledge. The fact that the academic perspective is only one viewpoint, and that it may need to be complemented by other forms of understanding by non-academic research subjects is largely ignored (Lather, 1986). The parameters within which academic dialogue takes place, therefore, are narrowly defined thereby inhibiting criticism of academic discourse itself, and prohibiting academics from understanding the world from the perspective of the 'other' outside the academy.

5 Emancipatory methodology

Resolving the dilemma posed by the colonising nature of research has been addressed by several feminist scholars and researchers (Bowles and Duelli Klein, 1983; Harding, 1991; Lather, 1991; Mies, 1984; Roberts, 1981; Smith, 1987), and more generally in the social sciences (Bernstein, 1983; de Koning and Martin, 1996; Oliver, 1992; Reason, 1988; Reason and Rowan, 1981). It is suggested that the alternative to illusory value-free knowledge is emancipatory knowledge. The aim of emancipatory research is to increase '… awareness of the contradictions hidden or distorted by everyday understandings', and in so doing to direct 'attention to the possibilities for social transformation inherent in the present configuration of social processes' (Lather, 1986: 259).

Ethical issues
The research industry is a massive one across all fields and disciplines; it takes place not only in universities or research institutes but in government departments, private companies, local and national service agencies, and in voluntary bodies. Cultural capital, of which research is a fundamental part, parallels industrial, financial and agricultural capital as a source of wealth and power. Unless it is shared with those who are directly affected by it, research data can be used for manipulation, abuse and control. The importance of democratising research arises therefore because knowledge is power.

Although conventional human rights thinking focuses on political rights in the more restricted political sense, there is also a need to recognise the importance of human rights in relation to the operation of public and private institutions and systems which exercise control over people's lives but which are not democratically appointed. Research-generating institutions and universities are such bodies, as they play a central role in validating and developing cultural forms and scientific knowledge which underpin social, economic and political policies in society.

Emancipatory research involves a recognition therefore of the moral right of research subjects to exercise ownership and control over the generation of knowledge produced about them, and their world. As Heron (1981) observes, this is a human rights issue. It constitutes part of people's right to political membership of their community. If people are structurally excluded from democratic engagement with research practice, they are precluded from assessing its validity in an informed manner. They are effectively disenfranchised from controlling the creation and dissemination of knowledge about themselves and/ or about institutions and systems within which they live and work.

> For persons, as autonomous beings, have a moral right to participate in decisions that claim to generate knowledge about them. Such a right does many things: (1) it honours the fulfilment of their need for autonomously acquired knowledge; (2) it protects them from becoming unwitting accessories to knowledge-claims that may be false and may be inappropriately or harmfully applied to others; (3) it protects them from being excluded from the formation of knowledge that purports to be about them and so from being managed and manipulated, both in the acquisition and in the application of knowledge, in ways they do not understand and so cannot assent to or dissent from (Heron, 1981: 35).

Although the moral or human right to know applies primarily to research on persons, it is also of significance in other fields including research in the physical sciences. The most obvious example arises in relation to research involving experimentation with the natural environment (as in the case of the nuclear industry) or the development of genetically modified foods; these, and indeed many other forms of research, much of which is not so high profile, have serious health and environmental implications not only for the living generation but for future generations. Concealment of the scope and impact of research may add to the power and influence of the companies and states that produce it, but it also creates a world order in which ordinary people are politically and informationally disenfranchised. Research and information enfranchisement must complement political enfranchisement.

Often a research information deficit can be the differentiating factor between having a meaningful or an alienating experience in an organisation. An immediate and concrete example arises in the field of education. Parents who know the basic research findings regarding such practices as streaming and ability grouping can exercise control over schools and teachers in a way that other parents cannot. Knowledge about the effects of different forms of ability grouping enables them to act in a way that protects the interests of their own child; they can exercise strategic choices such as moving the child to a more supportive school if they find her or him in the 'wrong' class. No such possibility exists for those who do not even know the implications of different forms of grouping in the first place. Similar examples could be taken from the health services where, for example, women and men are not aware of research findings regarding the long-term implications of taking different types of drugs and medication. Those who have access to (and can decode) the information are in control and can exercise choices in a way that those without it cannot.

Not only can people not make informed decisions if they lack information, neither can they participate effectively in public debates or policy partnerships. Even when and if people are given a partnership role, they may lack the technical knowledge to participate effectively. They can be physically present but technically absent, living in fear of a professional put down from those who are part of the research-informed. What is at issue is not only the exercise of democratic procedures in research production therefore; the effective democratic dissemination of research findings is also essential. Much research is closeted and used selectively by researchers, policy-makers or service-providers as the politics of the situation allows. Such practices ensure that people are managed and manipulated from the top and outside.

Reciprocity in the research relationship

Emancipatory research also involves developing a reciprocal relationship between the researcher and research subject. This requires a democratisation of the research relationship so that the research process enables participants to understand and change their situation. This is especially important for research in the area of equality, as research which is not oriented towards transformation effectively reinforces inequality by default. It allows inequality to persist by diverting intellectual and public attention elsewhere.

Reciprocity involves engaging participants firstly in the research planning and design, as it is only through such participation that marginalised groups can begin to control the naming of their own world. If research participation is confined to the interpretation or theoretical elaboration stage, it may be too late as issues which are not central to the group or community may have become the focus of attention in the first place. Involving research subjects in planning poses numerous challenges to researchers and theorists, not least of which is the information and expertise differential between the researcher and the subject. Mutual education is at least a partial solution to this dilemma; there is an especially strong onus on the researcher to facilitate and promote education given the power differential between them and the research subject (Heron, 1981). Integrating education with research imposes time and resource constraints on research, however, which cannot be easily set aside. And neither the funders nor the research subjects themselves may be interested in bearing the cost.

Reciprocity also demands that the research enables people to know and control their own world. This takes time, trust and negotiation; it is quite possible that the researcher and participants may not agree on the definition of the inequality, or indeed how it should be addressed. Kelly's (1996) research shows how working class community groups themselves interpreted unemployment according to quite different socio-political frames – ranging from radical to reformist to localist – although the formal class identity of all twelve groups involved was the same.

Recognising the very real practical difficulties posed by reciprocal research relations is not a sufficient reason to discount them. Operating out of principles of reciprocity, albeit imperfectly, would radically alter the ways in which research is planned and conducted; this is important in restructuring power relations and would be an important movement towards the democratisation of research in itself.

Dialectical theory building

Another feature of praxis-oriented research is its use of dialectical theory-building rather than theoretical imposition (Lather, 1991). Research respondents are not only involved therefore in the design of the research but also in the construction and validation of meaning. To undertake theory-construction in this manner represents an enormous challenge for researchers as it imposes a substantive educational commitment upon them (Heron, 1981). A dialogical approach to theory building is even more demanding, in many respects, than partnership in empirical research, as it involves the accommodation of two very different epistemological standpoints on the world, the academic and the local or particular. It demands theoretical construction in a language which is recognisable and meaningful across disparate communities; the theorist can no longer construct a view of the world without knowing and recognising the view of the 'other', howsoever the latter may be defined. What dialectical theory building involves therefore is the democratisation of theoretical construction; a reordering of power relations between the academy and the named world. Yet theoretical imposition is the natural predisposition of most researchers given traditional academic training. The author assumes the superiority of their 'framework'; grounding frameworks in the context of live understandings challenges this tradition and informs and enriches understanding.

Reflexivity

Systematic reflexivity is also a requirement for emancipatory research as it is only through the constant analysis of one's own theoretical and methodological presuppositions that one can retain an awareness of the importance of other people's definitions and understandings of theirs. Although reflexivity is necessary, it is not a sufficient condition for emancipatory research. An ethically disinterested reflexivity would not suggest any change in research practice. If reflexivity is to facilitate change it needs to be guided by principles of democratic engagement and a commitment to change.

6 Emancipatory research in practice: coalitions and partnerships

There are a number of practical problems posed by the emancipatory methodology, including the fact that it does increase the cost of the research. This is not necessarily something which will be supported by research funders, although it may change over time when the importance of dialogue and its educational outcomes are appreciated. There is also very little research training available in most educational institutions on emancipatory methodology although there are exceptions to this (Reason, 1988) especially in feminist-led courses in recent years.

A further dilemma for the operation of emancipatory research is establishing procedures whereby radical understandings can be utilised for challenging structural inequalities. Even if radical understandings emerge from research, which for example, happened in Kelly's (1996) work, there may be no mechanism within the emancipatory method to move this understanding into discourses and political practices which would enable it to become active in the struggle for equality and social justice. Emancipation cannot be conferred by one group (academics) on another (oppressed or marginalised people), no matter how well intentioned the researchers might be (Martin, 1994, 1996).

While Mies (1984) shows how particular research led to important policy changes in Germany in relation to policies on women and violence, what is not clear is what makes it possible for this to happen. Is egalitarian development left contingent on a particular set of historical and political circumstances? One fact which does appear to be important is to involve marginalised groups themselves at all stages of the research, including the policy-related implementation stage, if action is to be taken. For this to happen, research organisations have to enter into new relations of dialogue and coalition with community or other groups which may be anathema to their organisational or cultural traditions. Certainly universities and research institutes have rarely established procedures for entering into dialogue with research participants in marginalised groups and communities. While liaisons with such groups may be permitted, they are usually kept at the periphery of the organisation where they exercise marginal power, often in adult education departments or women's studies departments.

Within current emancipatory discourse, the choice about whether or not to use emancipatory methods is left to the researcher; there is no serious attempt to identify the kind of structural conditions necessary to ensure that emancipatory methods are implemented on an ongoing basis. To institutionalise a truly radical approach to research, however, would require the development of new structures at both university and departmental level (and ultimately at central university and research planning level). Similar challenges would arise for institutes and bodies undertaking research elsewhere. Procedures would have to be put in place whereby those who are marginalised and oppressed in society can enter into dialogue about all research undertaken in their name. They would not simply be dependent on the good will of individual researchers allowing them to enter into dialogue on their own terms. Rather, community groups or other representatives of marginalised groups would be involved on an ongoing basis in planning, monitoring and commenting on research. They would play a very different and more powerful role than if they are simply research subjects being given the opportunity to participate or dialogue about research at the will of the researcher.

This would require a radical change in the structuring of departments in the university and the management of research operations. It would involve the establishment of Research Coalitions with those marginalised groups and communities who are so often the objects of research. Such groups would move from being objects to subjects, from being respondents to being partners; they would have the opportunity to define research agendas relating to their own lives. No one would have the authority to name, codify and claim scholarly understanding and ownership of someone else's world without debate, negotiation and, ultimately, consent.

Under a Research Coalition arrangement, power would be shared. The researchers would have to explain and justify the nature of their proposed research and theory about marginalised groups to the groups themselves. This is not to deny the difficulties involved. The academic voice is validated by virtue of its scientific origin; it is structurally defined as superior to the local or community voice. Thus any research partnership between researchers and the community is not an equal one, in the sense that prior cultural relations define it otherwise. To say this is not to suggest that the power differential in Research Coalitions cannot be managed and controlled. It merely highlights the importance of enabling those who are not full-time researchers to have the capacity and skill to name their research agendas in the partnerships. A further difficulty arises from the volatile character and composition of community groups themselves. Such groups are not necessarily constituted in a democratic or representative manner; they often lack formal procedures of accountability to their own constituency. Their effectiveness as representative bodies has to be constantly monitored therefore. While this is not essentially a research problem, it is nonetheless an issue which has to be addressed in partnership contexts (Sabel, 1996).

If Research Coalitions were to be established, it is evident that the onus of responsibility for setting them up rests initially with those who exercise control over the research process. Negotiations and discussions need to be set in train to identify the needs and interests of both parties, and to resolve the barriers which need to be overcome. These include barriers relating to differences in research expertise, language usage, life experiences, and attitudes to, and experience of, research.

The experience of Local Area Partnerships in Ireland has shown that community representatives cannot be fully effective participants without resourcing (Lynam, 1997). If marginalised groups were to participate effectively in the research process, training, researching and support would be essential, although the knowledge differential is not only confined to them. Academics also experience a (frequently unacknowledged) knowledge differential about the daily lived reality of the groups about whom they write. Such living knowledge represents an important resource which the community groups would bring to the Research Coalitions.

To be effective Research Coalitions would need to be complemented therefore by Learning Partnerships. These would be mutual education forums for academics, researchers and community personnel, so that each could share their definitions and interpretations of issues and events. In this way research agendas could be assessed and prioritised.

The Research Coalitions and Learning Partnerships would inevitably facilitate action for change, as the communities where action is required would be directly involved in defining and interpreting their own situations. The research understandings available to them would be a powerful tool in negotiations with politicians and policy makers.

What is at issue here is the case for an extended epistemology within the academy (Heron, 1981: 27–31). Most empirical research is in the domain of propositional knowledge. The outcome of research is stated as a set of propositions, which claim to be statements of facts or truths about the world. These theoretical constructs or empirical statements are artefacts or constructs about the world; they do not constitute the world in and of itself. They provide a framing of the world, a context for giving meaning; they are not synonymous with the experiential knowledge of the world. Experiential knowledge involves knowing the world in a direct face-to-face encounter. 'It is knowing a person or thing through sustained acquaintance' (ibid: 27). Knowing poverty or racism through the medium of academic frameworks, and framing propositions about it empirically and theoretically makes an important contribution to human understanding. However, it is but one window on reality; it can only offer a limited perspective. While it is clear that academics do not claim to offer a 'complete understanding' of any phenomena, the reality is that academic definitions of situations have status and power over and above other understandings. The meaning of poverty or inequality as it is understood and acted upon at policy level is as researchers have defined it; it is not as poor people see it (O'Neill, 1992).

The need to democratise the creation of academic knowledge therefore arises from the simple fact that such knowledge is acted upon as the defining understanding of a situation. With the advancement of information technology, the likelihood is that this trend will grow rather than retract. The scope for creating massive data bases on people of both a quantitative and qualitative nature has been greatly enhanced by computer developments in recent years. With this, the scope for researchers to colonise the life worlds of those who are marginalised is likely to increase considerably unless democratisation of the research process is introduced.

While the democratisation of the research process is necessary across all fields, it is especially acute in the equality field. In general, those who carry the burden of inequality are far removed from the life-world of researchers. By virtue of their personal experience, however, they have a better vantage point for understanding the totality of the social world that creates inequality than those who enjoy its advantages. They have a much deeper understanding of how particular laws, policies and procedures operate to promote inequalities than those who are advantaged by same (Connell, 1993: 39–41; hooks, 1994).

The importance of establishing Learning Partnerships between researchers and the community arises not only from the point of view of respecting the fundamental human rights of those about whom we write, but also as a means of realising change. While critical theorists place considerable store on developing theories, including theories jointly created by researchers and participants, they do not make clear how such understanding will lead to change. Most academic productions remain confined to a narrow community of readers and listeners. No matter how radical the knowledge may be, its transformative potential is far from self evident unless it is available and disseminated in accessible form to those about whom it is written or whose lives are affected by it. Learning Partnerships arising from Research Coalitions would allow this to happen. They would ensure that an avenue of communication is established so that those who have most to gain from transformative action have the knowledge to act. The Learning Partnerships would provide a forum for challenging biases and deceptions thereby reinforcing the incentive to act. Those who have experiential knowledge of inequality and injustice can ally this understanding with academic knowledge to create a new and deeper knowledge of their world. This deeper understanding can challenge established 'wisdoms' and 'ideologies' around inequality and injustice. Learning Partnerships would provide the opportunity to link analysis directly into a community of participants with the potential to act.

Knowledge, no matter how radical in intent, is not inherently transformative. Even if critical intellectuals shift from being 'universalising spokespersons' for marginalised groups to being 'cultural workers whose task is to take away barriers that prevent people from speaking for themselves' (Apple, 1991: ix) this does not guarantee change. It is not self evident that deepening knowledge of injustices and inequalities, among marginalised communities or peoples themselves, will inevitably lead to transformative action outside of the research field; there is always an element of choice. Understandings need to be linked into a political forum so that knowledge does not become redundant and divorced from action. If Learning Partnerships are created between academics and community representatives, then it also seems necessary to develop Equality Action Plans on a collaborative basis. Action needs to be planned and implemented for changing structures at the political and related levels. Without integrating planning for change into the entire process there can be no guarantee that it will happen.

7 A challenge to the academy

What is being proposed here in terms of Research Coalitions and Learning Partnerships would be seen by many academics as a challenge to their intellectual autonomy. And it does pose serious questions about the nature of independence for the universities and research institutes if taken seriously. However, the professional ideology of 'freedom and independence' within the universities is itself in need of deconstruction. As Bourdieu (1988, 1993) has noted the nature of the freedom which academics exercise is in fact seriously circumscribed by numerous conventions and controls. There are many forms of subtle constraint and censorship which operate for intellectuals, although these are rarely named as such. To be published requires a high degree of conformity to the paradigmatic rules of the day within one's disciplines, and breaking out to create new forms of knowledge, either within existing disciplines, or through the creation of new disciplines can be heavily sanctioned.

> The secret resistance to innovation and to intellectual creativity, the aversion to ideas and to a free and critical spirit, which so often orientate academic judgements, as much at the viva of a doctoral thesis or in critical book reviews as in well-balanced

lectures setting off neatly against each other the latest avant-gardes, are no doubt the effect of the recognition granted to an institutionalized thought only on those who implicitly accept the limits assigned by the institution (Bourdieu, 1988: 95).

Freedom of expression is allowed, but the publication and dissemination of that expression is often dependent on working within the received wisdom. And this is even more true when trying to establish new forms of knowledge or understanding. While resistance to innovation may be concealed within established disciplines, more open resistance has confronted new disciplines such as Women's Studies and Equality Studies. There is a need therefore to establish the procedures and practices of those who control academic knowledge and discourse. This would help clarify the power relations within which intellectual life operates, and may be necessary before dialogue can be satisfactorily introduced.

What is being suggested here is that the forces of conservatism within the academy exercise a power over academic freedom which is too rarely named. The forces countering innovation operate both within and between disciplines; the control which medicine has traditionally exercised over nursing is an example of the latter, while the marginalisation of feminist research within male-dominated disciplines is an example of the former. At other times, the forces of conservatism arise from the simple organisational dynamics of academic careerism itself. Although academics may have tenured posts (as most full-time academics do in Ireland) the freedom which flows from this does not always encourage people to think critically; rather people become beholden to the concept of the career – moving upwards promotionally within the system. All too frequently the line of least innovation is the line of ascent. Organisational recognition comes more readily to those who conform to the dominant norms and paradigms. This breeds a culture of conformity, silence and academic orthodoxy which belies the very freedom granted by the academy. While it is clear that people do innovate and resist the forces of conformity within the academy in many different ways, it is also evident that this often happens at considerable personal cost, especially when the innovations challenge traditional values and practices among dominant groups.

Giving a role to marginalised groups to set out the terms in which knowledge about themselves and their world is created is merely to recognise that such groups have hitherto exercised little power in relation to the definition of knowledge. If there is to be a serious attempt to decolonise the knowledge and understanding of oppressed groups in society, then it seems essential to put mechanisms in place to ensure that emancipatory methods are not always an optional extra, something to be granted on a case-by-case basis at the behest of experts. Without structures there can be no guarantee that partnership-based dialogue will happen.

The academy needs to be reconstituted in its structural relations with marginalised groups if resistance is to be effective. Otherwise systems of dialogue will be completely one sided, with all the choices about initiating or ending dialogue being with the researcher. Allowing the researcher to decide on all occasions whether or not their interpretations of other people's worlds will be shared and/or challenged is to perpetuate the highly unequal power relations which now underpin the social construction of knowledge in academic life. This perpetuates a practice wherein the naming of one's own world, especially by marginalised people, is effectively in the hands of academic power brokers, no matter how well intentioned these might be.

8 Conclusions

Radical researchers occupy a contradictory class location in relation to the academy. On the one hand, like all other academics, they are part of a cultural elite which receives salaries and work privileges in excess of many other occupational groups by virtue of their claim to expertise. On the other, they are working as agents for change and social transformation to create a more egalitarian society, one which may not endow their own groups with the same 'freedom from necessity' to research and to write.

A genuine and ongoing commitment to change cannot be guaranteed in this type of situation by simply relying on some form of subjective reflexivity. While reflexivity is essential, it is but one element in the process of creating emancipatory research methodology. If the aim of critically inspired thought is to make theory, method and praxis inseparable from each other, then it is necessary to create structures which guarantee that this will happen rather than leave it to the good will or interest of individual researchers. Moreover, granting the researcher a veto on whether or not to utilise emancipatory methods on equality issues is to disempower the research participants in the very way that critical theorists have strongly criticised in other contexts. The only way in which people can exercise ongoing systematic influence on naming their own world is by being centrally involved at all stages of the research process, including design, interpretation and outcome-implementation. For this to happen, procedures for Research Coalitions would need to be developed between research bodies, universities (and their departments) and communities and groups who are being researched. In addition, Learning Partnerships need to be established to enable researchers to learn (in the doing of research) about the role of experiential knowledge in understanding and, to enable marginalised peoples to name their own world in their own words. Finally, if knowledge is to have transformative potential at a structural as well as an ideological level, then Equality Action Plans need to be developed from the research findings.

For Equality Studies and other cognate fields to have moral, intellectual and political credibility it is incumbent upon researchers to implement the emancipatory research methods as outlined. If it confines its emancipatory actions to the operational stage of the research and ignores the conceptualisation, design, interpretation and action stage, then it is belying the notion of emancipation in its more substantive sense. To operate a more radical form of emancipatory method does present many new and exciting challenges not only for research but for other work in the university as well. Clearly, if emancipatory methods are being employed in research this also calls into question the authenticity and suitability of current pedagogical and assessment methods, most of which are based on strongly hierarchical views of both teacher-student relationships and indeed of knowledge itself.

Many Irish universities and colleges of higher education claim service to the Community as one of their objectives. If this is the case, then there is a need to identify the many different communities with whom we are to work. In this paper, it is suggested that marginalised and

excluded groups in our society are part of the Community; indeed
very often such communities comprise the subject matter of social
scientific research, but rarely the research designers or partners. The
paper suggests that it is time that Research Coalitions were established
between the universities and socially excluded Communities to enable
the latter to control the naming of their own world.

References

Apple, M. (1991) 'Introduction' to P. Lather, *Getting Smart: Feminist Research
    and Pedagogy With / In the Postmodern*. New York, Routledge.
Arnot, M. (1991) 'Equality and Democracy: a Decade of Struggle over
    Education' in *British Journal of Sociology of Education*, Vol. 12, pp.
    447–466.
Arnot, M. and Barton, L. (eds) (1992) *Voicing Concerns: Sociological Perspectives
    on Contemporary Education Reforms*. Wallingford, Oxfordshire, Triangle
    Books.
Baker, J. (1987) *Arguing for Equality*. New York, Verso.
Baker, J. (1997) 'Studying Equality' in *Imprints*, Vol. 2, No. 1, pp. 57–71.
Benhabib, S. (1986) *Critique, Norm and Utopia: A Study of the Foundations of
    Critical Theory*. New York, Columbia University Press.
Bernstein, B. (1971) 'On the Classification and Framing of Educational
    Knowledge' in M.F.D. Young (ed.) *Knowledge and Control: New
    Directions for the Sociology of Education*. London, Collier-Macmillan.
Bernstein, R. (1976) *The Restructuring of Social and Political Theory*. New
    York, Harcourt, Brace Jovanovich.
Bernstein, R. (1983) *Beyond Objectivism and Relativism: Science, Hermeneutics
    and Praxis*. Pennsylvania, University of Pennsylvania Press.
Bourdieu, P. (1973) 'Cultural Reproduction and Social Reproduction' in R.
    Brown (ed.) *Knowledge, Education and Cultural Change*. London,
    Tavistock.
Bourdieu, P. (1978) *The Inheritors: French Students and Their Relation to Culture*.
    Chicago. Chicago University Press.
Bourdieu, P. (1984) *Distinction: A Social Critique of the Judgement of Taste*
    (trans. R. Nice). London, Routledge and Kegan Paul.
Bourdieu, P. (1998) *Homo Academicus*. Stanford, Stanford University Press.
Bourdieu, P. (1993) *Sociology in Question*. London, Sage.
Bowles, G. and Duelli-Klein, R. (eds) (1983) *Theories of Women's Studies*.
    London, Routledge and Kegan Paul.

Breen, R., Hannan, D., Rottman, D. and Whelan, C.T. (1990) *Understanding Contemporary Ireland*. Dublin, Gill and Macmillan.

Brown, P., Halsey, A.H., Lauder, H. and Wells, A.S. (1997) 'The Transformation of Education and Society: An Introduction' in A.H. Halsey *et al.* (eds) *Education: Culture, Economy and Society*. Oxford, Oxford University Press.

Callan, T., Nolan, B., Whelan, B.J., Hannan, D.F. and Creighton, S. (1989) *Poverty, Income and Welfare in Ireland*, General Research Series, No. 146. Dublin, The Economic and Social Research Institute.

Callan, T., Nolan, B., Whelan, B., Whelan, C. and Williams, J. (1996) *Poverty in the 1990s*. Dublin, Oaktree Press.

Chambers, R. (1983) *Rural Development: Putting the Last First*. Harlow, Longman.

Clancy, P. (1988) *Who Goes to College?* Dublin, Higher Education Authority.

Clancy, P. (1995) *Access to College: Patterns of Continuity and Change*. Dublin, Higher Education Authority.

Cobalti, A. (1990) 'Schooling Inequalities in Italy: Trends Over Time' in *European Sociological Review*, Vol. 6, No. 3, pp. 190–214.

Cocks, J. (1989) *The Oppositional Imagination: Feminism, Critique and Political Theory*. New York, Routledge.

Connell, R.W. (1993) *Schools and Social Justice*. Philadelphia, Temple University Press.

Cormack, B. and Osborne, B. (1995) 'Education in Northern Ireland: the Struggle for Equality' in P. Clancy, S. Drudy, K. Lynch and L. O'Dowd (eds) *Irish Society: Sociological Perspectives*, pp. 495–528. Dublin, Institute of Public Administration.

Davies, S. (1995) 'Leaps of Faith: Shifting Currents in Critical Sociology of Education' in *American Journal of Sociology*, Vol. 100, No. 6, pp. 1448–1478.

de Koning, K. and Martin, M. (eds) (1996) *Participatory Research in Health*. London, Zed Books.

Dowling, T. (1991) 'Inequalities in Preparation for University Entrance: An Examination of the Educational Histories of Entrants to University College Cork', in *Irish Journal of Sociology*, Vol. 1, pp. 18–30.

Fay, B. (1987) *Critical Social Science*. Ithaca, Cornell University.

Fischer, C., Hout, M. *et al.* (1996) *Inequality By Design: Cracking the Bell Curve Myth*. Princeton, Princeton University Press.

Fraser, H. (1995) 'From Redistribution to Recognition? Dilemmas of Social Justice in a "Post-Socialist Age"' in *New Left Review*, No. 212, pp. 68–93.

Giroux, H. (1983) *Theory and Resistance in Education*. London, Heinemann.

Gould, S.J. (1981) *The Mismeasure of Man*. New York, Norton and Co.

Gouldner, A.V. (1970) *The Coming Crisis of Western Sociology*. London, Heinemann.

Habermas, J. (1971) *Knowledge and Human Interests*. Boston, Beacon Press.

Habermas, J. (1984) *The Theory of Communicative Action, Vols. 1 and 2* (trans. T. McCarthy). Cambridge, Polity Press.

Halsey, A.H. (1994) 'Sociology as Political Arithmetic' in *British Journal of Sociology*, Vol. 45, pp. 427–444.

Hammersley, M. (1992) 'On Feminist Methodology' in *Sociology*, Vol. 26, No. 1, pp. 187–206.

Hammersley, M. (1995) *The Politics of Social Research*. London, Sage.

Hannan, D.F., Smyth, E., McCullagh, J., O'Leary, R. and McMahon, D. (1996) *Coeducation and Gender Equality*. Dublin, Oak Tree Press.

Harding, S. (ed.) (1987) *Feminism and Methodology: Social Science Issues*. Bloomingdale, Indiana University Press.

Harding, S. (1991) *Whose Science? Whose Knowledge?* Milton Keynes: Open University Press.

Harré, R. (1981) 'The Post-Empiricist Approach and its Alternative' in P. Reason and J. Rowan (eds) *Human Inquiry: A Sourcebook of new Paradigm Research*. Chichester, John Wiley and Sons.

Heron, J. (1981) 'Philosophical Basis for a New Paradigm' in P. Reason and J. Rowan (eds) *Human Inquiry: A Sourcebook of New Paradigm Research*. Chichester, John Wiley and Sons.

hooks, b. (1994) *Teaching to Transgress: Education as the Practice of Freedom*. London, Routledge.

Humphries, B. (1997) 'From Critical Thought to Emancipatory Action: Contradictory Research Goals' in *Sociological Research Online*, Vol. 2, No. 1: (www.socresonline.org.uk/socresonline/2/1/3.html).

Humphries, B. and Truman, C. (eds) (1994) *Rethinking Social Research*. Aldershot, Avebury.

Jagger, A. (1983) *Feminist Politics and Human Nature*. Totawa, NJ., Rowman and Allenheld.

Jayaratne, T.E. and Stewart, A.J. (1995) 'Quantitative and Qualitative Methods in the Social Sciences: Feminist Issues and Practical Strategies' in J. Hollan, M. Blair and S. Sheldon (eds) *Debates and Issues in Feminist Research and Pedagogy*. Clevedon, Open University Press.

Kelly, M. (1996) *Educational Television: Emancipatory Education and the Right to Learn Project*. Dublin, Radio Telefís Eireann in association with the Equality Studies Centre.

Kuhn, T. (1991) *The Structure of Scientific Revolutions*. Chicago, Chicago University Press.

Lather, P. (1986) 'Research as Praxis' in *Harvard Educational Review*, Vol. 56, No. 3, pp. 257–277.

Lather, P. (1991) *Getting Smart; Feminist Research and Pedagogy With / In the Post-modern*. New York, Routledge.

Lentin, R. (1993) 'Feminist Research Methodologies – A Separate Paradigm? Notes for a Debate' in *Irish Journal of Sociology*, Vol. 3, pp. 119–138.

Lugones, M. and Spelman, E. (1985) 'Have we got a theory for you! Feminist theory, cultural imperialism and the demand for the "women's role"' in *Women's Studies International Forum*, Vol. 6, No. 6, pp. 573–581.

Lynam, S. (1997) 'Democratising Local Development: The Experience of the Community Sector in its Attempts to Advance Participatory Democracy.' Dublin, University College, Equality Studies Centre, unpublished Masters thesis.

Lynch, K. (1995) 'Equality and Resistance in Higher Education' in *International Studies in Sociology of Education*, Vol. 5, No. 1, pp. 93–111.

Lynch, K. and O'Neill, C. (1994) 'The Colonisation of Social Class in Education' in *British Journal of Sociology of Education*, Vol. 15, No. 3, pp. 307–324.

McCullagh, C. (1995) 'Getting the Criminals We Want: The Social Production of the Criminal Population' in P. Clancy *et al.* (eds) *Irish Society: Sociological Perspectives*. Dublin, Institute of Public Administration.

Martin, M. (1994) 'Developing a Feminist Participative Research Framework: Evaluating the Process' in B. Humphries and C. Truman (eds) *Rethinking Social Research*. Aldershot, Avebury.

Martin, M. (1996) 'Issues of Power in the Participatory Research Process' in K. de Koning and M. Martin (eds) *Participatory Research in Health*. London, Zed Books.

Mies, M. (1984) 'Towards a Methodology for Feminist Research' in E. Albach (ed.) *German Feminism: Readings in Politics and Literature*. Albany, State University of New York Press.

Nolan, B. (1991) *The Wealth of Irish Households*. Dublin, Combat Poverty Agency.

Oliver, M. (1992) 'Changing the Social Relations of Research Production' in *Disability, Handicap and Society*, Vol. 7, pp. 1011–114.

O'Neill, C. (1992) *Telling It Like It Is*. Dublin, Combat Poverty Agency.

Poster, M. (1989) *Critical Theory and Poststructuralism: In Search of a Context*.

Ithaca, Cornell University Press.

Reason, P. (ed.) (1988) *Human Inquiry in Action: Developments in New Paradigm Research*. London, Sage.

Reason, P. and Rowan, J. (eds) (1981) *Human Inquiry: A Sourcebook of New Paradigm Research*. Chichester, John Wiley and Sons.

Reay, D. (1996) 'Insider Perspectives or Stealing the Words out of Women's Mouths: Interpretation in the Research Process' in *Feminist Review*, No. 53, Summer, pp. 57–73.

Roberts, J. (1981) *Doing Feminist Research*. London, Routledge and Kegan Paul.

Sabel, C.F. (1996) *IRELAND: Local Partnerships and Social Innovation*. Paris, OECD.

Sayer, A. (1995) *Radical Political Economy: A Critique*. Oxford, Blackwell.

Shavit, Y. and Blossfeld, H. P. (eds) (1993) *Persistent Inequality: Changing Educational Attainment in Thirteen Countries*. Boulder, Colorado, Westview Press.

Siraj-Blatchford, I. (1995) 'Critical Social Research and the Academy: the Role of Organic Intellectuals in Educational Research' in *British Journal of Sociology of Education*, Vol. 16, No. 2, pp. 205–220.

Smith, D. (1987) *The Everyday World as Problematic: A Feminist Sociology*. Milton Keynes, Open University Press.

Stanley, L, and Wise, S. (1983) *Breaking Out: Feminist Consciousness and Feminist Research*. London, Routledge and Kegan Paul.

Tomlinson, M., Varley, T. and McCullagh, C. (eds) (1988) *Whose Law and Order? Aspects of Crime and Social Control in Irish Society*. Belfast, Sociological Association of Ireland.

Weiler, K. (1988) *Women Teaching for Change: Gender, Class and Power*. Boston, Bergin and Harvey Press.

Young, I.M. (1990) *Justice and the Politics of Difference*. Princeton, NJ, Princeton University Press.

Notes

1 We are grateful to the *Economic and Social Review* for granting permission for this article to be reproduced here. It originally appeared in the *Economic and Social Review*, Vol. 30, No. 1, January 1999, pp 41–69.

2 While positive here refers primarily to quantitative studies, much of qualitative research operates out of similar principles in its research design

(Oliver, 1992; Jayaratne and Stewart, 1995).

3 In his analysis of *The Wealth of Irish Households*, Nolan (1991) noted that one of the biggest problems in examining wealth distribution was the lack of accurate and comprehensive data.

4 The *European Community Household Panel Survey* and the *Irish Household Budget Survey* are examples of this type of research. National data bases on poverty and related issues are collected through these.

5 An example of how academics may inadvertently structure the exclusion of marginalised groups occurred at a conference organised in TCD on July 18, 1997 on 'Travellers, Society and the Law'. All the lecturers were professionals and there was no space in the programme for the Travellers' perspective. In addition, the fee for the day was £100, so it was only those with access to resources could attend.

6 At the Irish Conference on Civil and Social Rights in the European Union, Dublin, May 7–8, 1997, a number of working class community activists were highly critical of one of the speakers who made no attempt to communicate his academic ideas in accessible language (the audience included community activists from various non-governmental organisations, researchers, policy-makers and administrators). The response to this criticism was (unfortunately) one of dismissal; the speaker justified his approach on the grounds that it was only possible to communicate (sic) his ideas in a particular type of language code.

7 While there are exceptions to this most notably intellectuals who are in the position of defining what is or is not in fashion, most academics, especially those without tenure, are not in that position.

8 An interesting example of this is the way in which inventories of academic activities and research publications are compiled; only lectures to one's academic peers are generally counted as being of high standing; the same principle applies to publications. While this is understandable from the perspective of the academy, it shows how the University systematically devalues dialogue with persons and bodies other than academics.

Chapter 3

Towards a new architecture of learning: Reflection on action as an experience of change

Michael Schratz

The ethnography of learning[1]

The educational assumptions that underlie action research relate to a family of ideas at the heart of which lies the idea of learning by reflecting on experience. The idea that reflecting on experience is a key to human learning is probably almost as old as language itself. Being able to speak to ourselves and to others about what we experience provides a means of editing and rewriting the scripts of everyday life, enables the building of a mental reference system for filing and storing significant memories, and allows us to build the narratives that give meaning and interest to our lives and those of others. Moreover, being able to replay life through talk provides the basis for much of what we find most engaging and compelling in human interaction.

It is important to be aware that 'learning from experience' is not merely a psychological mechanism; for, as an activity and a process, in itself it provides the foundation for much social life. The stories we tell in families, at work and elsewhere provide the basis on which we construct our sense of community and belonging. 'Learning', in short, is not simply the process of acquiring knowledge and skills; since it involves language it inevitably opens doors to multiple levels of discourse. It has both form and content; process and outcome; it is both social and cultural. As the anthropologist Jules Henry wrote, 'education in humans is essentially polyphasic' (Henry, 1960: 268), which is to say we almost never learn only one thing at a time. The multidimensionality and reflexive potential of language lies at the heart of a culture's capacity to develop and to change. It follows that to place people in reflective settings is not just to provide opportunities for them to learn, it is also to disrupt their lives.

To place people in the role of a reflective practitioner is to expect them to act as researchers. Particularly it is to ask that they see themselves as ethnographers, learning about the culture by learning how to act as a useful member of it (Lave, 1988). But taking this role inevitably places them in situations marked by transgression, for inevitably they find themselves being seen by those 'inside' as an anomaly, partly inside the situation and partly outside, not clearly located by the boundaries and the relationships that define the roles of everyone else. To be a participant researcher is not to be an apprentice member, for the researcher always has one eye on what they can take away from the situation for use in another context. They are both stranger and friend; their loyalties are split: they are spies and mirrors.

You need only read a little social or cultural anthropology to realise that being placed for some period of time in another culture in order to try to understand it can have an enormous impact on your understanding of yourself and your socialisation. 'Fieldwork', as anthropologists describe it, is a method which relates as much to identity as it does to technique. On reflection this is more curious than we might at first realise. The more alien the culture, the more likely it is that immersion in it will lead to basic understandings of yourself and your own culture. We might call it the 'Close Encounters Hypothesis', or perhaps 'The X-files hypothesis'! What fascinates us about the alien and the exotic is that it threatens to pull the rug from under those things that in everyday life we take for granted, but this very fascination can lead us into duplicity and tempts us to confuse lies with the truth.

Valorising trivia

Interestingly, the 'basic understandings' of social situations and cultures which anthropologists achieve, are often built on a reassessment of the significance of trivia (in the sense of 'commonplace'). What we first notice in any novel situation are the small things. When we travel we re-tune our perceptions, noticing advertising, the way people dress, street signs, the things in shop windows, the graphic design of newspapers. Until we readjust our perceptions and return to a 'normal' view, it is as though our perceptions are amplified. Colours may seem brighter, we are aware, and are able to recall with some precision, particular scents and smells, we hear different sounds that the locals may not notice – the church bells from a distant village, the sound of a bamboo flute in the hills, the many sounds in a Harlem air shaft.

The same is true (though perhaps in a more mundane sense) of social and workplace situations. As our minds race to read social interaction, to detect power and influence, insecurity and resentment, pride and guilt, so these perceptions too can become amplified and distorted. And because we quickly become a part of these interactions, so our perceptions of ourselves can be thrown out of their usual grooves. We notice what is trivial because we are forced to. For in a small way what we have to do is rebuild our lives. We have to learn, very quickly, how to act appropriately. We do this by working back through our perceptions to a level where we can take things for granted, and the more alien the situation the further back we have to go.

So, one of the valuable educational processes that action research encourages is a return to the trivial. This is not just a comment on the social nature of perception, for there is a moral colour to these observations of small things. They touch directly on our emotions and on the nature of human memory, but they also have an ethical dimension, for in a new context we usually find it hard to read the signs, to know when we have transgressed or misunderstood. Travellers may be tempted to romanticise small differences but ethnographers and migrants inevitably experience the next stage in this process which is a moral longing for the familiar (they miss all those things that were so much better back home). They become aware that there is a silence in their lives which was once filled with the small things from home, certain foods, flowers, music, the sound of a radio program, the customary ways in which people greet one another, laugh, celebrate and grieve. Again it is often the trivial things that loom largest, seemingly carrying an emotional tone far outweighing their apparent significance.

The basic structure of the educational situations involves conceptual (and cultural) separations between the world of learning – such as school, college, university – and the 'real world' in terms of the knowledge/discourse that is characteristic of each. In both cases we are trying to create a space within which we can talk about experience in a way disconnected from the immediate need for action but with immediate implications for changes in action. We are also, at heart, seeking to disrupt the assumption that the learning institution has the sole right to decide what is worth knowing, with a service monopoly in terms of providing teaching programs and opportunities for learning and research. As academics and as teachers we are moving to circumscribe our authority, not assuming that we know or understand all that our students are learning, but trying to place ourselves in a role where we can stimulate, refocus and sometimes rescue students as they set out on their own paths.

How data become knowledge

Validating and reporting in the world of learning has a lot to do with what has recently been called 'knowledge management'. Helmut Willke (1998), a German researcher in systems theory, has come up with a model for the architecture of knowledge, which I have adapted for this purpose (see figure 1).

Both in gaining and reporting data we are confronted with questions relating to (1) What becomes data? (2) What becomes information from (1)? (3) What becomes knowledge from (2)?

Moreover, in all instances (both in gaining and reporting data) the validity problem is involved: (1) How valid are the data according to the coding processes? (2) How systemically relevant are the data to become information? (3) How valid are the data to be built into the contexts of experience?

	(1) data	(2) information	(3) knowledge
Basic operation	coded 'observation' (through all senses)	systemically relevant data	building information into contexts of experience
restrictions	numbers/words/ images	information is systemically relevant	community of practice
challenge	innovative, hybrid forms	information transfer	participatory action

Figure 1: Data, information, knowledge

Therefore we can assume that the validity question is not of any great significance in an action research context (taking the validity question to be primarily about the extent to which the representations that research has of events are true to those events). According to the model above, action research has built into its process and procedures a series of validity checks in the stages (1) (2) (3) that in conventional research are only addressed *post hoc*. Action research that is 'invalid' won't work; that is, data would not become information if they are not systemically relevant to the people involved, and the information would not become knowledge if there is no community of practice. It usually uncovers contention rather than encourages consensus.

In recent research (Schratz and Steiner-Löffler, 1998a), we used photography as a means of pupils' self-evaluation with a view towards their changing their social situation in school. However, a teacher (from a statistics oriented paradigm) challenged the 'validity' of the photos the children had brought with them as data. When the children had gone through a participatory action research process collecting visual data with their cameras they had to make them systemically relevant to each other and, through the community of practice in jointly taking the photos, they built the information they gained into their contexts of experience in school. When the photos were presented, for that teacher they were coded as 'images' and therefore not 'valid data' (for him only numbers are 'valid' data!) Therefore they did not become relevant so as to become 'valid' information, let alone knowledge! In order to show the power of visual images I give some background information on such an approach.

In search of a visual language

Research in general and evaluation in particular are dominated by methods drawing on the spoken or written word. Culturally and historically this has to do with the tradition of academia, which has built its foundations on the written word. When we, Ulrike Steiner-Löffler and I, started experimenting with different activities by including pupils and students in school developmental work, we soon realised that traditional research methods cannot easily be put into practice. Pupils at a younger age find it difficult to use standardised forms of feedback or to write elaborate reports on this matter. The power relationship proves to be too much in favour of the adults when children are confronted with verbal argumentation. 'They should first learn their lessons well enough before they start demanding changes' is a statement we heard from a teacher when we worked with a school.

Therefore we tried to find other possibilities of looking into the 'inner world' of schools from the pupils' perspective. It was particularly important to get an idea of how they experience school from the inside, yet we found very little literature in the area of research methods which pupils can be in control of. We were attracted by Rob Walker's suggestions on the use of photographs in evaluation and research; he was interested in using this method because it 'touches on the limitations of language, especially language used for descriptive purposes. In using photographs the potential exists, however elusive the achievement, to find ways of thinking about social life that escape the traps set by language' (Walker, 1993: 72). His aspiration in using black and white photographs was to find a silent voice for the researcher. For him, looking at photographs creates a tension between the image and the picture, between what one expects to observe and what one actually sees. Therefore, images 'are not just adjuncts to print, but carry heavy cultural traffic on their own account' (Walker, 1993: 91).

These ideas have been further developed in Schratz and Walker (1995), who write that there has been a curious neglect of the visual imagination in the social sciences. 'Despite an enormous research literature that argues the contrary, researchers have trusted words (especially their own) as much as they have mistrusted pictures' (1995: 72). For them the use of pictures in research raises the continuing question of the relationship between public and private knowledge and the role of research in tracing and transgressing this boundary.

> In social research pictures have the capacity to short circuit the insulation between action and interpretation, between practice and theory, perhaps because they provide a somewhat less sharply sensitive instrument than words and certainly because we treat them less defensively. Our use of language, because it is so close to who we are, is surrounded by layers of defence, by false signals, pre-emptive attack, counteractive responses, imitations, parodies, blinds and double blinds so that most of the time we confuse even (perhaps, especially) ourselves (Schratz and Walker, 1995:76).

After having studied the theoretical background we were convinced of the power of pictures in doing research and decided to try out how the instrument of photo-evaluation works when it is put into the hands of pupils. Moreover, we were particularly fascinated by the idea of using photo-evaluation with pupils to research into the area of school culture (Schratz and Steiner-Löffler, 1998a). As a result we confronted the pupils with the idea of finding evidence for the question, 'Where do you feel happy in school and where not?' This aspect seems to be an important indicator for the quality of school culture seen through the pupils' eyes (MacBeath, 1999).

According to constructivist theory we do not regard human behaviour as following a trivial cause-and-effect relationship (Glasersfeld, 1997: 124). We rather tend to see it in its entirety, its elements interwoven in a network of interrelationships in which each influences all others. Therefore it is the study of the social significance, that is, how things, events, and rules of interactions become meaningful within the overall framework of reference, which signifies the changes of the overall system and structures of the system (Simon, 1993: 26). There is not only one 'reality' in an organisation like schools, but multiple realities. Visual images offer a challenging opportunity to bring to the fore the different layers of reality of the pupils' world in schools. To do so, the camera forms a special lens which can be focused on the single elements of school life by changing between the foreground and the background and thus enabling unimportant details, the 'trivia', to become the main focus of interest.

Parts of the micro system of a school can be 'deranged' by isolating elements from the whole, because they can be viewed from a different angle. Thus, for example, in the picture taken by the pupils, the head's office is no longer the management centre of the school, but commented on as 'not an enjoyable place because behind that door lurk dangers'. For them the staff room is not, as it is for the teachers, the only retreat to their professional community, but 'this is the place where boring lessons come from'. As in everyday life, there is no 'real' reality (Watzlawick *et al.*, 1969) and no comprehensive human consensus, but only islands of agreement in a sea of different opinions (Simon, 1993: 61). Handling knowledge in an action-oriented learning process can help in finding where these islands are and, more importantly, how they can be used to enhance future development both personally and institutionally.

Understanding change forces

I want to close by looking at the forces which are at work in the dynamics of change processes and particularly how we can influence this dynamic. The nearer changes approach our personal sphere the more they tend to irritate us – even more so, they lead to anxiety! In such a situation, the degree of discomfort created by changes varies from person to person. I find useful an explanatory model which allows for the spread of human reactions, based on Riemann's *Grundformen der Angst* (1977; *Basic Forms of Fear*). Fritz Riemann's fascinating idea exists in the design of an ***anthropological*** model on the background of a ***cosmic*** analogy:

> We are born into a world ruled by four powerful impulses. The earth circles the sun in a certain rhythm – therefore it moves around the central constellation of the narrow system of the earth. Riemann calls this movement a revolution. At the same time, the earth turns on its own axis – it rotates. Therefore, there are two further opposing – or complementary – impulses taking place at the same time – which not only keep the earth (system) moving, but move it along certain paths – gravitational force and centrifugal force. Gravitational force holds the earth together – is directed centripetally inwards, towards the centre and exercises a certain force of suction which strives to hold together and attract. Centrifugal force strives – in a centrifugal manner – to escape from the centre with an outward force which 'strives to let loose and to be set free'. Only a balance of these four impulses guarantees the law of order in which we live and which we call the cosmos. Should one movement predominate or fail, then the arrangement would be disturbed or destroyed and would lead to chaos (Bertl, 1997: 17–18).

If we apply Riemann's four cosmic elements to human beings and their fundamental needs, we arrive at the following correspondences:

- centrifugal force corresponds to the need for change – in a psychic context;
- gravitational force corresponds to the need for continuity and order;
- rotation – i.e. rotating on one's own axis – is compared to one's striving for individualism – for freedom and for distance;
- the so-called revolution – the manner in which the earth circles the sun – can be compared to our need for belonging to a (greater) entirety and for human closeness.

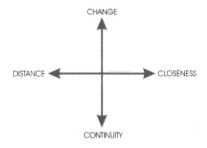

Figure 2: The psycho-dynamic of groups

Thus we have two dimensions (with the extreme poles closeness/ distance and continuity/change) which we cross with each other to obtain four basic human types. It is our experience that these four types are of great significance for the psycho-dynamic of groups. Therefore, we will regard them more closely. They are:

- the type of person who prefers to keep their distance and is aloof – dominated by striving for change and distance;
- the devoted, helping type, who seeks continuity and closeness;
- the orderly type of person who strives for continuity and distance;
- and the exuberant type, who is constantly in search of change and closeness.

Each individual character is composed of constituents of all four variations, but one is more predominant than the others. Yet another phenomenon must also be considered: with regard to the theory of attraction of diametrically opposite patterns, we long for a 'totally different' pattern. A person who is tired of being in the continuity/ closeness corner would, perhaps, love to be a 'lonesome hero' now and again (of a distance/change type), without much emotional involvement, relaxed and independent; and a representative of the exuberant type of person probably longs to be an orderly type now and again – someone who draws clear lines, gives support in every situation and promises only few surprises.

Riemann's classification and the corresponding personality patterns are often mentioned in literature on the subject and have been further developed (see especially Thomann and Schulz von Thun (1988: 149) and Schley (1994)). The following diagram (after Schratz and Steiner-Löffler 1998b: 165 after Schley, 1994: 59), shows the vigour and dangers of the four fields with regard to a common development process.

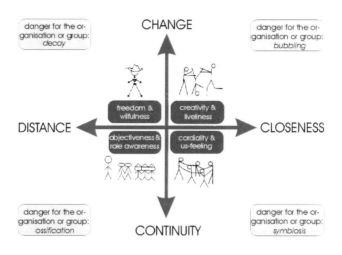

Figure 3: Significant types in the psycho-dynamic of groups (after Schratz and Steiner-Löffler, 1998b; after Schley, 1994)

The positive aspects in each square – for example 'heartiness and companionship' – are in opposition to the dangers which are involved if each type exercises their personality to the full – in this case, the result would perhaps be 'courteous peaceableness'.

How can a new architecture of learning benefit from this model? If one encourages a group of teachers to experiment with the model for themselves, for example, then the mere fact that the varied qualities and needs of each individual are made apparent by classifying these needs into the cross has an enlightening effect. The most important aspect of such a task is the message that *all* the quadrants are equally important for the quality and development of an organisation.

(Possibly, however, the merits of *one* of the quadrants are needed in each phase of development.) Therefore, one should never absolutely disregard the merits of *one* type in favour of another! However, this is easier said than done, since the person in charge of the activity has, himself or herself, 'preferences and fundamental orientations which are in affinity with certain quadrants'; and that means danger, unconscious coalitions with (personally) intimate persons.

It is particularly difficult to preserve the necessary equidistance when dealing with new challenges in times of change. It is easy to imagine what a burden it could be for someone of the continuity/distance type to be continually 'outed' as eternally old-fashioned, rigid, cold and uncreative (even if only in under-tones) when from the change/ closeness corner there are communicative activists bubbling over with new ideas! Individuals of the two other fields (continuity/closeness and distance/change) are perhaps not as badly affected by the classification of the quadrants, since their position shows at least one factor which would suggest that they could be a model school developer – either closeness or change – only the continuity/distance types are deprived of both factors. Quite often it is just such people, however, who hold on firmly to joint agreements concerning development even when the representatives of the change/closeness groups are already taken up with new ideas and are no longer particularly interested in the 'old-new' agreements.

References

Bertl, S. (1997) *Lehrpersonen als forschende Praktiker.* Unpublished doctoral thesis, University of Innsbruck.

Glasersfeld, E. von (1997) *Wege des Wissens. Erkundungen durch unser Denken.* Heidelberg, Carl Auer.

Henry, J. (1960) 'A cross cultural outline of education' in *Current Anthropology*, Vol. 1, No. 4.

Lave, J. (1988) *Cognition in Practice: Mind, mathematics and culture in everyday life.* Cambridge, Cambridge University Press.

MacBeath, J. (1999) *Schools Must Speak for Themselves: the case for school self-evaluation.* London, Routledge.

Riemann, F. (1977) *Die Grundformen der Angst.* München, Reinhardt.

Schley, W. (1994) *Organisationsentwicklung in der Schule. Seminar für BeraterInnen für standortbezogene und autonome Schulentwicklung.* Pöllauberg, Unpublished manuscript.

Schratz, M. and Steiner-Löffler, U. (1998a) 'Pupils Using Photographs in School Self-Evaluation' in J. Prosser (ed.) *Image-based Research: A Sourcebook for Qualitative Researchers.* London, Falmer.

Schratz, M. and Steiner-Löffler, U. (1998b) *Die Lernende Schule: Arbeitsbuch pädagogische Schulentwicklung.* Weinheim, Beltz.

Schratz, M. and Walker, R. (1995) *Research as Social Change.* London, Routledge.

Schratz, M. and Walker, R. (1998) 'Towards an Ethnography of Learning: Reflection on Action as Experience of Experience' in *Studies in Cultures, Organisations and Societies,* Vol. 4, pp. 197–209.

Simon, F. B. (1993) *Meine Psychose, mien Fahrrad und ich: Zür Selbstorganisation von Verrücktheit.* Heidelberg, Carl Auer.

Thomann, C. and Schultz von Thun, F. (1988) *Klärungen für Therapeuten: Gesprächshelfer und Moderatoren in Schwierigen Gesprächen.* Reinbek, Rowohlt.

Walker, R. (1993) 'Finding a Silent Voice for the Researcher: Using Photographs in Evaluation and Research' in M. Schratz (ed.) *Qualitative Voices in Educational Research.* London, Falmer.

Watzlawick, P., Beavin, J.H. and Jackson, D.D. (1969) *Menschliche Kommunikation: Formen, Störungen, Paradoxien.* Bern, Huber.

Willke, H. (1998) Systemisches Wissensmanagement. Stuttgart, Lucius and Lucius.

Note

1 The first two sections are based on parts of a paper which appeared under the title 'Towards an Ethnography of Learning', written with Rob Walker (see Schratz and Walker, 1998).

Chapter 4

Response to keynote presentations

Bernadette Ní Áingléis

It is with gratitude to the Educational Studies Association of Ireland together with the School of Education in both Trinity College Dublin and Dublin City University that I am delighted to accept the invitation to respond to the keynote addresses. I do so from the perspective of an interested educator and a novice researcher. I do so also from the perspective of one who is continuously searching for meaningful ways to engage schools in reflexive inquiry with the promise of enhanced teacher personal/professional development and whole school enrichment. Systematically thinking about what we do as professionals and discussing it, helps to clarify our thinking and justify our practices. It is also a powerful facility which helps check the taken-for-granted assumptions and beliefs underlying professional practices. In so doing, new educational theories are generated which have the potential to inform and enrich our professional judgements. The very process of deconstruction and reconstruction of personal/professional educational theories is, in my view, a vibrant catalyst for lifelong and life-wide learning. It is an energising task.

Our three keynote speakers have presented us with some challenging models to set about the task.

Michael Schratz highlights the issue of knowledge management and how data which are generated, negotiated and interpreted within a community of learnings can facilitate participatory processes in learning. This is a particularly useful model for understanding educational theory development under the schoolhouse roof.

Democratic, participatory processes, as Michael advocates, have the potential to generate the necessary ambience to ensure that data 'moves' from being mere 'data' to becoming information, and, finally, to becoming knowledge. Knowledge generated in this way would seem to be entirely meaningful within the microethnographic context of a classroom or a school, and relevant to the particular situated learning context. I think Michael also hints at the need to build new theories of knowledge from classroom research, lest we risk producing all 'ground' and no theory, or all action and no research. We should not resist any opportunities to theorise when working within a democratic, interpretive action research form of inquiry.

As educators, I think we should encourage and foster the conditions which facilitate teachers in transformative, theory-building, theory-deconstruction and theory-rebuilding. In so doing, the continuous building of critical theories of knowledge by classroom practitioners themselves (theories relevant to learning and teaching) might go some way to elevating the status of teacher-generated knowledge and theory in the wider research world.

The question remains, however, as to how action research might contribute to developing a commonality of knowledge principles, which would be acceptable to and scientifically validated by both professionals within the immediate school ecosystem, and those outside it. Furthermore, we might ask ourselves how action research might ease the conflict of purposes sometimes perceived between its use as a mechanism for the rendering of account and the fundamental purpose of school-based self-evaluative inquiry which is the improvement of the quality of learning and teaching. Perhaps it is not so much a matter of conflict but rather a lack of clarity about the purposes and the potential of action research in school development and teacher professionalism.

The potential of action research to create networks of educative relationships in classrooms, in schools, and between schools, communities, education centres and universities and in fostering communicative action has been highlighted by both Kathleen Lynch and Jack Whitehead. The concept of networking is, in my view, particularly important in developing shared understandings of what constitutes good teaching, effective learning and a sound professional knowledge base. For practitioners, networking or the Illichian concept of learning webs, provides essential critical, supportive structures, when one is attempting to validate everyday classroom practices and the theories which underpin them. Opportunities to talk about classroom life in order to give meaning and direction to practices also facilitate sharing and dissemination of good practice. It builds self-confidence and heightens self-image. It also helps to develop deeper understandings of what authentic partnership in learning and teaching is all about.

Our three speakers have highlighted that a culture of partnership within schools, in classrooms between teachers and students, between classes in schools, between school and home and community, and between schools and other centres of learning generates enthusiasm, harnesses energies and makes people feel valued. However, educative partnerships cannot be taken for granted. They have to be nurtured and worked at. For it is only within a trusting, dialectical culture that practitioners might risk pushing back the boundaries of their practice, critically self-evaluating, and preventing what Kelly (1955) terms 'hardening of the categories'.

Issues of ownership and the control of knowledge which Kathleen alluded to in her address would seem to rest entirely with the self-reflective practitioner who confidently seeks to address the gap between the belief of practice and the reality of practice. More importantly, the self-evaluating teacher is in a favourable position to address the perceived incongruence between professional expectations and one's own value system. Who the researcher is (the private person/the trained professional) cannot be separated from the research process or the knowledge generated. Researchers and research participants have unique voices.

The concept of the emancipatory potential of action research is a key theme throughout. Methodologies which are emancipatory might be understood as a facility which gives 'voice' to many silent learners (in particular, students and parents) and encouragement to teachers, who until now might have shuddered with absolute fear at the thought of doing research and having to become familiar with the language of academia and of the dominant orthodox research community.

It is particularly encouraging and exciting to hear of school communities travelling down roads less travelled in research. I mention here especially learning organisations which integrate information and communication technologies (ICTs), such as film, photography and video in school self review and teacher professional development. Hearing how Jack Whitehead's research communities have used multimedia and the Internet is illuminating and refreshing. Against the backdrop of the Department of Education and Science's *Schools IT 2000*, we warmly welcome hearing of good practice in this area and disseminating it to schools. Image-based research using photography or film would seem to hold much promise in the development of user-friendly school self review and development strategies. The power of images to engage human hearts and heads and minds in meaning-making is undeniably true. The work of Michael Schratz and Rob Walker (1995), Jon Prosser (1998) and my own recent research (English, 1998) bears this out. In my own image-based research, 'hard', valid data emerged from the creative inquiry by pupils, teachers and parents in their evaluation of a home-school reading project. Key research instruments used were a camera and photo-elicitation interviews. The language of feelings, values and perceptions was inseparable from the process and the outcomes. It was also entirely relevant and meaningful to the research participants (students, teachers and parents), user-friendly and empowering. Exciting media such as film, video and photography have enormous potential, in my view, in school self-review strategies and in curriculum delivery and enrichment. Such media successfully capture the character of the school and other key schooling processes unique to each school and which are crucial in understanding school effectiveness. What was particularly significant about the image-based research in which I was involved was the contribution which the methodologies made to the development of children's creative problem solving and critical thinking skills and the sheer enjoyment of learning how to learn in partnership with the school community.

The challenge, however, remains as to how action research methodologies might become sufficiently robust to incorporate the multi-level professional responsibilities which exist at various levels in schools. The complexity of merging multi-level knowledge should not, I feel, be underestimated in action research and in professional development theories.

A more immediate challenge is imminent, however. All three keynote speakers at this ESAI conference have focused our attention on it: the social responsibility inherent in research communities to disseminate outcomes and findings which emanate from teacher-school-community-researcher inquiry. We need to do so in ways which will be accessible to those at the 'chalk face', and couched in a language which will enable and empower practitioners to question and probe the depths of their own theories (in practice and espoused), in order to validate and inform them and be informed by them. This is a major challenge.

Theory, method, praxis may indeed be inseparable. So too, in my books, are knowledge, responsibility and the total human being.

References

English, B. (1998) 'Pupil, Teacher and Parent Perceptions of a Paired Reading Project within the context of Partnership in Curriculum'. Unpublished MSc dissertation, Dublin City University.

Kelly, G.A. (1955) *The Psychology of Personal Constructs, Vols. 1 and 2.* New York, W.W. Norton and Co.

Prosser, J. (ed.) (1998) *Image-based Research: A Sourcebook for Qualitative Researchers.* London, Falmer.

Schratz, M. and Walker, R. (1995) *Research as Social Change: New Possibilities for Qualitative Research.* London, Routledge.

Part 2

CASE STORIES

Chapter 5

Rethinking nursing knowledge through action research

Siobhán O' Halloran

Introduction

On reflecting upon the origin of nursing, both historical and contemporary literature sketch a phenomenon of human evolution as old as society itself. From this perspective it seems somewhat unusual that during this journey nursing has not yet given voice to a cohesive body of scientific knowledge to support its practice. Current nursing programmes argue for the development of nursing knowledge through research based practice. Clearly the integration of knowledge and practice begs a fundamental question as to what knowledge is valid in that practice. In this paper I hope to emphasise the experience of action research as a mechanism for generating nursing knowledge and thus argue that innovative inquiry into the practice of nursing is required. The theme of the debate is to consider action research as an authentic voice for bringing tacit knowledge to the forefront of nursing dialogue. Within this context it is argued that to focus on action is legitimate quite simply because, as a practice discipline, nursing is grounded in action. Therefore the generation of knowledge to support and inform the practice of nursing must by its very nature emerge from that practice. I acknowledge that the process of uncovering this knowledge is inextricably linked to the society in which it exists with particular respect to cultural authority. From this stance I believe there is a need, in the process of generating knowledge, to admit the interconnectedness of power and knowledge. There is also a need to recognise that any reorganisation of knowledge, no matter what the discipline or profession, is closely linked to the social position of the carriers of that knowledge. To this end the derivation of knowledge from action research seems to be capable of responding to the socio-political arena within which practice occurs. My own experiences of action research are employed in an attempt to give life to the issues raised.

Context

When we begin to question the development of knowledge for nursing practice it may prove useful to note Naisbitt and Aburdenes' (1990) observation that events rarely if ever occur in a vacuum, but rather in a social, political, cultural and economic context. What any profession is therefore arises from history, its place in the system, the interplay of social forces which shape its development together with the power play of different groups that have a vested interest in its advancement. In posing a similar question regarding the relationship between theory and action research inquiry, Winter (1997) commented that the personal, practical question is also a political, institutional, and cultural one. As a point of departure it appears appropriate to consider the broad environment within which nursing is evolving.

On a world platform twentieth century societal challenges include shifting demographics, environmental development, and changes in lifestyle, together with a market economy which embraces both cost control and regulation. The recent Irish strategy for the re-orientation of the healthcare system argued for broad changes across health and personal social services (Department of Health, 1994). The underlying concepts of health and social gain influenced all aspects of the strategy and reflected the visionary goals articulated in the World Health Organisation's Targets for Health (WHO, 1985). These developments represented far-reaching challenges for nursing around the world. In reflecting these societal and world trends An Bord Altranais (Irish

Nursing Board) (1994a) illustrated the following influences on the changing role of nursing:

- complex influences
- demographic and epidemiological factors
- Information Technology
- biomedical and psycho-social knowledge

In the last quarter of this century nursing in Ireland has recognised that the increasingly complex nature of health care demands more than apprenticeship training. The *Report of the Commission on Nursing* (Department of Health and Children 1998: 5.9, 5.22) recommended an overhaul of the current system of training for nurses which will culminate in the establishment of an undergraduate programme in the year 2002. While these events are welcomed, however, acknowledgement should be given that control of nursing practice by nurses is central to the profession's ability to continue to define itself and deliver the unique service of caring offered to society.

Nursing consequently is witnessing significant changes in the relationship between practice and education. Much educational reform is reflected in the process of affiliation with institutes of higher education. This is apparent in changing accreditation arrangements, changing organisational structures, together with the changing shape and content of nursing curricula. During the process of this change, third level institutes have the potential to replace hospitals as the location of professional knowledge. It is worth noting that in the process of change the development of nursing knowledge is being strongly influenced by the norms and values of institutes of higher education. It is also not beyond the realm of possibility that the socialisation of knowledge in this equation has the potential to occur at the expense of needs identified within the arena of practice. Indeed it can be argued that practical knowledge has the potential to become delegitimised in the ensuing relationship. A professional discipline is a branch of learning, which is concerned not only with the development of knowledge, but also with the actual implementation of knowledge in practice (Donaldson and Crowley, 1978). Commitment to the development of knowledge is interrelated with a social mandate to provide a particular service to society. From this perspective Cervero (1992) argues for reclaiming practical knowledge as a legitimate and worthwhile part of professional knowing. In an attempt to redress the situation Winter (1998) has advanced action research as a mechanism for decentralising the production of knowledge, and removing the monopoly of universities, governments, and scientific research establishments, thereby giving a voice to practitioners and community. This is what makes action research crucially important.

The issue

Nursing as an activity is unique in assisting individuals to cope with and adapt to life experiences. The value of much knowledge in nursing might be justified by its usefulness in understanding human experience. This is why nursing represents a peculiar unity of theoretical knowledge and practical know how within the domain of modern science. Expertise in nursing exists when the nurse has developed the ability to use appropriate nursing knowledge and skilled judgement in the delivery of patient care. The ability requires not only the use of technical knowledge but also the development of an intellectual capacity to contextualise and apply this knowledge in diverse practice settings. Although this form of knowledge may not be directly observable or measurable, the skill component may be communicated as in, for example, active listening skills displayed in an empathetic manner. Despite awareness in nursing of the need for a unique body of knowledge, there is no conclusive evidence that comprehensively describes the knowledge required to conduct the business of nursing. If one goal of nurse education is to encourage factors which enable the development of practical knowledge, then the discovery of personal meanings and strategies which enable individuals to construct their own knowledge in self-enhancing ways must be considered paramount. The following case study attempts to illustrate the dilemma facing nurse educationalists and offers action research as a promising approach for exploring and negotiating this transition.

A case study

The setting for the study was one particular School of Nursing in Southern Ireland. The School offers an eighteen-month post-registration programme of studies in mental handicap nursing. The course curriculum has been developed in accordance with the Rules and Criteria for Training Student Nurses (An Bord Altranais, 1994b). These regulations stipulate the duration, structure and content of both theoretical and practical components of the course. The rules allow six weeks, which are unspecified during the eighteen-month programme, which can be interpreted and utilised as considered appropriate by local schools of nursing. Individual schools also have a degree of autonomy in developing the process of courses, that is, methods of teaching and learning to be employed. In determining how the period of time could be developed it is worth noting that all student nurses must successfully complete a final summative examination, which is both administered and assessed by An Bord Altranais.

The initial idea for this project arose from the need to develop and identify the manner in which the six unspecified weeks could be used within the constraints of a professional curriculum. Action research was considered an appropriate methodology within which to consider the issue. Interest in action research has gained momentum in nursing and nurse education as reflected in the plethora of publications in the last decade (East and Robinson, 1993; Meyer, 1993; Greenwood, 1994; Sparrow and Robinson, 1994; Hart and Bond, 1996; Ramussen, 1997; Soltis Jarrett, 1997; Lindsey, Shields and Stajduhar, 1999). Hart (1996) attributes the popularity of action research to its affinity with nursing when the latter is defined as a social process essentially concerned with people and their actions and interactions, and also as possessing a discrete knowledge base rooted in humanistic values. The interest appears to be part of a wider critique of positivism on a number of grounds including the inability of positivism to embrace the social context in which people construct meaning together and its treatment of human beings as passive subjects. The popularity of action research also rests on the premise that the primary role of nursing is to assist the curative properties of nature; therefore nurses need pragmatic modes of inquiry. Another strength of action research is its conceptualisation as a cyclical process. This fits with a quest for perpetual development, built into the idea of professionalism and programmes designed to foster the development of professional practitioners.

The aims of this study were to explore post-registration student nurses' understanding of self-direction and to link this with the process of curriculum development. To meet these aims, it was considered appropriate to employ Kurt Lewin's (1946) model of action research as interpreted by Elliott (1991). The sample consisted of fifteen post registration student nurses currently participating in a single nursing course. During the reconnaissance phase of the cycle, data was collected in three phases as depicted in figure 1.

Data collection Phase 1	Data collection Phase 2	Data collection Phase 3
Problem solving exercise	Focused interviewing	Analytic memos

Figure 1: Methods of data collection

Use of the problem solving technique required students to articulate existing beliefs and share views to help them arrive at what Belenky *et al.* (1986) called constructed knowing. McKernan (1994) suggests that as an action research strategy, it helps elicit alternatives in the form of value choices and subsequent examination of these choices and their consequences for behaviour and action. I wrote a question on a flip chart and invited responses, and all responses were recorded unconditionally. Twenty suggestions emerged from the strategy as depicted in figure 2.

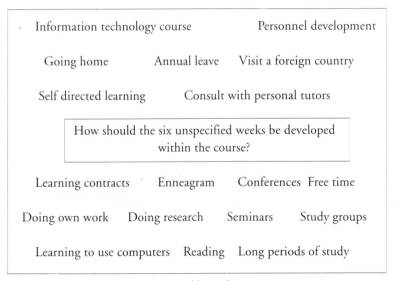

Figure 2: Problem solving exercise

To prevent selecting my own ideas I asked participants to generate solution criteria through the process of internal discussion (Figure 3). McKernan (op. cit.) argues that this is an appropriate way to evaluate ideas generated. The exercise seemed to prompt open minded inquiry and democratic exploration congruent with the ideology of action research.

1 Comply with Rules and Criteria for the Education and Training of Student Nurses (An Bord Altranais, 1994b)
2 Generated by students
3 Congruent with organisational ethos
4 Fit with schedule of clinical placements
5 Acceptable in terms of contract of employment
6 Relevant to professional development

Figure 3: Solution criteria generated

Participants then selected and rank ordered solutions in accordance with solution criteria as illustrated in figure 4.

---

1   Week one Thursday and Friday off (remaining weeks one day off)

2   Two half days per week

3   Full day off each week (Friday)

4   Week one Thursday and Friday off, remaining weeks two half days off

5   One full week off consecutively

Figure 4: Rank ordered solutions

The reasons for identified solutions were:

1   Additional free study time would promote the assimilation of current information.
2   Preference for long study periods.
3   Some students prefer to study in their own environment.
4   More time needed to use external libraries.
5   Additional study time would help to boost morale, self confidence and interest.
6   It would make more time available for students to liaise with personal tutors.
7   The concepts currently being presented are new and difficult.
8   We need more time to ourselves to sort out 'what is what'.

Brief thematic analysis of the participants' solutions and reasons revealed 'need for time' as a central structured unit of data. I then asked participants to verify the issue, and all agreed that the need for time to engage in self-direction should be central to curriculum development. The process of checking the findings with participants strengthened the credibility of the findings, as it was a measure of whether or not participants recognised the experience as their own based on the data. Self directed time was incorporated into the weekly timetable for the duration of the course.

The second phase of data collection aimed to elucidate the participants' understanding of self-direction through the process of 15 informal interviews. The role of interviewer in a study of this nature is fraught with complexity. Being in daily contact with the participants both as principal tutor and teacher made it inappropriate for me to attempt to develop an alternative role identity. I also believe that this would have been contradictory to the collaborative nature of action research. In reflecting on the dilemma it could be concluded that I could not, realistically speaking, avoid influencing the conversations. My role may have been seen as co-authoring the findings which resulted from the interviews. Data obtained from these interviews were analysed using the constant comparative method as described by Strauss and Corbin (1990). Broad categories identified in the first interviews were subsequently expanded. Reduction of the data generated three tentative core conceptual categories, and each tentative core category comprised a number of higher order categories as demonstrated in Table 1.

Analytic memos were simply notes which I kept to organise my thoughts on a cycle of action research. I used them to provide a framework which could illuminate the type of data needed at each stage of the cycle. They acted as a vehicle for bringing together readings on action research, self-directed nursing knowledge, and information gathered throughout the research process.

Collaboration between researcher and practitioner in a spirit of reciprocal respect and influence is central to an action research approach. I presented the findings of the study to the participants by outlining the three tentative core categories and the relevant supporting higher order categories in each instance. I invited participants to confer in order to prioritise the findings of the study in accordance with direct need. The participants returned the need for a module of study on information technology as a resource necessary to support the continued development of self-direction within the current context. Pursuing this mode of action fits with McNiff's (1988) contention that by making participants more aware and critical of practice, open to the process of change and improvement, theories emerge together with rationales which allow for reasoned justification and the development of professional knowledge.

Table 1: The findings

Tentative core categories	Higher order categories
Expression for the benefits of self	The benefits to individuals in terms of content explored The benefits to individuals in terms of constructing own knowledge
Expressed need for resources	The need for time The need for computers The need for library facilities The need for space
Self-direction as a transitional dynamic	Difficulty in adjusting to self-direction Foundation as a necessity Direction as a necessity The shift in direction

Reflection on action

As the boundaries of action research remain undefined, the criteria for judging the quality of such studies becomes elusive. In considering the boundaries of this study I think there is a need to embrace the notion of positionality or standpoint epistemology described by theorists such as hooks (1994) and Lincoln (1995). Lincoln's (1995) post-structural, postmodern argument is that texts are always partial and incomplete, and socially, culturally, historically, racially and sexually located; they can therefore never represent any truth except those truths that exhibit the same characteristics. In essence this research engaged both students and educators in a process which became mutually inclusive in challenging conventional notions of education. The work emulates the post-structuralist shift in focus from reliance on all embracing theories to positions of discourse, contestation and local action thereby responding to exciting opportunities. The work also seems to mirror Winter's (1998) conception of action research as a means of seeking one's own voice, a voice with which to speak one's experience and one's ability to learn from that experience.

Critics of action research could argue that the current investigation resulted in a study of the management of change. Action research however differs from change theory in that it utilises principles of change theory to effect change in a system while at the same time systematically investigating the process, and results as a form of scientific inquiry. If one accepts Sykes' (1987) contention that research is an attempt to discover new or collate old facts by critical investigation, then this study by its very nature must be considered research. Moller (1998) has argued that the scientific status of action research is characterised by confusion and disagreement. The author discriminates between action research identified as professional work and action research as a research strategy. The former is best described as critical inquiry or action learning. In many respects the process encapsulates Freire's (1970) ideology of presenting back to people in a reasonable form what they are looking for in a confused manner. I view the study as the beginnings of a more comprehensive action research project to explore and build on self-direction as a key construct in knowing nursing.

Throughout the last fifty years action research as a facet of the interpretative paradigm has enjoyed various levels of acceptability. In some instances the approach has been criticised for not being scientific enough to be labelled research. This is compounded by the fact that it deals principally with local problems thereby lacking the breath necessary to ensure generalisability in the short term. Contradictory explanations emerging from different studies can be problematic for practitioners who require unambiguous answers to pragmatic problems. This debate is countenanced by the idea that such an approach is capable of offering explanations, as in this instance, which have a degree of ecological validity.

The wider debate

Taylor (1994) contended that the inability of nursing to define its knowledge base is in part related to its inability to decide on the central essence or being of nursing. Because we don't have an agreed meaning of nursing the developing body of nursing knowledge is quite vulnerable to the shifting tides of information accumulation. De Silva *et al.* (1995) crystallise the issue by illustrating Plato's belief that people cannot understand the world around them without understanding what it is they know and, more importantly, without understanding how the things they know are interrelated. An alternative approach to characterising the knowledge base for a profession is to ascertain the personal knowledge of working professionals. Consequently the knowledge question becomes a question of meaning. How do I find meaning in what I know? The central tenet at this point is to suggest that a philosophical shift from trying to define a knowledge base for nursing to trying to embrace a method capable of capturing the meaning of being in nursing may represent one way forward in terms of articulating the process of knowledge construction to be included in curricula.

Future challenges

Taylor (1994) argued that throughout history knowledge generation has undergone changes which have been grouped into ways of knowing. The value of exploring ways of knowing is to present a context within which to judge the appropriateness of nursing knowledge. Gaining an insight into the process of knowing will not enlarge the body of factual knowledge in nursing. However it will serve to focus critical attention on what it means to know, and what kinds of knowledge are valid for inclusion in nursing curricula. Clearly it is only through the examination of current belief structures that both practitioners and educationalists can search collaboratively for a unique body of nursing knowledge.

There are challenges in this debate. The political challenge is central. I have argued for the democratisation of nursing knowledge. This approach appears in some respects to focus on maximising individual differences in an attempt to build communities of knowers. As such it makes a prior assumption regarding the relatively harmonious nature of these differences. Inherent in this challenge is an appreciation of the interconnectedness of knowledge and power. This requires a complex understanding of the nature of power and its potential impact on promoting practice sites as a focus for knowledge production. Reorienting the derivation and organisation of knowledge from practice gives rise to user-derived knowledge, much of it tacit in nature, which has the potential to threaten the dominant authority of higher education. This is particularly so since tacit knowledge has not previously been accorded the status of scientific knowledge. The dominant paradigm is extremely powerful in determining the nature of what counts as knowledge, how it is generated, and how it is disseminated, as well as the underlying beliefs which influence such decisions. Humanistic analysis therefore must attempt to address the dynamics of organisational relationships within specific socio-political contexts. Walker (1997) has pointed out that nursing has neither in the past nor in the present day lacked philosophers. But has nursing had enough skilled engineers of change? And have those engineers, while focused on transformation, engaged in dialogue with the philosophers of nursing?

The second challenge relates to the epistemological basis of nursing. In this forum reality exists as multiple, sometimes conflicting mental constructions of everyday work experience that are situation and context determined. Practitioners respond to their environment, as they perceive it to be. Knowledge is constructed which is not true or false but instead represents a viable understanding of experience in practice. The essential elements of theoretical pluralism and interpretative stance permeate the process. The discipline and profession of nursing then combine not to construct the application of knowledge to practice, but rather to question the legitimacy and effectiveness of nursing work within the context of an increasingly diverse and rapidly changing health care arena. By presenting the experience of nursing as the prime generator of nursing knowledge, knowledge is seen to emerge in and from practice. Ultimately practice becomes the architect of authentic nursing knowledge. This represents a key challenge, as deference to externally validated knowledge has been part of the tradition of nursing.

The third task is to consider the moral agenda in relation to knowledge generation. Pivotal issues include What constitutes knowledge? Who controls it and how? In this instance, rather than rationalising the case for tacit knowledge as the cornerstone of professional practice, the challenge becomes one of why this should be the case. At the heart of this challenge is the social mandate attached to any profession. In pursuing this position the Marxist question needs to be posed: To whom the good? A science of nursing has been a long-standing preoccupation with the profession. Indeed, few occupations become so obsessed with this debate as those who doubt their position in the first place. The idea of advocating craft knowledge as a vehicle for improving patient welfare warrants novel and innovative enquiry into the impact of that knowledge. In the development of this knowledge there will also be a need to ensure that its character is strong enough to handle the ethical paradox inherent in fulfilling a social contract of care, while at the same time operating within a performance outcome-oriented public management ideology. To this end there is need to construct a body of evidence to illustrate the effectiveness of knowledge while at the same time capturing the essence of that practice as it is lived. To have currency, this knowledge will require full expression in the language of certainty rather than emotion.

Conclusion

Restructuring nursing knowledge from this new world view challenges practitioners and educators to advance nursing as a human science from a standpoint that addresses the study of human experience as it is lived. Transformation through evolution will occur as the profession seeks to envision and espouse new philosophical perspectives, in an attempt to articulate ways in which practitioners and students of nursing can construct knowledge within the context of a practice discipline. By encouraging a critical analysis of the nature of knowledge and offering alternative paradigms for the development of that knowledge we may aid the development of a new, more personal and humanistic nursing science for the future.

References

An Bord Altranais (1994a) *The Future of Nurse Education and Training in Ireland.* Dublin, An Bord Altranais.

An Bord Altranais (1994b) *Rules for the Education and Training of Student Nurses.* Dublin, An Bord Altranais.

Belenky, M., Clinchy, B., Goldberger, N. and Tarule, J. (1986) *Women's Ways of Knowing: The development of self, voice and mind.* New York, Basic Books.

Cervero, R.M. (1992) 'Professional Practice, Learning and Continuing Education: An integrated perspective' in *International Journal of Lifelong Education,* Vol. 1, No. 2.

Department of Health (1994) *Shaping a Healthier Future: A strategy for effective health care in the 1990s.* Dublin, Department of Health.

Department of Health and Children (1998) *Report of the Commission on Nursing: A blueprint for the future.* Dublin, Stationery Office.

De Silva, M., Sorell, J. and Sorell, C. (1995) 'From Carpers Patterns of Knowing to Ways of Being: An ontological philosophical shift in nursing' in *Advanced Nursing Science,* Vol. 18, No. 1, pp. 113–120.

Donaldson, S.K. and Crowley, D.M. (1978) 'The Discipline of Nursing' in *Nursing Outlook,* 26, pp. 113–120.

East, L. and Robinson, J. (1993) 'Attitude Problem' in *Nursing Times,* Vol. 89, No. 48, pp. 42–43.

Elliott, J. (1991) *Action Research for Educational Change.* Milton Keynes, Open University Press.

Freire, P. (1970) *Pedagogy of the Oppressed: Cultural action for freedom.* Massachusetts, Centre for the Study of Social Change.

Greenwood, J. (1994) 'Action Research: A Few Details, A Caution and Something New' in *Journal of Advanced Nursing,* 20, pp. 13–18.

Hart, E. (1996) 'Action Research as a Professionalising Strategy: Issues and dilemmas' in *Journal of Advanced Nursing,* 23, pp. 454–461.

Hart, E. and Bond, M. (1996) 'Making Sense of Action Research Through the Use of a Typology' in *Journal of Advanced Nursing,* 23, pp. 152–159.

hooks, b. (1994) *Outlaw Culture: Resisting representations.* New York, Routledge.

Lincoln, Y. (1995) 'Emerging Criteria for Quality in Qualitative and Interpretive Research' in *Qualitative Inquiry,* Vol. 1, No. 3, pp. 275–289.

Lindsey, E., Shields, L. and Stajduhar, K. (1999) 'Creating Effective Nursing Partnerships: Relating community development to participatory action research' in *Journal of Advanced Nursing,* Vol. 29, No. 5, pp. 1238–1245.

McKernan, J. (1994) *Curriculum Action Research: A handbook of methods and resources for the reflective practitioner.*. London, Kogan Page.

McNiff, J. (1988) *Action Research: Principles and Practice.* London, Routledge.

Meyer, J. E. (1993) 'New Paradigm Research in Practice: The trials and tribulations of action research' in *Journal of Advanced Nursing*, 18, pp. 1066–1072.

Moller, J. (1998) 'Action with Principals: Gain, strain and dilemmas' in *Educational Action Research*, Vol. 6, No. 1, pp. 69–80.

Naisbitt, J. and Aburdene, P. (1990) *Ten New Directions for the 1990s Megatrends 2000.* New York, William Morrow.

Ramussen, S. (1997) 'Action Research as Authentic Methodology for the Study of Nursing' in S. Thorne and V.E. Hayes (eds) *Nursing Praxis.* California, Sage.

Soltis-Jarrett, V. (1997) 'The Facilitator in Participatory Action Research: Les raisons d'etre' in *Advances in Nursing Science*, Vol. 20, No. 2, pp. 45–54.

Sparrow, J. and Robinson, J. (1994) 'Action Research: An appropriate design for nursing research' in *Educational Action Research*, Vol. 2, No. 3, pp. 347–356.

Strauss, A. and Corbin, S. (1990) *Basics of Qualitative Research.* Newbury Park CA, Sage.

Sykes, J. (ed.) (1987) *The Concise Oxford Dictionary.* Oxford, Oxford University Press.

Taylor, B. (1994) *Being Human: Ordinariness in Nursing.* London, Churchill Livingstone.

Walker, L., (1997) 'Challenge of Creating Impact: Linking knowledge to practice outcomes.' Conference Proceedings, Knowledge Impact Conference 11. Chestnut Hill, Massachusetts, Boston College School of Nursing.

Winter, T. (1997) 'Action Research, Universities and "Theory".' (A revised and abridged version of a talk originally presented at the Annual CARN Conference, 1997). Available on http://www.uea.ac.uk/care/carn/conf97.

Winter, R. (1998) 'Finding a Voice – Thinking with Others: a conception of action research' in *Educational Action Research*, Vol. 6, No. 1, pp. 53–68.

World Health Organisation (1985) *Targets for Health for All by the Year 2000.* Copenhagen, Regional Office.

Chapter 6

Action research: a means of changing and improving the clinical learning environment

Agnes Higgins

'It isn't the changes that do you in, it's the transitions'
(Bridges, 1998).

Introduction

Nursing is a practice-based profession, with clinical learning activities forming the heart of nursing's professional programme of study. It is through clinical experience that students learn to integrate theory and practice (McCrea *et al.*, 1994), discover the artistic aspect of nursing knowledge (Davies, 1993), and learn about the process of caring and the value system associated with practice (Dotan *et al.*, 1986). An Bord Altranais (1994) states that 'the major goal of nurse education and training is to help students develop the competencies necessary for effective practice' (p. 18). Consequently, the quality of the clinical learning environment is fundamental to achieving the desired aims of educational programmes. As a means of generating nursing knowledge and improving practice, action research creates unlimited opportunities for nurses.

This chapter focuses on an action research study undertaken in one organisation with a view to improving the quality of the clinical learning environment for student nurses. The study took place against the background of the review of nurse education and training (An Bord

Altranais, 1994) and the upgrading and accreditation of the preregistration psychiatric nursing programme to diploma level.

The focus of the chapter is on the process involved in bringing about the change and some of the issues that action research as a change process raises for practitioners. A more detailed description and account of the outcomes of the study are to be found in Higgins (1997).

The clinical learning environment

Over the years the clinical learning environment has been the centre of numerous studies, with various researchers attempting to identify factors that influence and impinge on student learning. Research suggests that 'good learning environments' are characterised by frequent contact and supervision by qualified staff (Lewin and Leach, 1982; Reid, 1985; Shailer, 1990); democratic and open communication between staff and students (Marson, 1982; Reid, 1985); and the provision of varied and frequent learning opportunities (Shailer, 1990; Savage, 1996). Treating students as learners as opposed to workers (Davies, 1993; Nehring, 1990) and challenging students to be independent and assume responsibility within their level of capabilities are also indicators of 'good' learning environments (Windsor, 1987; Nehring, 1990).

Despite this research the reality of everyday practice appears to be far removed from the ideal. Research both in Ireland and England suggests that in most cases students spend most of their time unsupervised (Jacka and Lewin, 1987), with the primary sources of direction and feedback being other students (Campbell *et al.*, 1994). Research also suggests that the hidden curriculum dominates students' learning, with students quickly internalising that 'getting the work done' takes precedence over learning (Fretwell, 1982; Melia, 1983; Treacy, 1987). Research findings on the provision of ward learning opportunities such as tutorials, hand over reports and attending multi-disciplinary meetings are equally unfavourable (Wheeler, 1988; Owen, 1993; Savage, 1996).

In some parts of the organisation where the study was carried out students frequently expressed dissatisfaction with the quality of education, support, supervision and direction given to them in clinical environments. In trying to describe the difficulties, one student said, 'I just walk and keep walking [around the ward] as I don't know what I am supposed to be doing.' Hence the initial aim for the study was to explore the difficulties that nursing staff encountered in educating and supporting students in the clinical area, and collaboratively develop a plan of action that might effect an improvement.

Merits of action research for the context

Despite the fact that research has identified factors which contribute to quality education in the clinical area as far back as the 1980s, they appear to be ignored in practice. There is now a growing body of other research that enumerates the reasons why nurses ignore research findings: either they are not aware of the research, don't understand it, or are unwilling to implement it (Hunt, 1987; Le May *et al.*, 1998; McIntosh, 1995; Staunton and Crotty, 1991). Rolfe (1996) wonders why few academics consider that the problem may not be the practitioners but the inadequacy of theory generated from the positivist research paradigm. This is a paradigm where the researcher is viewed as an expert carrying out research 'on' people with, as the primary objective, the generation of knowledge for its own sake rather than as a means of improving practice. It is a paradigm that gives the impression that if one wishes to improve practice all that is required is to 'twiddle a few knobs' in the research setting (Waterman, 1995), and is a paradigm that fails to acknowledge the social, political, cultural and organisational issues that influence change (Corner, 1991; Clarke, 1995).

A central feature of action research is the rejection of research as an 'esoteric activity indulged in by researchers in isolation from the people they study' (Webb, 1989: 404). Instead, the researcher seeks to empower people by creating a mutually beneficial, collaborative relationship with the participants. Given the importance of exploring the problem in the natural context and allowing interpretations and explanations to come from the people involved as opposed to a prior theory or hypothesis, action research seemed the most appropriate way forward for my study. I also believed that with action research there was a greater chance that the real problem would be diagnosed and in the process the political, organisational and cultural issues that influence change uncovered and addressed, thus resulting in some real change, no matter how small.

I also hoped that the collegial and collaborative approach of action research would enable the complex and unpredictable world of practice to be acknowledged and the values and beliefs of practitioners explored. Schön (1991) contends that people work with two types of theory – espoused theories that are used to explain and justify behaviour, and theories-in-use, which govern actual behaviour. By using an action research approach I hoped that by engaging the practitioners in a 'dialectical critique' they would be enabled to uncover their theories-in-use and espoused theories (Streubert and Carpenter, 1995: 258). For it is only by having brought to consciousness, and clearly articulated and exposed the contradictions between both kinds of theory, that openness to a 'new order' is possible. However, as Greenwood (1994: 17) suggests, peeling the 'causal onion' requires care as people's theories-in-use often serve a self-esteem and self-preservation function in cultures where conformity to 'the norm' is valued.

The final issue relates to the nature of the adult learner and andragogical principles (Knowles, 1984). As the success of the project was largely dependent on the practitioners learning new ways of doing things it was crucial that the practitioners' wealth of personal and professional experience be acknowledged and used as a source of learning. The practice-focused style of action research facilitates this, thus dispelling the myth that those who create theory are of higher status than those who implement it.

Status of the researcher

Rolfe (1996) suggests that the various typologies of action research can be viewed on a continuum. At one end is the traditional approach originally proposed by Lewin (1947). Within this approach the researcher, usually a professional expert from outside an organisation, designs the study, collects and interprets the data, following which recommendations are made to the employing organisation. The researcher does not initiate or carry out the change but supports the change agents who belong to the setting. This is similar to Titchen and Binnie's (1993) outsider model. At the other end of the continuum is participative and co-operative enquiry (Rolfe, 1996) or the insider model (Titchen and Binnie, 1993), where all those involved contribute to the exploration of the problem and possible solutions. In the study my position could be likened to that of an outsider as I worked in the school of nursing and as such was not directly involved in the day-to-day issues of clinical practice. However, by involving people in all stages, I anticipated that a mutual collaborative relationship would develop and that I would gradually move to being an insider.

Data collection

Action researchers set no limits to the methods used to generate data and include both quantitative and qualitative methods. In keeping with the philosophy of action research, and in an attempt to gain an insight into people's different realities and illuminate the issues under investigation, I used a triangulation of the following methods:

- brainstorming exercises
- group discussions
- informal interviews
- formal taped interviews
- questionnaires
- diary

I hoped that the possible deficiencies of any one method would be minimised by the strengths of the others. I would also be able to cross check the findings, with the intention of increasing the credibility and validity of the study.

Data analysis

One of the difficulties with action research is the failure of researchers to provide any theoretical framework to guide the process of data generation and data analysis. While the overriding intention of data gathering in action research is to gain an understanding of the situation and guide subsequent actions, collecting data by interviews and analysing transcripts can be a daunting task in the absence of a theoretical framework to guide the process. As part of this project involved detailed interviews with staff and students regarding their experiences, grounded theory as proposed and described by Glaser (1992) was used to guide data collection and data analysis. Data from the group discussion, informal interviews and qualitative data from the questionnaires was analysed using a simple content analysis. Due to the small sample size (n=14) quantitative data from questionnaires was analysed using simple statistics.

Action research cycles: telling the story

Action research does not proceed in a fixed linear fashion, but is typified by concurrent activities of data collection, reflection, analysis and action. Hence telling the story in a concise and coherent manner without losing sight of the confusion and human dimension that was such a part of the process was a major challenge. Given the open systemic nature of organisations and the diversity of people involved, a variety of issues arose during each cycle that influenced progress and demanded that we return to previous stages. The study involved four major cycles of reflection and action with each cycle incorporating to a greater or lesser extent the following phases:

- entering into dialogue with the staff
- gathering data whereby the researcher and participants act as a research team
- analysing data and feedback to the participants to ensure collective understanding of the data and issues identified
- developing action plans in collaboration with the participants

- implementation of action plans to resolve the issues
- evaluation of action

Entering into dialogue with the staff

In order to gain people's consent and commitment and begin the process of collaboration and partnership a lengthy negotiation was undertaken. As none of the staff had ever participated in an action research study I spent a lot of time explaining what action research was about, resolving anxieties regarding what would happen to the data and reassuring the staff that I was not just checking up on them. As I was asking staff to reflect on their own practice and expose both their strengths and weaknesses, gaining their consent was a major challenge. This difficulty was further compounded by the very nature of action research. Given the fact that the methodology and focus in action research tends to evolve as the process develops it was very difficult to provide people at the outset with a complete description of the research process which left some people a little uncomfortable. The other difficulty with action research is that you are asking people to be critical and reflective of their practice in a context which they may feel is unsafe, and with people who are at different levels in the work hierarchy. Consequently I had to spend time creating an environment where people felt safe and confident to express their opinions. To have moved too quickly in the early stage of data gathering may have resulted in an inaccurate or limited description of the problem.

Gathering data whereby the researcher and participants act as a research team

Initially the focus of data collection was on qualified nurses and students in one clinical area. As the study unfolded throughout the total organisation, other key stakeholders became involved. As stated, data was collected using a variety of methods with the methods employed varying depending on the focus of the issues under investigation.

Analysing data and feedback to the participants

In most cases staff were not involved in completing the data analysis (which was their choice). Once the data was analysed it was fed back to the participants to ensure collective understanding before moving on to the next stage. Analysis of the data resulted in what you could call the development of a local theory. While some of the difficulties identified in creating a quality learning environment had previously been cited in the literature, other context-dependent issues emerged, such as how the culture, work practice and beliefs of individuals contributed to the problem.

Developing action plans in collaboration with the participants

I believe the key to the success of action research is the fact that the complex and unpredictable world of practice must be acknowledged and incorporated into the plans made. While the literature on clinical learning provides us with lists and prescriptions of solutions, in most cases we modified ideas from the literature or developed our own creative solutions that suited our particular context.

Implementation of action plans to resolve the issues

Supporting people through the implementation of the plan and planning for the unforeseen were core aspects of this phase. However, what most writers on action research fail to tell us is how difficult, messy and political this stage is, as it challenges every interpersonal and negotiation skill one has. When I thought I had negotiated my way through the multiple realities and achieved a consensus another reality appeared which required further negotiation. It was also at this stage that the open systemic nature of the organisation came into perspective. Even though I was working with a particular group (nursing staff), changes in their work practices had implications for other groups which also required consideration.

Evaluation of action

An important part of any action research process is the evaluation of actions taken. In this study the evaluations served two major functions. The feedback not only resulted in some changes being made to the original action but also served to increase motivation and commitment to the changes taking place.

Cycle 1

Cycle 1 of the study was undertaken in one unit of the hospital with the aim of exploring the difficulties staff encountered with educating and supporting students in the clinical area. In order to explore the issue and define the problem from the staff's and students' perspectives, I collected data through brainstorming techniques, group discussion and unstructured taped interviews. Analysis of the data clearly revealed that although the staff were committed to education they lacked a co-ordinated and structured system for educating and supporting students. Lack of qualified staff is frequently cited in the literature as a reason for the poor quality in clinical education. Ironically in this study the high ratio of qualified nursing staff to students (16:3) did not work in favour of the students. It appeared that because no one person was assigned responsibility for student education, students were often forgotten. Through the process of collaboration and negotiation with staff a mentorship scheme for student nurses was developed, implemented and evaluated. The mentor was a qualified nurse who was assigned to the student for the purpose of supporting, facilitating and assessing the students' learning during their clinical placement.

Although telling the story is simple, the cycle took approximately nine months. Based on the positive outcomes of this and smug with confidence we moved on to the second cycle.

Cycle 2

The initial aim for cycle 2 was to expand the mentorship scheme to the total organisation. By this time nurse education was in transition with the educational programme being accredited at diploma level. In an attempt to commence the collaborative process on a wider scale a curriculum development group which was no longer active (as it had completed its task two months previously) was reconvened. The decision to reconvene the group was based on a number of factors. The group had previously worked with me on developing part of the diploma curriculum; hence they were familiar with many of the changes occurring in nurse education. More importantly the group consisted of an assistant director of nursing and senior clinical staff who were major stakeholders in the change process. As they were the 'gatekeepers' in the clinical area their involvement was paramount if commitment to the change was to be generated and sustained on a wider scale. I also hoped that by involving them, they would act as both change agents and supporters of the change in their own work areas.

Our initial plan was to develop a series of educational programmes for the total organisation. However after a few weeks working on this plan it became apparent from informal discussions with the junior staff nurses that the context had changed and staff were much more concerned with day to day issues such as how the diploma programme would affect them in terms of status, future promotions, staff shortages and staff replacement. In an attempt to gain a deeper understanding of staff concerns we retraced our steps, returned to reconnaissance and redefined our aim.

Cycle 3

The mentorship scheme was put on hold in order to explore staff's concerns regarding the introduction of the diploma programme. At this time the curriculum development group became co-researchers as they each took responsibility for a particular clinical area and explored staff concerns through the use of group discussion. Engaging in this consultative exercise with the junior staff proved fruitful in many ways. It served to identify the multiple realities that existed within the organisation and highlighted to the group the importance of addressing ourselves not just to the world as we saw it, but also to the world others see. Feedback from the consultative process also provided the group with a detailed list of issues that required exploration and discussion, much of which could have been overlooked. Although some of the issues and questions raised were not directly related to the educational environment for student nurses or the initial problem, we were conscious that staff's concerns needed to be responded to if motivation to the change was to be maintained. Once all the emerging issues were addressed, implementing the action for this cycle of the project was commenced. The action consisted of a series of educational sessions to address staff's concerns which were developed and planned, this time in consultation with the staff. Feedback from the educational sessions was very positive. However, during the course of the workshop a variety of other issues emerged which required further consultation with the staff. The open systemic nature of the project also came into focus at this time, and resulted in the consultation process ceasing, as staff were preoccupied for a period of time with a variety of other national professional issues. This aspect of the project took over four months. Prior to completing the consultative processes on all the issues the next cycle was commenced.

Cycle 4

The focus for this cycle was on the original idea, which was to implement a mentorship scheme in the total organisation. Once again issues in the wider external environment strongly influenced how the collaborative process was initiated and developed. At this time the Department of Health created three new posts within the organisation: a nursing development officer's post and two clinical placement co-ordinator posts. The primary focus of these posts was on the development of clinical practice and co-ordinating student learning in the clinical areas. As these people were to be involved in the clinical area it was important to develop a collaborative relationship with them to ensure that we were working towards a common goal. Hence the remainder of the study was carried out in conjunction with these staff. To advance the aim of developing a mentorship scheme the next action step taken involved consultation with the nursing officers to discuss the proposal and criteria for becoming a mentor. They were all in favour. Following this, each unit where students were going on placement identified members of staff who fulfilled the criteria and who were willing to assume the role of mentor. Once the mentors were identified the process focused on consultation regarding their role and how it related to the clinical placement co-ordinators. All mentors were involved in an educational programme to prepare them for the role. Following implementation through the use of interviews and questionnaires a detailed evaluation of the mentorship scheme was also completed. Despite some difficulties with busy or absent mentors most of the students reported very positive experiences and valued the role the mentor played in creating a challenging, supportive and educational environment. In an attempt to incorporate mentorship as part of the educational ethos of the organisation, a quality standard in line with the organisational model of quality was written and an audit tool developed in consultation with the mentors. Education for staff beyond the first cohort was also organised.

Although I have presented the study in four discrete cycles, in the course of living the project it must be said that the process was much more cyclical, iterative and overlapping and the logic or structure was not as evident. What appeared at the outset to be technically simple proved to be a socially complex process, a process that involved many phases of negotiation, reflection, feedback, recycling plans, coping with multiple realities, micropolitics, frustration and on many occasions, sheer muddle. It could be said that during the course of the study many paths that were not directly related to the primary objective were pursued; however it was only through this process that the multiple realities were revealed. Indeed to have ignored the other agendas and issues could have sabotaged the change process. As McNiff (1988) rightly points out, one of the strengths of action research is that it allows the researcher to address different problems at one time without losing sight of the main issue.

Rigour of the study

Action research has been criticised for trading some aspects of scientific rigour for relevance. Clarke (1992) goes so far as to suggest that the blurring of boundaries between the researcher and participants which is such a part of action research renders it unscientific. If one views rigour from the positivist perspective then this study requires questioning. The small sample size and the confinement to one specific hospital makes any findings both context and participant specific. My own bias indeed may have influenced how the interviews and group discussions were conducted and analysed. There is also the question of whether at an unconscious level I pursued information that confirmed my own view, or as O'Dea (1994) suggests, whether I selected data that facilitated the telling of a more coherent or patterned story. Therefore it is possible that another researcher would have produced different findings. The validity of the findings may have been further reduced by the fact that I was the students' tutor and may have been perceived as the 'critical eye' checking up on staff.

Consequently, fear of repercussions, if anonymity of the mentor was not maintained, may have influenced what students said during the course of their evaluation interviews. Had it been another interviewer the findings may not have been as positive.

Conclusion

Despite having some reservations about the rigour of action research and the credibility of the findings in this study, I believe that action research is a path worth pursuing. As a neophyte discipline, nursing has historically drawn on positivism to guide its research which has resulted in many of the findings being perceived by nurses as being irrelevant to their practice and therefore not implemented. For theory, practice and research to be congruent a critical praxis must emerge. By addressing key issues in the swampy lowlands of practice (Schön, 1991), multiple realities emerged and the emphasis remained not on a search for ultimate truth but on a search for a practical truth which helped people to act 'more intelligently and skilfully' (Elliott, 1991: 69). This is not to suggest that action research is a panacea for all ills and that other forms of research should be abandoned. I believe scientific enquiry should be guided by the problem one wishes to address and each paradigm offers different kinds of insights, all of which are relevant and appropriate. The question is not which is the 'best method' but which is the most appropriate approach given the nature of the phenomenon one wishes to investigate.

References

An Bord Altranais (1994) *The Future of Nurse Education and Training in Ireland.* Dublin, An Bord Altranais.
Bridges, W. (1998) *Managing Transitions: Making the most of change.* London, Nicholas Brealey.
Campbell, I., Larrivee, L., Field, P., Day, R. and Reutter, L. (1994) 'Learning to Nurse in the Clinical Setting' in *Journal of Advanced Nursing*, Vol. 17, No. 2, pp. 243–252.

Clarke, L. (1992) 'Qualitative Research: Meaning and Language' in *Journal of Advanced Nursing*, Vol. 17, No. 2, pp. 243–252.

Clarke, L. (1995) 'Nursing Research: Science, Vision and Telling Stories' in *Journal of Advanced Nursing*, Vol. 21, No. 3. pp. 584–593.

Corner, J. (1991) 'In Search for More Complete Answers to Research Questions. Quantitative versus Qualitative Research Methods: is there a way forward?' in *Journal of Advanced Nursing*, Vol. 16, No. 6, pp. 718–727.

Davies, E. (1993) 'Clinical Role Modelling: Uncovering Hidden Knowledge' in *Journal of Advanced Nursing*, Vol. 18, No. 4, pp. 627–636.

Dotan, M., Krulik, T., Bergman, R., Eckerling, S. and Shatzman, H. (1986) 'Role Models in Nursing' in *Nursing Times*, Vol. 87, No. 7, pp. 55–57.

Elliott, J. (1991) *Action Research for Educational Change*. Milton Keynes, Open University Press.

Fretwell, J. (1982) *Ward Teaching and Learning*. London, Royal College of Nursing.

Glaser, B. (1992) *Emergent versus Forcing Basics of Grounded Theory Analysis*. California, The Sociology Press.

Greenwood, J. (1994) 'Action Research: A few details, a caution and something new' in *Journal of Advanced Nursing*, Vol. 20, No. 1, pp. 13–18.

Higgins, A. (1997) 'Mentorship: A Supportive and Educational Strategy for Student Psychiatric Nurses in the Clinical Environment.' Unpublished Master's thesis, Dublin City University.

Hunt, M. (1987) 'The Process of Translating Research Findings into Nursing Practice' in *Journal of Advanced Nursing*, Vol. 12, No. 1, pp. 101–110.

Jacka, K. and Lewin, D. (1987) 'The Clinical Learning of Student Nurses' *NERU Report No. 6*. London, Nursing Education Research Unit, King's College, University of London.

Knowles, M. (1984) *The Adult Learner: A Neglected Species*. Houston, Gulf Publishing.

LeMay, A., Mulhall, A. and Alexander, C. (1998) 'Bridging the Research-Practice Gap: Exploring the Research Cultures of Practitioners and Managers' in *Journal of Advanced Nursing*, Vol. 28, No. 2, pp. 426–437.

Lewin, K. (1947) in Rolfe, G. (1996) 'Going to Extremes: Action Research, grounded practice and the theory-practice gap in nursing' in *Journal of Advanced Nursing*, Vol. 24, No. 6, pp. 1315–1320.

Lewin, D. and Leach, J. (1982) 'Factors Influencing the Quality of Wards as Learning Environments for Student Nurses' in *International Journal of Nursing Studies*, Vol. 19, No. 3, pp. 125–137.

Marson, S. (1982) 'Ward Sister – Teacher or Facilitator? An Investigation into Behavioural Characteristics of Effective teachers' in Journal of Advanced Nursing, Vol. 7, No. 4, pp. 347–357.

McCrea, J., Thompson, K., Carswell, L. and Whittington, D. (1994) 'Student Midwives' Learning Experiences on the Wards' in *Journal of Clinical Nursing*, Vol. 3, No. 2, pp. 97–102.

McIntosh, J. (1995) 'Barriers to Research Implementation' in *Nurse Researcher*, Vol. 2, No. 4, pp. 83–91.

McNiff, J. (1988) *Action Research: Principles and Practice.* London, Routledge.

Melia, K. (1983) *Learning and Working: the occupational socialisation of nurses.* London, Tavistock.

Nehring, V. (1990) 'Nursing Clinical Teacher Effectiveness Inventory: a replication study of the characteristics of "best" and "worst" clinical teachers as perceived by nursing faculty and students' in *Journal of Advanced Nursing*, Vol. 15, No. 8, pp. 934–940.

O'Dea, N. (1994) 'Pursuing Truth in Narrative Research' in *Journal of Philosophy of Education*, Vol. 28, No. 2, pp. 161–171.

Owen, S. (1993) 'Identifying the Role of the Nurse Teacher in the Clinical Area' in *Journal of Advanced Nursing*, Vol. 18, No. 5, pp. 816–825.

Reid, N. (1985) *Wards in Chancery.* London, Royal College of Nursing.

Rolfe, G. (1996) 'Going to Extremes: Action research, grounded practice and the theory-practice gap in nursing' in *Journal of Advanced Nursing*, Vol. 24, No. 6, pp. 1315–1320.

Savage, E. (1996) 'Student Nurses' Reported Views on the Influence of Staff Nurses in Creating a Ward Learning Environment.' Unpublished Masters thesis, University College Cork.

Schön, D. (1991) *The Reflective Practitioner.* London, Temple Smith.

Shailer, B. (1990) 'Clinical Learning Environment Audit' in *Nurse Education Today*, Vol. 10, No. 3, pp. 220–227.

Staunton, A. and Crotty, M. (1991) 'The Impact of Research on Clinical Practice' in *Senior Nurse*, Vol. 11, No. 6, pp. 16–19.

Streubert, H. and Carpenter, R. (1995) *Qualitative Research in Nursing: Advancing the Humanistic Imperative.* Philadelphia, Lippincott Company.

Titchen, A. and Binnie, A. (1993) 'Research Partnership: Collaborative Action Research in Nursing' in *Journal of Advanced Nursing*, Vol. 18, No. 6, pp. 858–865.

Treacy, M. (1987) 'In the Pipeline: A Qualitative Study of General Nurse Training with Special Reference to Nurses' Role in Health Education.' Unpublished PhD thesis, University of London.

Waterman, J. (1995) 'Dinstinguishing Between Traditional and Action Research' in *Nurse Researcher*, Vol. 2, No. 3, pp. 14–23.

Webb, C. (1989) 'Action Research: Philosophy, Methods and Personal Experience' in *Journal of Advanced Nursing*, Vol. 14, No. 5, pp. 403–410.

Wheeler, H. (1988) 'Evaluating Study Modules in Basic Nurse Education Programmes' in *Nurse Education Today*, Vol. 8, No. 4, pp. 77–84.

Windsor, A. (1987) 'Nursing Students' Perceptions of Clinical Experience' in *Journal of Nursing Education*, Vol. 26, No. 4, pp. 150–154.

Chapter 7

Action research, multiple intelligences, and the politics of educational knowledge

Ann FitzGibbon and Anne Fleischmann

The focus of this chapter is the potential link between the theories of multiple intelligences and action research with reference to the politics of educational knowledge. We describe our collaboration over three years in the areas of curriculum development and teacher education and our efforts to encourage students' and teachers' experiences of, and reflections on, their separate and collective practices.

We suggest that teaching methodologies using action research and multiple intelligences frameworks should be located within the context of the politics of educational knowledge, since both address issues to do with the production and ownership of knowledge, albeit in different ways. One tradition of action research – emancipatory action research – is closely connected to critical social science, which itself addresses issues of the relationship between knowledge, power and control, and holds a belief in the individual's central role in social transformation. However, action research methodologies do not of themselves ensure outcomes of emancipation (see, for example, Gore and Zeichner, 1995). In a multiple intelligences approach, the need for individuals to claim responsibility for their own learning is central; a key purpose of teaching is to enable individuals to come to know their own strengths and modes of learning, with the aim of helping them to become self-directed learners. Emphasis is placed on the individualisation and democratisation of education.

A teacher preparing to use a multiple intelligences approach as a teaching strategy is in a transitional phase, moving from one model of teaching to another which focuses centrally on student learning. This requires the teacher to re-examine preconceptions and beliefs regarding concepts of intelligence, and issues of power and control in classrooms. Juxtaposing action research and multiple intelligences approaches in the context of the politics of knowledge permits exploration, among other possibilities, of the nature of power and transitions in the areas of teacher education and classroom practice.

There is much reference in the literature to how action research and multiple intelligences approaches lend themselves to teacher development. For example, McNiff (1988) considers that action research affords an opportunity for teachers to become uniquely involved in their own practice, to enhance their professionalism, and to provide justification for their work. Cohen and Manion (1994: 188–189) recommend action research on the grounds that teachers would be equipped '... with new skills and methods, ... analytical powers ... self awareness', a point echoed by Gore and Zeichner (1995: 204) who further link such practice to teacher empowerment, stating that '[w]ith action research there is a clear recognition of teachers as knowledge producers and of the need for teaching to be put back in the hands of teachers' (p. 205). They also sound notes of caution, however, warning that the potential for genuine teacher development can be undermined when, for example, action research focuses on helping teachers better to reproduce university-sponsored research practices at the expense of teachers' identifying their own theories; and (b) 'means and end thinking', thus limiting teachers' reflection to technical questions, ignoring the wider social and institutional contexts of teaching.

Campbell *et al.* (1996), in their review of the literature of multiple intelligences, report that learning to use, and using a multiple intelligences approach, result in teacher development. Reference is made again to the changing role of the teacher in a multiple intelligences classroom, such change being identified as the increasingly facilitative nature of the role of the teacher, and the recognition that production of knowledge is not the prerogative of the teacher solely.

In our professional work, we aim to include action research and multiple intelligences approaches in any courses that we teach, since we recognise, and hope, that courses involving these approaches would have implications for practice beyond the boundaries of any one teacher's classroom. Within our courses and presentations, therefore, we aim to present the concept of multiple intelligences using an action research approach. Our work is informed by the deeply held belief that in presenting the concepts of multiple intelligences, our approach must reflect those concepts, and therefore we suggest that each intelligence should be used as a frame for exploring a concept. We aim to use, for example, methodologies using imagery (reflective of spatial-visual intelligence) and rap (reflective of musical intelligence) when exploring the visual and musical intelligences.

We present the theories as a possible approach for teachers and students and are interested in the response of participants. Such an opportunity arose when we presented our work at the Action Research Conference whose proceedings this book documents. In that session we attempted to demonstrate the practical realities of both concepts, by encouraging participants to reflect on the concepts from their own immediate experience of engaging with these ideas as an initial stage of an action research process. We also invited the audience to assess their experience at the end of the session, and we refer to this data later in the chapter as an indication that the session had value for the professional learning of participants. The methodology we used during this session was:

- an examination of the present situation – also called reconnaissance (Elliott, 1991; Lewin, 1947);
- the experience of learning through a selected intelligence;
- reflection on and evaluation of this experience;
- action planning for the future.

Our understanding of theories of action research and multiple intelligences

It would be helpful here to give a brief account of how we understand theories of action research and multiple intelligences.

Action research

The origin of action research is usually attributed to Kurt Lewin who set out his first ideas on action research in 1934 and stated the basic principle of 'no action without research, no research without action' in the 1940s (see Adelman, 1993: 8). Although, as indicated earlier, different traditions have developed within action research, most researchers would accept that it includes concepts of developmental stages, reflexivity, and practitioners as researchers; as well as an assumption that the process should lead to decisions and actions (Lewin, 1947; Corey, 1953; Calhoun, 1994; Cohen and Manion, 1994). There also seems to be an emerging consensus about the purposes of educational action research in terms of personal and social renewal leading to organisational change. Calhoun (1994), for example, recognises three scenarios for the use of action research in an educational setting, namely individual teacher research, collaborative action research, and school wide action research. Similarly, Sagor (1998), summing up his overview of action research literature, states that '... teacher-directed action research can be divided into three separate, yet overlapping, categories: action research for *teacher development ... school development ... organisation development ...*' (p.171; emphasis in original). Although researchers recognise that the same process tends to be used within varied settings, the emphasis on the detail of basic concerns of action research is often different.

Multiple intelligences

In *Frames of Mind*, Gardner (1983) describes the work that led him to suggest that all human beings are capable of at least eight different ways of knowing the world. These he rather provocatively called intelligences, a point he recognised at a recent conference in Birmingham, UK (O'Sullivan, 1998). He did not claim that the concept of multiple intelligences was new, but rather that it was one whose time had come. People may have a different range of intelligences, and also different strengths in any one intelligence. Gardner defines intelligence as a

> biological and psychological potential; that potential is capable of being realised to a greater or lesser extent as a consequence of the experiential, cultural and motivational factors that affect a person (Gardner, 1995: 202).

Social contexts are thus taken into account. Intelligence is a constructed concept, as Sternberg points out (1985: 336): '... a concept we invented in order to provide a useful way of evaluating, and occasionally, ordering people in terms of their performance on tasks and in situations that are valued by the culture ...'. Berliner and Biddle (1995: 44) agree: '... intelligence is a hypothetical entity and cannot be observed directly ... it is convenient to think that intelligence exists but we cannot be certain that it actually exists...'.

Gardner developed a set of criteria to characterise what he describes as an intelligence. Initially he codified seven, based on research data derived from a number of sources. These seven intelligences are:

- Linguistic: sensitivity to the sounds, structure, meanings and functions of words and language.
- Logical-mathematical: sensitivity to, and capacity to discern, logical or numerical patterns; ability to handle long chains of reasoning.
- Spatial: capacity to perceive the visual-spatial world accurately and to perform transformations on one's initial perceptions.
- Bodily-kinaesthetic: ability to control one's own body movements and to handle objects skilfully.
- Musical: ability to produce and appreciate rhythm, pitch and timbre; appreciation of the forms of musical expressiveness.
- Interpersonal: capacity to discern and respond appropriately to the moods, temperaments, motivations, and desires of other people.
- Intrapersonal: access to one's own feeling life and the ability to discriminate among one's own emotions, knowledge of one's own strengths and weaknesses.

(adapted from Armstrong, 1994: 6)

He introduced the eighth intelligence in later writings – naturalist intelligence, described as:

> a capacity to discern and respond appropriately to nature in its widest definition; to appreciate all forms of nature; to have an instinctive understanding and knowledge of nature (Hoerr, 1997: 2)

Another possibility now being considered is spiritual intelligence. At the Howard Gardner Summer Conference in Boston, July 1997, he described it as being '"the eighth and a half", not yet the ninth', and indicated that he was considering calling it 'existential intelligence'.

Gardner argued (1993) that the existence of multiple intelligences challenged the education system in the United States, which he perceived as heavily biased towards only linguistic and logical-mathematical intelligences. The education system also assumed that everyone learned in the same way, and that a uniform, universal measure sufficed to test students' learning. The same bias appears to be present in many educational systems today, including the system in Ireland. This point is increasingly recognised by some stakeholders; for example, a report to ascertain the views of parents on the points system based on the current traditional Leaving Certificate, summarised in a recent *Irish Times* supplement, indicated that the parents consulted were overwhelmingly of the opinion that the Leaving Certificate 'does not take into account other intelligences and natural aptitudes [than logical-linguistic]' (O'Loughlin, 1998: 2).

Gardner's ideas were developed for educational uses by several authors (for example, Armstrong, 1994; Lazaer, 1994, 1999), as well as colleagues at Harvard (for example, the Zero/Spectrum Project: Chen *et al.*, 1998). Issues concerning possible changes in the dynamics of the classroom, the role of the teacher, and the nature of knowledge are mentioned in passing in these publications, rather than analysed in depth. However, both Campbell *et al.* (1996) and Chen *et al.* (1998) record the self-development of teachers and changes in social dynamics in classrooms as a result of engaging in multiple intelligences approaches.

There are far-reaching implications for teachers in introducing multiple intelligences frameworks to the classroom. Lynch (1992: 146) captures these well in her review of the value of Gardner's theory for teachers:

> For educationalists with an interest in equality, Gardner's theory offers a new insight into how the system persistently produces failure. It shows that, in terms of curricula and syllabuses, our schools are biased in favour of those schooled in the canons of mathematical logic and practised in the field of language. It challenges us, therefore, to think of new ways in which we can recognise all human intelligences.

Gardner is very clear about the parameters of his theory:

> ... it is not the kind of theory that is going to be proved correct or incorrect by a single study or even a programmatic set of studies from a single experimental laboratory ... it is based on empirical findings and, like Darwin's synthesis [on evolution] ... will survive or be overthrown on the basis of future reflection on, and reorganisation of, the same and new bodies of data (Gardner, 1994: 577).

So it appears that the active encouragement of the use of action research as a frame for introducing the concept of multiple intelligences is in keeping with Gardner's philosophy, as the possibility exists for many small scale studies which could then be explored using a form of meta-analysis.

Gardner's theory has been criticised on a number of counts. Levin (1994), for example, calls for the theory to be tried out under everyday conditions (which is a real possibility when linked with action research). Levin is especially disappointed in the image of the school of the future as described in *Multiple Intelligences* (Gardner, 1993), in that the roles of adults, and not children, are spelled out, especially in regard to concepts such as classroom relationships, training, and mechanisms for negotiation. Sternberg's criticism (1990) suggests that Gardner's definition of intelligence is flawed and would be better considered as a talent, a point initially firmly refuted by Gardner (1991). Subsequently, however, Gardner suggested (O'Sullivan, 1998) that, in order to cope with the demands of an increasingly complex society, different cognitive representations are needed by individuals to tune into, for example, the sounds and sights of nature, each of which have their own signing (communicating) system. Such representations, he says, he would previously have termed 'intelligences'.

The debate continues.

Our perception of the relationship between action research and multiple intelligences

Embedded within both areas are concerns of equity (in terms of realising the educational potential of each individual), reflexivity and improving the learning and problem-solving process within the educational situation. It must be stated, however, that action research need not be oriented towards interests such as equity, as it may strive to realise its main focus of excellence in the classroom, ignoring other factors such as wider social development, which also inevitably involves issues of social justice. Action research would be useful as a process for schools which intend using a multiple intelligences approach (Chen *et al.*, 1998), since both, as noted above, are concerned with teacher development and influencing wider education systems.

Our experiences of using multiple intelligences approaches

Our concerns
We both share common concerns about education which have prompted us to explore the potential of multiple intelligences:

- concern about the underachieving child in the classroom;
- personal frustration with aspects of our own education;
- emphasis on learning using many frames;
- the need for variety in presentation of educational inputs;
- the value of reflection for the teacher and the student.

Our environments for using a multiple intelligences approach differ, as did our initial contacts with the theories. Ann FitzGibbon learned about these ideas in a 'top down' way, while Anne Fleischmann learned about them 'from the bottom up'. Ann was introduced to Gardner's work whilst on sabbatical in the United States in 1984. Working in a traditional academic environment, the concepts 'leaked' into her practice gradually as opportunities arose in the course of her teaching. Anne was seconded from her second level teaching post by the Department of Education and Science to a project that focused on the underachieving student. This involved working with teachers, students and parents at primary and post-primary levels, and this work did not lead to any form of accreditation. We designed together a programme which we taught for accreditation as a module leading towards the Master of Studies programme in the Department of Education, Trinity College (see below).

We now give a brief summary of our work in our separate locations.

Anne Fleischmann's project: the Nagle-Rice Project, 1993–1998

The aim of this project in year 1 was to identify the effective actions of creative, concerned teachers, that appeared to be benefiting those students who were not fitting easily into the traditional education system. Anne used an action research mode (McNiff, 1988) to identify the actions that the eleven teachers involved in the project felt were beneficial. At that stage she encountered Gardner's work and found that it addressed three major needs of the project:

- how to make sense of the variety in teacher approaches and student responses;
- how to discover the actual strengths of students, and to engage those strengths in the teaching-learning process;
- how to offer an appropriate variety of approaches to teachers who later joined the project.

For the next four years the project adopted a multiple intelligences approach as the main focus, with action research as a sub-theme. Twenty schools joined the project at various stages, and many teaching styles and students' learning styles were evident. This meant that the project could not offer a uniform approach, which strengthened the need for an action research approach, since reflection and evaluation were particularly important in such a fluid situation.

What did we learn from this project?

We have learnt a good deal. Some of our major learnings include the following:

- The multiple intelligences/action research frame is sufficiently robust to nurture a positive classroom atmosphere based on strengths rather than on problems, even in an examination-driven system.
- The multiple intelligences/action research frame encourages the development of a more tolerant classroom atmosphere, because questions move from an elitist kind – 'Who is clever?' – to a more inclusive kind – 'How are we clever?'
- Students of all ages involved in the project (ages 7–65) showed that they could evaluate their learning and experiment in different ways (Fleischmann, 1995).
- A multiple intelligences approach is appealing and makes sense to students, teachers and parents (Fleischmann, 1995).
- Every difficulty transformed into a positive learning event, as it led to new perspectives and new discoveries.

Some major problems as perceived by teachers in the project were:

- lack of time for planning or for trying out new approaches;
- lack of definite subject 'packages' or programmes suited to an Irish situation;
- the dominant influence of traditional examinations on curricula and classroom methodologies.

Some major problems as perceived by Anne Fleischmann were:

- lack of a safe space for teachers within which to try out new approaches;
- the difficulty of developing and maintaining an alternative view of intelligence as a process within the pressurised examinations-oriented system;
- the traditional notion of teacher as expert, which made it difficult for teachers to reconceptualise their roles as facilitators of learning.

What was effective?

The following approaches appear to have supported educational change:

- involving students in an exploration of their own learning;
- having students 'exhibit their own learning' for some group or visitor;
- having short term goals for students and teachers alike;
- having parent evenings where the teachers and students explained the benefits of a multiple intelligences approach;
- demonstrating the intelligences in action;
- having a multi-faceted approach;
- disseminating a newsletter with the views and experiences of participants.

Possible limitations to effectiveness

The following appear to have had a limiting effect on learning and on supporting educational change:

- a task centred approach rather than a people centred one;
- the major focus was on discovering student strengths, with much less emphasis on identifying teacher strengths;
- limited contact between participating schools and teachers.

It is interesting to note the number of instances which relate to issues of the politics of knowledge, as in, for example, when teachers see the need to move from being the only 'expert', and students see the need to take responsibility for their own learning.

Ann FitzGibbon's work: In-service modules for professional accreditation

The teachers who took the accredited module within the Faculty inservice structure made similar comments in evaluation phases of the project. For assessment of the module, they were required to design, teach and evaluate a series of lessons in their own schools. The problem of the extra time required for planning and correction became an issue: however, as one teacher commented: '… students familiar with learning through multiple intelligences are likely to be better equipped to adapt their learning patterns to meet their own needs in different situations.' For her, at least, the effort seemed to be worthwhile.

As the module is taught over three weekends, participants were encouraged to explore some element in the classrooms during the intervening periods. Their feedback was largely positive about the potential transferability of what they were learning. For example, a teacher of languages tried using an imagery approach when teaching irregular verbs; the response from her classes was so positive that she continued to develop this approach. Her reports to her peer group encouraged others to develop experimental strategies (FitzGibbon, 1999).

The conference presentation

We noted above that we used the conference presentation as an informal opportunity to test our own theories that a combination of multiple intelligences/action research approaches to teacher education would be educationally beneficial. We invited participants to evaluate their experience of the presentation. We adopted an action research methodology for the presentation.

First we invited participants to carry out a reconnaissance in the 'here and now', exploring each intelligence and tracking their own levels of involvement. Two 'questionnaires' were offered to the participants. One engaged primarily linguistic intelligences by posing the question: 'How did you react to the description of the session as involving experiential learning and to the request that you play an active part throughout?' The second focused on logical intelligence, and asked: 'What did you learn by using a key strategy that harnesses each intelligence and by naming the many ways in which you have been accessing such abilities?'.

Thirty-nine evaluations were returned to us at the end of the presentation. Twelve participants chose to complete the second possibility and twenty-seven the first. This feedback strengthened our own worry that the very structure of the conference (as is true of many conferences) reflected the reality of Irish education in general with its focus on linguistic forms of representation and on propositional forms of knowledge. We were allocated one hour to present our ideas, and this allowed us time to give a linguistic analysis of the potential benefits of action research and multiple intelligences, but not to invite participants to engage with their own experience sufficiently well that they would internalise the ideas at the level of their own personal theorising. We recognise this as a major issue in any potential development of this approach in real-life workplaces.

People generally seemed to find the experience enjoyable, informative but too rushed, and not enough discussion of the 'intellectual basis of multiple intelligences and action research', further evidence for us that teachers tend to expect to use linguistic analysis rather than experiential engagement as their primary form of knowing. People clearly recognised the educational potential for classrooms, as well as the possible difficulties in introducing such strategies into an examinations-dominated system, and the dangers of children being labelled.

Participants identified the following as negative or problematic:

- '... exclusionary to people hesitant to such open discussion of feeling ...'
- dislike of group sharing
- danger of alienation of some students

'Interesting' aspects were identified as

- increased awareness that no one has the monopoly on wisdom;
- the need for democracy in education;
- the idea that language used reveals one's own intelligences; 'I expected a cerebral approach in the university – nice to have parts of my life more integrated.'

Conclusion

Our own awareness of the politics of educational knowledge was placed in high relief from our experience of this presentation. We became aware of teachers' expectations about their own forms of knowledge, which are rooted in wider cultural epistemological traditions. While people might espouse at a theoretical level the values of democracy and self-direction that underpin multiple intelligences and action research approaches, there is not immediate readiness to engage at a level of lived experience. This, we feel, is a major problem for any inservice providers, and one that needs to be overcome. Before teachers can encourage their students to engage in their own learning from experience, teachers themselves have to do so. It is comfortable enough to invite others to engage; it is not so comfortable to do this oneself. And that, we feel, is part of the politics of knowledge – questions need to be raised concerning issues of Whose knowledge? How is knowledge legitimated? Who decides? We feel that our work goes some way to raising those questions, and to strengthening the legitimacy of the questions. This is a beginning; and we recognise that we are only at the beginning, and still have far to go.

References

Adelman, C. (1993) 'Kurt Lewin and the Origins of Action Research' in *Educational Action Research*, Vol. 1, No. 1, pp. 7–24.
Armstrong, T. (1994) *Multiple Intelligences in the Classroom*. Alexandria, VA., ASCD.

Berliner, D.C. and Biddle, B.J. (1995) *The Manufactured Crisis: Myths, Fraud, and the Attack on America's Public Schools.* Reading, MA, Addison-Wesley.

Calhoun, E. (1993) 'Action Research: Three Approaches' in *Educational Leadership,* Vol. 51, No. 2, pp. 62–65.

Campbell, B., Campbell, L. and Dickinson, D. (1996) *Multiple Intelligences in the Classroom.* Tucson, AZ. Skylight Press.

Chen, J., Krecheveshy, M. and Viens, J. with E. Isberg (1998) *Building on Children's Strengths: The Experience of Project Spectrum.* New York, Teachers College Press.

Cohen, L, and Manion, L. (1994) (4th Edition) *Research Methods in Education.* London, Routledge.

Corey, S.M. (1953) *Action Research to Improve School Practices.* New York, Teachers College Press.

Elliott, J. (1991) *Action Research for Educational Change.* Milton Keynes, Open University Press.

FitzGibbon, A. (1999) Personal communication: Education Centre course, Waterford.

Fleischmann, A. (1995) 'Spotting Their Intelligences' in *Action Researcher,* No. 4, pp. 28–31.

Gardner, H. (1983) *Frames of Mind.* New York, Basic Books.

Gardner, H. (1991) *The Unschooled Mind.* New York, Basic Books.

Gardner, H. (1993) *Multiple Intelligences.* New York, Basic Books.

Gardner, H. (1994) 'Intelligences in Theory and Practice' in *Teachers' College Record,* Vol. 95, No. 4, pp. 576–583.

Gardner, H. (1995) 'Reflections on Multiple Intelligences – Myths and Messages' in *Phi, Delta Kappan,* November, pp. 200–209.

Gore, J. and Zeichner, K. M. (1995) 'Connecting Action Research to Genuine Teacher Development' in J. Smyth (ed.) *Critical Discourses on Teacher Development.* London, Cassell.

Hoerr, T. (1997) 'The Naturalist Intelligence, succeeding with Multiple Intelligences, teaching through the Personalist Intelligences' in *ASCD for Multiple Intelligences Newsheet,* 1–2.

Lazaer, D. (1994) *The Seven Way Path.* Tucson, AZ, Zephyr Press.

Lazaer, D. (1999) *The Eight Way Path.* Tucson, AZ, Zephyr Press.

Levin, H. M. (1994) 'Commentary: Multiple Intelligence Theory and Everyday Practices' in *Teachers' College Record,* Vol. 95, No. 4, pp. 570–583.

Lewin, K. (1947) 'Group decisions and social change' in T.M. Newcomb and E.L. Hartley (eds) (1947) *Readings in Social Psychology.* New York, Henry Holt.

Lynch, K. (1992) 'Intelligence, Ability and Education: Challenging Traditional Views' in *Oideas*, Spring, 38, pp. 134–148.

McNiff, J. (1988) *Action Research: Principles and Practice*. London, Routledge.

O'Loughlin, T. (1998) 'Getting to the point about points' in *Education and Living, Irish Times*, November 24th.

O'Sullivan, C. (1998) Personal notes taken at 'Be a Super Learner' Conference, Birmingham, November 27th–29th.

Sagor, R. (1998) 'Collaborative Action Research for Educational Change' in A. Hargreaves (ed.) (1998) *Rethinking Educational Change with Heart and Mind*. Alexandria, VA, ASCD.

Sternberg, R.J. (1985) *Beyond IQ: a triarchic theory of human intelligence*. New York, Viking.

Sternberg, R.J. (1990) *Metaphors of Mind: Conception of the Nature of Intelligence*. Cambridge, MA, Cambridge University Press.

Chapter 8

External constraints, internal resistances: changing cultures, mindsets and practices
A response to Ann FitzGibbon and Anne Fleischmann

Joan Hanafin

Introduction

Action research is a particularly suitable approach for initiating and exploring practices in Multiple Intelligences (MI) classrooms, not least because misconceptions abound about the nature of such classrooms. Two examples from my own teaching on MI and action research to post-graduate students during the last year suggest the extent of such misconceptions. First, many students equate MI theory-in-use with a whole range of what they term 'progressive' education practices (MI *is* constructivism; MI *is* active learning). Second, a student embarking on an action research project framed her project on an initial step of 'running a battery of MI tests on pupils in order to establish their intelligence profiles'. These examples beg a number of questions.

1 What are the distinctive qualities of MI classrooms? What makes MI classrooms different from other kinds of classrooms where innovative, reflective and good practices take place?

2 What differences do MI classrooms make to the learning experience? What claims can we make for MI theory-in-use? What is the added value of MI classrooms?

3 What evidence do we have to support such claims?

4 What is the contribution of action research to implementing and evaluating MI theory-in-use?

Exploration of the interlinked nature of action research, multiple intelligences and the politics of educational knowledge provides a valuable contribution to our understanding of the interface of teacher professional development, multiple intelligences theory (MI) and action research.

Qualities of MI Classrooms

I have argued elsewhere (Hanafin, 1997a) that MI theory-in-use commits us to *taking action* arising out of appraisal (and re-appraisal) of professional acts. Such action includes supporting practices which recognise diversity and plurality in student learning as well as in teacher style, and finding diverse and pluralist approaches to assessing student performance. Many such actions have been identified in the classroom-based literature on MI. Initially, approaches such as teaching *to* and teaching *through* the intelligences were suggested. Latterly, the *Entry Point* approach as a theory of learning derived from a theory of mind has gained currency. Such an approach uses up to six gateways or windows to gain access to or shed light on a topic. Allied to this is the use of the *Teaching for Understanding* framework, proposed as a means of planning and organising topics in ways which prioritise learner understanding and attempt to give learners ownership of classroom knowledge. Finally, the use of authentic assessment practices and, specifically, the use of *portfolio assessment* has been widely discussed in the literature on MI theory-in-use.

Good and creative teachers have always used diverse ways of approaching a topic, have always prioritised learner understanding, and have always found exciting and authentic means for learners to demonstrate such understanding. These practices stand independently of an MI framework. It is my view that the essential contribution of MI theory to classroom practice remains, therefore, the reconstruction of intelligence and the consequent premising of action based on such reconstruction. I believe that this reconstruction is not only the cornerstone of MI theory-in-use, but also presents the greatest challenge to practitioners. I have found recently that student teachers attempting to move towards the establishment of MI classrooms frequently focus on limitations relating to external constraints such as timetabling, space, and lack of collegial or principal support. In second-level schools, for example, timetabling in 40-minute slots is reported as a hindrance, as is the formal layout of classrooms and the problems of increased noise levels for those in adjoining classrooms.

While accepting the real constraining nature of these external factors, I believe it is necessary to focus on internal resistances as much as on external constraints. Peeling away the layers of deeply-held beliefs about intelligence is a painful, slow and difficult task for most of us, probably much more painful, slow and difficult than introducing an entry point approach or a teaching for understanding framework in our classrooms. We see evidence of this all the time in the continued use of descriptors such as 'weak pupils' and 'lower-ability pupils' (pupils who inevitably attract added impediments such as being 'poorly motivated', or 'lower achieving'). Overcoming this internal resistance (a resistance grounded in and supported by structural institutional resistances) will provide the greatest challenge to the realisation of MI classrooms. In their paper, Ann FitzGibbon and Anne Fleischmann note a variety of external constraints experienced by teachers ('lack of time for planning', 'dominance of the traditional examinations', 'extra amount of time for planning and correction required'). They also note internal resistances, acknowledging (from the director's point of view) 'the difficulty of maintaining an alternative view of intelligence within such a pressurised system'.

MI added value

What claims can we make for MI theory-in-use and for the contribution of action research in that context? Some include: the building of a positive atmosphere based on strengths rather than on problems; the achievement of a more tolerant classroom atmosphere; and the ability of participants to evaluate their learning and experiment in alternative ways. Claims made for MI theory-in-use include greater participation and achievement by learners, as well as more democratic organisational structures. I have suggested (Hanafin, 1997b) that MI theory-in-use has the potential to contribute to greater equality in classrooms and have submitted that Kathleen Lynch's (1996) macro-framework of access, participation, outcome, and condition can be mapped at a micro level onto the MI classroom. This may be operationalised in the ways in which learners access classroom knowledge (through the use, for example, of entry points), participate more and achieve better outcomes. Ultimately, opportunities are provided for greater respect in classrooms (Marie Flynn, personal communication).

Action research and evidence for claims

In making claims for MI theory-in-use, it is important for the reasons outlined above to advance evidence for any such claims. Specifically, if we assert that particular benefits for learners, teachers, assessment practices, and school organisational structures accrue from MI practices, then it is necessary to demonstrate how we know this. An action research approach is ideally placed to do this because of its insistence on the collection of data to evaluate action and to support claims made for the success or otherwise of such action. Within the action research context, the importance of practitioners framing their own questions as problems for inquiry is noted. The importance of collecting data from primary sources is also noted. For example, if we say that learners' self-esteem is improved in MI classrooms, then supporting data should come from the learners rather than be mediated through teachers' perceptions.

Quality

Can we say that MI theory-in-use improves the learning experience and adds to quality in education? Much of the early literature on quality is concerned with outcome measurement, and the phrase 'if it can't be measured, it isn't quality' is often heard. More recent work on quality has concerned itself with process and the inherent difficulties in measuring process are widely discussed. Much of what is claimed for MI theory-in-use may be understood in an 'outcomes' framework of quality (higher achievement, greater motivation, more involvement, improved self-esteem) and evidence can be produced to substantiate such claims (from classroom observation, teachers' diaries, students' logs, tests, ongoing assessment, performances of understanding). Perhaps the most significant contribution of MI theory-in-use, however, is concerned with benefits which are processual, crucially the respect which accrues from practices based on changed constructs of intelligence and which leads to learners 'knowing' differently their value in their educational environment. It is likely that those who have reconstructed understandings of intelligence interact and organise differently in classrooms compared with those who hold more traditional beliefs on the nature of intelligence. Although process is more difficult to measure than outcome, I believe that it is possible within an action research framework to substantiate claims for better quality in this regard. For example, learners can demonstrate in many ways (visually, linguistically, kinaesthetically) their understandings of the respect afforded them in their educational environments for the diversity of ways in which they know and learn.

Multiple intelligences, action research and professional development

The excitement of the professional development experience which results from involvement with action research and Multiple Intelligences theory is evident in the work presented in FitzGibbon's and Fleischmann's paper. I recognise this excitement from my own experience as director of the MI, Curriculum and Assessment Action Research Project at the National University of Ireland, Cork. Working with teachers in such a context is a rich developmental experience for all concerned. A nagging question which arises during work of this kind concerns the extent to which the richness of the developmental experience is a function of the particularity of the context rather than a function of the generality of a professional development experience of this kind. A group of committed, motivated, self-selected practitioners experimenting with a 'problem' such as 'How do I go about making my classroom an MI classroom?' will inevitably generate interesting classroom experiences as well as worthwhile professional development experiences. In other words, how much of the success of projects like these can be attributed to the particular Multiple Intelligences/action research framework and how much to the dynamic professional growth that occurs within a supportive group context.

Conclusion

Anything which leads to the inclusion of more learners in classrooms and greater respect for human diversity is to be welcomed. It is evident from the work presented in the paper by Ann FitzGibbon and Anne Fleischmann that this is possible through MI theory-in-use. It is also evident that action research provides a valuable framework for implementing and evaluating such action as well as making an important contribution to presenting evidence for claims evinced.

References

Hanafin, J. (1997a) 'Unfreezing the Frame: Implications of Multiple Intelligences Theory for Curriculum Assessment' in *Issues in Education*, Vol. 2, Dublin, ASTI.

Hanafin, J. (1997b) 'Teaching for Difference and the Equality Challenge: Intelligence, Learning and Assessment' in *College Courier*, p. 15, July.

Lynch, K. (1996) 'The Limits of Liberalism for the Promotion of Equality in Education' in E. Befring (ed.) *Teacher Education for Equality*. Oslo, ATEE.

Chapter 9

Introducing a multi-skilling training programme for time-served craftpersons in a pharmaceutical manufacturing company

David Taylor

This chapter describes an action research project which I undertook in an effort to understand how the management and communication processes in a large organisation could be improved, so that relationships would be strengthened throughout the organisation and productivity enhanced.

Context for the research

The company

This study was undertaken in the Irish subsidiary of a European pharmaceutical manufacturing company. The company is responsible for the bulk manufacture and packaging of prescriptive medication in a wide variety of delivery methods from ointment, creams and gels, to tablets, powders, vials for injection and pre-loaded syringes. The finished product is filled and packaged on high speed automated machines.

The company employs 302 permanent and approximately 30 temporary personnel. It is organised along traditional lines and is managed by several functional departments: Manufacturing, Engineering, Quality Assurance/Quality Control, Finance and

Administration (including IT), Logistics, Environment and Safety, and Personnel.

Structure and culture

The company has a functional structure and the culture is strongly task oriented. The complex and technical nature of the pharmaceutical industry demands a range of skills that are most easily organised into functional areas. A functional structure also lends itself to regulatory requirements that activities be highly proceduralised.

The strong task orientation of the culture resulted in departmentalisation of tasks and a reluctance to engage in cross functional initiatives. Change initiatives have been treated with suspicion and have been slow to gain support and momentum.

Maintenance department

To facilitate the smooth running and the maintenance of manufacturing processes and filling and packaging equipment the company employs 28 time-served craftpersons in the Maintenance Department. The Maintenance Department is part of the Engineering function and also includes a maintenance manager and five engineers. The maintenance craftpersons are divided into three groups: process, filling/packing and utilities. Each group consists of craftpersons with particular expertise and experience in their own areas reporting to a maintenance engineer. Within each area craftpersons tend to specialise in particular processes and equipment, and there has traditionally been little or no transfer between groups. Craftpersons have been paid according to a 15 point time served incremental scale.

There are 28 craftpersons in the maintenance department. They are all male and range in age from 21 to 53. There are 23 mechanical fitters, 4 electricians and one instrumentation technician. All the craftpersons are members of the Union and are time served having completed an apprenticeship of four or five years. Only two of the group served their apprenticeship in the company.

Until recently, there have been strict demarcation lines between the trades of mechanical fitter and electrician and each trade tended to guard their respective roles, responsibilities and tasks. This often resulted in unrealistic allocations of personnel for simple mechanical/ electrical tasks with a resultant increase in costs.

The methods and work procedures practised by the craftpersons have been established for a number of years and there was always great reluctance to embrace change or participate in continuous improvement projects. These problems were recognised by the engineering management and by the younger members of the crafts group who felt they were not getting the opportunity to practise their skills and also felt there was no incentive to learn new skills. The training manager felt that the present training regime was insufficient for a modern progressive company and wished to introduced some elements of a learning organisation. These issues were often discussed in informal meetings.

Rationale for the study

Following three months of negotiations a new agreement was signed by the representatives of the crafts trade union and the company in March 1996. The areas covering conditions of employment as well as new roles and responsibilities and flexibility were agreed, but a multi-skilling programme was agreed in principle only. The multi-skilling model was intended to replace the existing 15 point time served payment scale with a four point payment system based on skills attained. Progression through the new scale was based on the achievement of a pre-determined set of knowledge and skills following a series of agreed training programmes, both on and off the job. The attainment of a particular level was agreed at a formal review conducted by the local engineer and the individual craftperson.

The design of the up-skilling programme and its implementation, including the payment structure, was to be agreed and initiated in September 1996. A working party comprising members of the craft group and management was established and a multi-skilling model was developed and implemented on a pilot basis.

However, evidence of problems with the system arose after the initial skill reviews in September 1996. The engineers expressed concern over the length of time it was taking for each review and the craftpersons were not happy with inconsistencies in the reviews among the different engineers. This was discussed by the working party and it was agreed that the problems were probably because this was the first time the reviews had been conducted. It was anticipated that the next reviews in six months' time would be more efficient.

In the event, over the following six months an increasing number of complaints and concerns were expressed to the training manager, ranging from insufficient training, cancellation of training courses, no time for training, to lack of any training whatsoever. There were suggestions that the whole programme was too complicated. The second review took place in March 1997, but this also was accompanied by expressions of dissatisfaction from the craftpersons and the engineers. At this stage, I was requested by the engineering manager to assess the overall programme and to present proposals for altering or amending the system in order to help alleviate the concerns of both the craftpersons and the engineers.

The study

Contemplating the task ahead of me I decided that this would be best approached as an action research project. It was a live project that affected people. It required the co-operation of all parties concerned and it was going to be an evolving project. The perceptions of the up-skilling programme by the different parties were based on comments, informal discussions and personal conclusions resulting from a number of years' experience working in an industrial environment. A study based on sound research would provide me and the company with an opportunity to test these observations and develop an up-skilling programme which would have the potential to meet the needs of all concerned.

I discussed my proposal for the study with the engineering manager and he agreed to participate, provided that the craftpersons agreed, and the study itself did not interfere with the objectives of the up-skilling project. I explained my proposal to the craft representatives, and how the project would be conducted, and they were willing to co-operate provided their comments and observations remained confidential. I took care to assure all parties that ethical considerations would be strictly observed, and I produced ethics statements to this effect.

Action research

The research methodology

I chose to investigate the multi-skilling programme using a qualitative methodology and I decided to use an action research approach. My reasons for choosing action research were that it identified a clear issue (Elliott, 1991); it aimed to generate new understandings of the issue (Cohen and Manion, 1994); it was collaborative (Atweh *et al.*, 1998); it accommodated participants' different viewpoints (Altrichter *et al.*, 1993); it aimed to improve a current situation (Webb, 1991).

I chose the action plan outlined by John Elliott (1991), an adaptation of Lewin's original action-reflection cycle (Lewin, 1947). Elliott usefully adds a reconnaissance stage after each cycle in the spiral. This is important because it not only asks the researcher to collect and describe the facts of the situation, but also to explain the facts in the context in which they occurred. Elliott also states that the general idea should be allowed to shift and that evaluation of the effects of an action should not proceed until its implementation is evaluated.

I interpreted Elliott's model as follows;

Identification of the general idea
Although I identified an initial problem, Elliott states that this idea should be allowed to shift as the study progresses.

Reconnaissance
This would involve fact finding and the gathering of information.

Analysis of the fact
This would include an analysis of all information, an explanation of the facts and the formulation of an hypothesis.

Formulation of an action plan

This would include a revised statement of the general idea and also include the action steps.

Implementation of planned action steps

I would carry out the plan in a systematic way.

Analysis of the outcomes

To include a review of the implementation procedures.

Amend plan if required

I would listen to feedback and modify plans accordingly.

Implement the next action

I would continue with the work.

Data collection

Elliott (1991: 77) recommends various techniques and methods for collecting data. I chose the following:

Diary

I kept a reflective diary to record the sequence of events and any perceptions and comments from participants. I also used the diary to make notes to check on specific facts or to ask follow up questions to help confirm my impressions of participants' underlying feelings or possible motives (see also Bell, 1987: 80.

I found the diary useful for keeping notes about my feelings at different stages throughout the study. I discovered that keeping a diary requires discipline. I have learnt for future studies to record relevant facts and feelings as soon as possible after the event. I would also keep the diary strictly for the study as on this occasion I tended to intermingle the entries with unrelated notes and reminders – frustrating when referencing the diary afterwards.

Documents
I examined

- the company mission statement on training
- standard operating procedures for training
- training records
- documents relating to the initial upskilling model
- training evaluation forms
- specific equipment training manuals

Interviews
The main technique used for data collection was semi-structured interviews. I found this useful for obtaining different types of information from different participants. I also found the technique of asking open ended questions encouraged a relaxed atmosphere. The semi-structured interview process was useful, bearing in mind Simons' advice (1982: 23) that '… an interview should be a conversation piece, not an inquisition'.

Through conducting the interviews, I came to appreciate the importance of my relationship with the participants. To improve the training process I had to be seen as part of the process. I came to see this as the most important feature of action research.

The interview process
I explained the procedures and techniques of action research to the participants at the proposal stage of the study. I had already guaranteed anonymity to participants, but all agreed that their interview transcripts could be included in the final report of the study.

In selecting the actual interviewees I approached a cross section of the maintenance personnel to ensure as much as possible a representative group. It was important that the information reflected the contributions and the feelings of both the maintenance management and the craft group. The following personnel agreed to take part:

- the maintenance manager
- an engineering supervisor
- a craftperson
- the craft group union shop steward
- the union branch secretary

I hoped that this group would provide a range of 'typical' and 'atypical' experiences (Morse, 1991: 131).

All the interviews were held in a meeting room attached to the company training centre. Each interview was tape recorded and transcribed. Each interviewee was given a copy of the transcription for verification of accuracy.

To analyse the interview transcripts I used Burnard's (1991) method of thematic content analysis (see below).

Rigour of the study

Qualitative research has been criticised by empirical researchers on the grounds that there is lack of control over the validity and reliability of the findings. Addressing this criticism, Lincoln and Guba (1985) propose a model that is appropriate for qualitative research suggesting that trustworthiness can be measured by examining truth value, applicability, consistency and neutrality.

Truth value
In qualitative research there may be multiple realities because of the various perspectives of the participants. The truth value of this study was measured by asking each participant to check the transcripts of their interviews and also to comment and agree on the categories I had identified. I was concerned that only two craftpersons were included in the study but I was aware that one of these (the union representative) discussed the categories with his colleagues. The selection of a union representative as a participant in the study was a deliberate decision by myself because I felt that the traditional values of collectiveness and solidarity displayed by the craft union group would ensure that the content, deductions and recommendations of the study

would be agreed collectively with the union representative with consent for their inclusion in the final draft (see McNiff 1988: 112 on the need for theories to be grounded in practice and agreed by collaborative validation procedures).

Applicability

This criterion is used to determine whether the findings can be applied in other contexts or with other similar groups. Because I was using an action research methodology I did not consider whether the findings could be applied in other contexts. I am confident however that the observations made in the study and the resultant upskilling model would be more than useful to organisations and craft groups who are considering a multi-skilling initiative.

Consistency

This criterion assesses whether the findings would be consistent if the enquiry was replicated with the same participants or in a similar context. In action research where the research situation considers multiple realities and the researcher attempts to examine and explain underlying feelings, this notion of consistency has to be viewed less rigidly. However I am confident that given the same objectives and in a situation with the same internal and external considerations the results would be similar.

Neutrality

This criterion refers to the freedom of bias in the research procedure and results, which is anathema to quantitative research. Action researchers are an integral part of the study and accept that bias in unavoidable and view it as the beneficial influence of critical experience. On this point Meighan comments (1986: 279):

> They carry out their research in particular moments in history, in particular material circumstances, and they cannot suddenly switch off their personal predilections and purposes and stop being human in the name of 'objective research'. To imagine therefore that a first priority in starting out on a piece of social research is for the researcher to confront the problem of whether

she or he has an 'objective' approach and technique or one based on values, commitment and personal motives, is a rather pointless concern.

Through my study I came to critique the idea that traditional research categories of analysis are appropriate to action research, which seems to demand its own internal criteria and standards of judgement (see Whitehead, 2000).

The study

In this section I want to give an outline of how I conducted the research, now considering options other than Elliott's (1991) action plan (see above). I hope this move demonstrates my own capacity to reflect on practice and modify my own practice by adopting strategies that are more appropriate to my research purposes.

The general idea

The general idea for the study was to examine the up-skilling programme with a view to agreeing and implementing improvements. To reassure myself that this was a valid idea I now adopted Whitehead's (see McNiff, 1988) six questions (in this instance, the first three questions):

What is my concern?
I am concerned that the up-skilling programme is not meeting the expectations of the craft group or the maintenance management.

Why am I concerned?
The up-skilling programme is an integral part of the New Deal for Maintenance Craftpersons and if it fails there is a danger that the craft group or the maintenance manager may cancel the whole deal. This would have a detrimental effect on relationships and would have serious consequences for future change initiatives.

What do I think I could do about it?

As the manager responsible for training in the organisation I have an integral role in any training initiative, making decisions regarding the design and implementation of training initiatives. I have established my own credibility through fifteen years experience as a training practitioner, and I have a good working relationship with both the craft group and maintenance management team.

Reconnaissance

Interviews

I commenced the study with interviews. Each participant was asked the same questions in the first part of the interview. The second part of the interview was informed by the responses to the initial questions. I never referred to answers given by the other respondents but I did make suggestions, based on my own training experience and also on my interpretation of the underlying feelings behind the responses, and asked the interviewee for comments. The interviews were not conducted in one sitting. I returned to each interviewee on at least one occasion to ask questions prompted by responses from the other participants.

Data collection

The type of data collected was prompted by particular comments made by the participants in the interviews. This was important to check on statements made by the participants. For example, if an interviewee commented that the training reviews were taking too long I felt it was important to check that statement by analysing the review documentation and asking the engineering supervisors how long each review lasted.

The analytical model

I analysed the data using Burnard's (1991) method of thematic content analysis (pp. 462–464). This method provided me with a logical and comprehensive set of procedures for analysing what at times seemed like an expanding collection of unrelated facts.

The method involves producing a detailed, systematic recording of the themes and issues addressed in the interviews. These are then linked together to form a list of categories. Burnard suggests 14 different stages for the analysis of qualitative data. I followed all the stages except those relating to an associate double-checking the categories to confirm the validity of the findings. I felt this was an unnecessary step as an associate may validate my list of categories but the real validation comes from the participants. If the participants do not agree with the list of categories presented by the researcher then the data has to be revisited. Before deciding on any action steps I had agreed the categories with all the participants and although they placed different emphases on certain categories they all agreed with their inclusion in the report.

My stages, as described by Burnard, were:

1 Read all data, transcripts, field notes and memos.
2 Re-read the data and generate general themes.
3 Re-read the transcripts and identify specific headings and categories.
4 Sort the categories into precise groups.
5 Re-sort and remove any extraneous categories.
6 Transcripts and categories are examined identifying the data relating to each category.
7 Data is collected and monitored for context.
8 Data is linked to category headings.
9 Respondents are asked to check and validate the categories.
10 All data is collected before writing the research findings.
11 Research findings are written up with reference to the literature.

Burnard (1991: 464) suggests presenting the findings using verbatim examples of the responses to illustrate the various categories and a separate section to link these findings to the literature. This is the approach I adopted.

Analysis of the findings

The initial analysis of the interview transcripts resulted in 56 themes. These were then grouped under headings and the categories examined and re-sorted to produce 13 new categories (as on the left hand side below). The initial 13 categories were then regrouped into 4 new categories (on the right).

'communications' 'attitudes'	'becomes	**'communications'**
'levels of trust' 'different age groups' 'overtime' 'inter-union co-operation'	becomes	**'mutual trust'**
'type of multi-skilling' 'flexibility'	becomes	**'type of multi-skilling'**
'bogged down in details' 'reviews' 'time for training' 'type of training' 'responsibility for learning'	becomes	**'the training model'**

Figure 1: Categories generated through analysis of transcripts

The following is a brief summary of the data collection analysis:

Communications
The problem as I saw it was that the negotiations were continuing after the deal was agreed. The craft group were only performing to the level of commitment as interpreted by the shop stewards and not necessarily as expected by the maintenance management. There was no direct communication with the craft persons themselves and this

was resulting in the conflicting view of the expectations of both stakeholders.

To overcome this barrier it was agreed that the level and method of communications would need to be improved.

Mutual trust

This category could be summarised in five statements:

1 The craftworkers felt that the company could use the new payment system to freeze the pay levels by 'holding' individuals on the lower levels;
2 promised training might not materialise because that is what happened in the past;
3 older craftworkers could be left behind;
4 some maintenance tasks could be handed over to the production operatives and therefore reduce the dependence on the craft group;
5 the programme could be used to cut overtime and therefore reduce the earning potential of the individuals.

Type of multi-skilling

It was evident from the interviews that there was still some confusion concerning the type of craftworker the new operating environment would require. It was not necessary to produce fully multi-skilled technicians. The engineering department did not require mechanical craftpersons fully trained in the skills of electricians, or vice versa, and the company would not have the resources to provide the necessary training. Up-skilling would be a more appropriate description of the company requirements and it was agreed that this would be the description used in all future discussions and proposals.

The training model

It was evident from the interviews that the engineering manager was not happy in that he appeared to have to negotiate every new initiative with the craft group shop stewards. There was also concern that the system was too complicated. Time for training was a concern of the craft group and responsibility for their own learning was a concern of the maintenance management.

The action plan

This action research study was only part of the overall process of improving the up-skilling programme. Action research is a rational approach to analysing a situation and usually arrives at rational suggestions, but I had to be careful not to regard my own research as the only aspect which led to the success of the overall initiative. For example, other groups had a key influence. Union officials were visiting other companies to examine their multi-skilling programmes; the engineering manager had his own vision of the 'technician of the future'; and there were also operational and cost considerations. In summary, it is important to emphasise that the action steps agreed for the overall initiative were not only because of my action research study. This was one of a combination of processes involved in arriving at agreed strategies for improvement. The important fact is, however, that among a series of discussions, formal union/management meetings, meetings among the craft group and meetings between the craftpersons and the engineering management, my research made an important contribution: the categories described above were discussed and a range of possible solutions was debated.

As an outcome of all these processes, the following strategic action steps were agreed and endorsed:

1 Engineering training co-ordinator
It was agreed that the next stage in the development of the up-skilling programme would require the attention of a full time person to co-ordinate the activities of the working group. The initial suggestions centred around the possibility of appointing a member of the maintenance department to the position. It was agreed that it would be more appropriate to employ an experienced training professional.

2 Up-skilling review group

The second action step was to re-constitute the up-skilling working group. The members of the new group should consist of the new training co-ordinator, a representative of the maintenance engineering supervisors and four craftpersons who were not union representatives of the craft group. It was also agreed that among the tasks of the working group should be a plan to improve communications and explain the development model to all involved, to examine and improve the delivery of training and to simplify the training review system.

3 Self-directed learning

This action step was to change the emphasis of the training delivery method. The preferred delivery method to date was a limited number of off the job training modules and on the job training whenever the opportunity arose.

There was also concern that the craftpersons were not taking responsibility for their own development. It was pointed out by the craft group that neither the training system nor the working arrangements facilitated this type of learning. Following discussions it was agreed that the future training programmes should consider the operational restrictions and should place a major emphasis on self-directed learning. An appropriate model would be developed by the training co-ordinator with assistance from the other members of the working group.

4 New review process

It was agreed that the final action step was to design a new review process. Analysis to date had shown that all parties agreed that the current system, although comprehensive, was cumbersome, over complicated, not transparent, and time consuming. Of serious concern to the craft group was the fact that it appeared to be open to inconsistencies in its application.

It was agreed that the new review should be easy to administer and understand, should facilitate a consistent and standard approach and should rely as much as possible on objective rather than subjective evidence.

Evaluation of the action steps

I have sub-divided the analysis into the three areas that I feel appeared to present the major concerns during the initial reconnaissance stage: communications and trust, local ownership of training, and more transparent reviews.

Communications and trust

The appointment of the full time training co-ordinator illustrated to the craft group that the company were committed to the up-skilling programme. There was some scepticism in the early stages but this was overcome when the co-ordinator gained the trust and respect of the craftpersons and the engineers. This was achieved by continuous discussions and consultations with all the craftpersons and engineers and not confining meetings only to the shop stewards and the maintenance management as had been the practice in the past.

A new development matrix with adjusted skills percentages for progression through the scales contributed immensely to the improvement of trust in the system as the original criteria were seen to be unrealistic and could be used as a mechanism for maintaining the wages of the craftpersons at the current levels. The application of standard systems across the site and the introduction of set skills criteria for each work area also made the programme more transparent and easier to understand.

The working group organised regular briefings and presentations for both the craft group and the engineers.

Local ownership of training

The development of generic training models (such as electrics and pneumatics) and the introduction of self-directed learning had immediate effect. The decision to introduce self-directed learning was taken by the engineering management and the shop stewards before the formation of the working group. This resulted from a recognition that it was in the craftperson's own interest to learn, as this would affect their earnings. The company provided the infrastructure, in the form of individual development plans and generic training modules, and it was up to the craftpersons to agree their plan with the engineer and arrange time slots for training.

The number of craftpersons availing of the generic training modules exceeded expectations and analysis of their usage shows that all modules have been studied at some stage, with the most popular being control systems and pneumatics, which reflects the technology of the process and packaging equipment. The other surprising development is the number of craftpersons who were studying the modules in their own time. Finally, analysis of overtime activities showed that the amount of training conducted during these hours had reduced significantly. This was attributed to a more systematic training plan and the allocation of training time into the maintenance schedules.

More transparent reviews

The craft group considered the reviews as one of the most important aspects of the up-skilling programme. Success in the reviews would determine an individual's earnings and it was vital that the reviews were seen as fair and consistent. The engineers were also unhappy with the review system as it took too long to administer and was very cumbersome. The engineering manager was determined that the reviews would be objective and reflect the actual performance of the craftperson and would not indicate a perception of their capabilities.

The new review documentation system, which consisted of one page, was much easier to understand and could be completed by the craftpersons before the review, if they so desired. This had not been possible under the old system. This had the effect of removing any element of discretion by engineers and resulted in a new degree of trust in the system.

A set of ground rules for reviews also helped to remove the feeling of inconsistencies in the system as all participants were now clear on the rules and criteria for progression through the scales.

The final improvement in the review system was the introduction of a review appeals committee.

Reflections

Throughout this study I have often asked myself whether the up-skilling programme would have developed to the present stage without the benefit of the study. The honest answer is probably, yes. However, I have to conclude that the study brought a sense of order to the analysis and the agreed action steps. As a problem solving approach, I also found that action research adopts a very systematic approach (see also French and Bell, 1995: 140).

It is however important to compare the impression this report may give to the reader and the actual sequence of events. On reading the report it would appear that the events were conducted in a systematic fashion with data collection, analysis, discussion of findings and agreed action steps all occurring in sequence and following well-defined models and plan. The reality was somewhat different. There was a plan and I found Elliott's (1991) action research model very practical and adaptable, but Elliott's notional sequence of steps were often intermingled, delayed and interrupted. I feel that this is the consequence of conducting research in a live situation and also in an environment where priorities often change. Without a model I feel it would have been difficult to focus when the opportunity came to return to the study. Cohen and Manion (1994) also agree with this when they state that models can be of great help in achieving clarity and focusing on key issues. McNiff *et al.* (1996) remind us that plans act as indicators only and keep us focused, but the realities of practice may turn out to be quite different.

I found Burnard's (1991) method of thematic content analysis invaluable in sifting through the vast amount of information collected in the interviews. Without the data generated from the interviews I feel the proposed changes to the up-skilling programmes would have been based on different interpretations of the feelings, actions and comments of the stakeholders. Despite the benefit of the study these perceptions and feelings would have to be considered, but I felt the analysis model provided all the participants in the study with an objective method of considering the comments and providing evidence to justify the chosen action steps. This is commented on by Nonaka (1991) who stated that successful companies depend on tapping the tacit, and often highly subjective insights, intuitions and hunches of individual employees and making those insights available for testing and use by the company as a whole.

Having used action research I can see the model becoming another tool in my kit bag of procedures for identifying and analysing problems and issues. Whether I will have the discipline to document all the stages and consequences of agreed actions, or whether it applies in other situations, is not important. What is important is that it works and involves people in solving their own problems. As a research tool used for gathering information to improve the knowledge and effectiveness of the training professional it certainly acknowledges the contributions of the participants and the experience and know-how of the practitioners. I feel that quantitative research still plays an important part in assisting in the education of today's professional, and in improving the practice. Action research should not be seen as the only answer to solving problems that require specific knowledge for a specific problem in a specific situation.

If researchers are concerned about staying true to their core mission of advancing knowledge about universal management issues and making that knowledge publicly available, both through publications and the educational process, then by examining an issue from multiple points of view they might gain a richer and ultimately more useful way of understanding that issue. By combining more than one research paradigm it is possible that researchers may be able to advance general knowledge and practical tools beyond what would be possible through following only one research paradigm.

References

Altrichter, H., Posch, P. and Somekh, B. (1993) *Teachers Investigate their Work: An Introduction to the Methods of Action Research*. London, Routledge.

Atweh, B., Kemmis, S. and Weeks, P. (1998) *Action Research in Practice: Partnerships for Social Justice in Education*. London, Routledge.

Bell, J. (1987) *Doing Your Research Project*. Bristol, Open University Press.

Burnard, P. (1991) 'A method of analysing interview transcripts in qualitative research' in *Nurse Education Today*, Vol. 11, pp. 461–466.

Cohen, L and Manion, L. (1994) (4th Edition) *Research Methods in Education*. London, Routledge.

Elliott, J. (1991) *Action Research for Educational Change*. Milton Keynes, Open University Press.

French, W.L. and Bell, C.H. (1995) *Organizational Development: Behavioral Science Interventions for Organization Improvement*. New Jersey, Prentice Hall.

Lewin, K. (1947) 'Frontiers in Group Dynamics: Concept, Methods and Reality in Social Science' in *Human Relations*, Vol. 1, pp. 5–41.

Lincoln, Y.S. and Guba, E.G. (1985) *Naturalistic Inquiry*. Newbury Park, Sage.

McNiff, J. (1988) *Action Research: Principles and Practice*. London, Routledge.

McNiff, J., Lomax, P. and Whitehead, J. (1996) *You and Your Action Research Project*. London, Routledge.

Meighan, R. (1986) *A Sociology of Education*. London, Holt Education.

Morse, J.M. (1991) *Qualitative Nursing Research: A Contemporary Dialogue*. London, Sage.

Nonaka, I. (1991) 'The Knowledge Creating Company' in *Harvard Business Review*, November–December, pp. 312–330.

Senge, P.M. (1990) *The Fifth Discipline: The Art and Practice of the Learning Organisation*. London, Century Business.

Senge, P.M. (1991) 'Transforming the Practice of Management': a paper presented at the Systems Thinking in Action Conference, Massachusetts Institute of Technology, November 14th.

Simons, H. (1982) 'Conversation Piece: The Practice of Interviewing in Case Study Research' in R. McCormack (ed.) *Calling Education to Account*. London, Heinemann Education.

Webb, C. (1991) 'Action Research' in D.F.S. Cormack (ed.) *The Research Process in Nursing*. London, Blackwell.

Weisbord, M.R. (1991) *Productive Workplaces*. San Francisco, Jossey-Bass.

Whitehead, J. (2000) 'How Do I Improve My Practice? Creating and legitimating an epistemology of practice' in *Journal of Reflective Practice*, Vol. 1, No. 1, pp 91–104.

Chapter 10

Action research in an industrial setting

Senan Cooke

Background to the research

In 1996 the executive management of an indigenous manufacturing company in the south of Ireland took a strategic decision to introduce team briefing as part of the official company communications programme. In my role as manager of training and communications, I had overall responsibility for designing, launching, implementing, co-ordinating and evaluating the programme. I decided to consult widely and involve everyone who might have an influence on the success of the programme. In order to do so I undertook an action research project to help me discover how to build a sustainable communications programme.

I chose action research because it combines the rigorous approach of the professional practitioner with the social perspective, understanding and experience of the in-dweller. Schön (1983) emphasises that to establish base-line facts there is a need to engage in the swampy lowlands of practice where situations are confusing messes incapable of technical solutions and insensitive to quantitative measurement.

Employee perceptions, attitudes and beliefs can make or break any human resource initiative, in particular any one that requires openness and co-operation. Various attitudes and perceptions are to be found on the shopfloor among the many work and social groups which make up the social fabric of any organisation.

The need for sensitivity in this initiative was heightened because communications in the company in 1996 was a delicate issue. A strike in the early 1990s had been divisive and bitter, and had left a legacy of caution. Any initiative had to be introduced thoughtfully and with due regard for appropriate consultation strategies. Management recognised that communication was a key aspect, and had been assuming greater responsibility for ensuring that the work force was kept fully informed. Control of formal employee communications in the company however was shared between management and union. The issue became how to gain the commitment both of the union and management to join forces and ensure the free flow of information throughout the organisation. One of the key strategies identified for this was team briefing.

The research setting

The setting is an indigenous manufacturing company producing high quality gift products mainly for the export market. It is situated in the south of Ireland on two sites within 30 miles of each other. The company employs approximately 2,000 people across the two sites. It also employs 600 people in the US and 500 in the UK. It is a partner with a major UK company and employs 7,000 people in total. The company has been undergoing transformational change since the late 1980s when the first major rationalisation occurred.

There are six distinct functions within the organisation: manufacturing, finance, marketing, logistics, human resources and quality. Individually they have their own distinct practices, perspectives, language and ways of looking at the world. Significant strides have been made through cross functional team building and through management restructuring to create a more integrated operating structure.

The need for good communications

Communications has been a critical issue with management over the last ten years as the organisation has had to cope with continuous crisis.

To many of the key decision makers, communications had become the thread in the suit, the wool in the jumper, that is, the permeating force that holds the company together through the development of good relationships. Good communications would, it was hoped, help towards developing an informed and questioning workforce, which in turn would create a single focus around achieving and retaining competitiveness to sustain the viability of the company into the future.

Further, change in the working environment was gathering pace and making work practices and decision making ever more complex. A high degree of business literacy was required at all levels within the organisation to ensure that the change process was understood and managed successfully.

It is important to note how the present communications system operated, in order to appreciate the complexity of the changes that would be involved in the proposed team briefing initiative.

Because of the recent troubled history of the firm, management had by degrees taken over full responsibility for company wide communications initiatives in an attempt to keep employees informed of current and pending situations. At the same time, the union representative body also had a mandate for ensuring smooth communications. The shop steward played a key role in a highly democratic union structure. A close relationship and strong communications links, built up over years, existed between shop stewards and the membership. The issue was how to bring all parties together in a spirit of commitment to participatory work practices to ensure the success of this initiative.

The action research project focused on gaining the confidence of management, employees, union and members in an effort to ensure ongoing improvement. I therefore had to take all the conflicting emotions into consideration and manage the resultant strains and tensions. The proposed team briefing initiative was generally regarded as a positive step in improving communications and enhancing relationships on a company-wide basis.

From the start it was recognised that the team briefing initiative would involve gaining the support and commitment of all participants. It could not be mandated, but would involved hearts and minds. It was anticipated that the team briefing process would primarily involve the communication of important information between the front-line manager and the shopfloor employee. This would develop over time into a key relationship within the company. It meant however that the profile of the front-line manager had to be raised to ensure that they were regarded as someone who had important knowledge which could be shared with colleagues. Until now, the general body of employees received information from union representatives, executive and senior managers, the company magazine, electronic notice boards, e-mail, and the grapevine – a powerful medium in any company. Often, the very last and perceived least reliable source of information for them was their immediate front line manager whose primary role they tended to perceive as delivering on production targets. How now to encourage the manager to become a briefer?

Initial planning for team briefing

Space for reflection and dialogue between front line managers and team members needed to be created and the team briefing process promised to be a useful strategy for this. In designing and implementing the team briefing programme it was essential that an intensive consultative process was undertaken. Through the action research process, many views and perceptions were accepted and incorporated into the final agreed model. It was anticipated that team briefers could be educated in helping their staff access information appropriately.

The team briefing programme was initially planned for staff members only. The issue therefore was the training of front line managers to become briefers of their work teams. This plan was based on the premise that a new relationship could be developed between the front line manager and the team.

An action research approach was chosen as the best way of ensuring the production of the most effective team briefing system. The main research strategy would be face to face interviews. This would enable immediate clarification of issues, and provide decision makers with essential feedback on opinions, suggestions and any impending difficulties in employee relations.

A key aspiration in deciding on the introduction of a team briefing programme in the company at that point was to establish a platform on which a new relationship could be built between managers and employees. It was hoped that over time a new work environment would be characterised by ongoing dialogue between management and employees on a continuous basis. The team briefing process would establish a new rapport. It was imperative that the briefers and briefees should make a success of the programme and every effort would be made to get it right first time.

The team briefing programme was named 'Inform' and, in the event, it has become an outstanding success in the history of employee relations in the company over the past ten years. It is operating very successfully today. It has met all the expectations laid down by executive management. A recent survey (July 1999) on the effectiveness of the current communications strategy in the company with executive and senior management rated it the most important component of the formal communications network which operated in the company. The programme is subject to continuous review which is in keeping with the action research methodology used to design and introduce it in the first place. Innovations are being constantly introduced to maintain its freshness and effectiveness. The current full participation of briefer and briefee can be in part credited to the comprehensive research and consultative process engaged in at the design and implementation stage.

The collaborative nature of action research was a source of valuable insight and direction for the designers and implementers. A cyclical approach represented building blocks to facilitate improvements at every stage and the involvement of all the key players in the evaluation process. The validity of the information and planning followed in the eventual operation of the system. Personal inputs were visibly represented in the programme structure, content and delivery. The team briefing programme was accepted as people's own production and they made it work.

The research

Aim of the research

The aim of the action research project was to develop and implement a team briefing programme to impact positively on the free flow of information throughout the company. It was also expected to provide a regular formal opportunity for the front line manager to take the primary responsibility for keeping shop floor employees fully informed.

The starting point for the research was best practice principles on team briefing promoted by the Industrial Society and which had been the subject of many research surveys and validation exercises in other organisations. Using the Industrial Society model, the main participants were invited to customise a team briefing system that would meet their needs and the needs of the organisation for the foreseeable future.

Reasons for choosing action research

Action research is collaborative and participatory. These elements were essential for this project. It was vital to secure the participation of all, and to emphasise corporate responsibility for the success of the programme. Everyone was involved in the process of information gathering, analysis, design, implementation and evaluation. This approach also enhanced the customisation of the programme. This commitment is widely reported in the literature. Senge (1990), for example, speaks of the learning organisation in which work-based learning is fundamental. Employees are today more involved in the broader aspects of their work than ever before. Action research is a particularly appropriate methodology, since it shares the same kind of philosophical and pragmatic values that drive contemporary business.

It is worth pausing here to reflect on the kinds of values that drive contemporary business, and that are also manifested in the action research process.

A first value is that action plans and programmes which are designed to solve real problems should be based on valid public data generated collaboratively by clients and consultants. A second value is that action in the real world should be accompanied by research on that action in order to build up a body of knowledge in terms of the outcomes and whether they did solve the identified problems. Only by systematically evaluating action is it possible to know what the real effects of the actions might be.

In this respect, traditional academic knowledge is wanting (see Schön, 1995). Any effort to understand a complex work environment will involve an understanding of the issues under review. For this, traditional academic knowledge is inadequate, since the form of traditional knowledge tends to appear as conceptual theories, abstract models and functional techniques. Traditional researchers seldom have an opportunity to apply their skills in an actual corporate setting. They often find it difficult to understand the values held by employees, the business terminology and the informal organisation; and they are not always able to penetrate below the surface of events.

An action research approach, on the other hand, with its systematic problem-solving approach, enables digging out the truth and establishing a platform upon which lasting improvements can be made. In the context of this project, where team briefing was at issue with its potential for long-term sustainable change, this approach appeared to be appropriate.

The model

John Elliott's (1991) model was chosen for its simplicity, and ease of management and control. The basic action reflection cycle is:

- identify the general area
- reconnaissance
- general planning
- developing the first action step
- implementing the first action step
- evaluation
- revising the general plan

Elliott suggests that the most important criterion for selecting a 'general idea' is whether the situation it refers to impinges on one's field of action and is something one would like to change or improve. This model was entirely appropriate to my research needs.

Data gathering and analysis

The following data gathering techniques were used:

maintaining a self-reflective diary
This enabled compiling a record of events, facts, comments, reflections, dates, nuances on a day-to-day basis as the research developed.

Document analysis
Rich sources of information were available within the organisation in the form of reports arising from audits, surveys and research carried out by various consultants over the years.

Questionnaire
To engage the commitment of senior management and create an organisation-wide team briefing programme it was essential that a cross section of managers gave their views and experiences on all key aspects of the programme. The questionnaire included open and closed questions and was designed to inform on strategy, philosophy, objectives, design, launch, implementation, management and evaluation of the programme.

Analytic memos
The memos were particularly useful at the reconnaissance phase. The organisation included a wide mix of employees, including professionals, artists, craftsmen, technicians, general workers, administrative personnel. Sub-cultures existed in different areas and in various social and work groups. Sometimes company initiatives infringed on the perceived autonomy of the various work groups and barricades were installed immediately while sensitive negotiations were carried out. The memos capture many rich anecdotal references which informed

the research and were also invaluable in winning advocates and participants in the process.

Interviews

Interviews were held to evaluate the first action reflection cycle and they provided the necessary feedback to adjust and redesign elements which were causing difficulty. This was particularly relevant for the briefers and with the formation of the content for the briefs. Face to face interviews became the main data gathering technique of the project.

The process of developing the team briefing initiative

The initiative spanned several months, and involved a number of different activities. The action was constantly monitored, and findings discussed among relevant participants and validated through, among other techniques, triangulation procedures. The main elements of the process were as follows.

1 Reconnaissance stage

This stage involved gathering data about the current situation, to inform future action. The main data gathering techniques were as follows:

Reflective diary

I maintained a reflective diary, and encouraged others to do the same. These diaries provided rich sources of information which was used to inform the progress of the research.

Document analysis

Throughout the life of the research project, and especially in its earlier stages, documents were studied. There was a wealth of information in, for example, surveys carried out during the 1980s by external consultants. As well as providing a historical basis for the events of recent years, study of documents also provided ideas on how to develop good communications within the current situation as it was informed by the legacy of the past.

Survey-interviews

A series of 30-minute interviews were held with executive managers, senior managers and managers who would become team briefers within the company communications system. At the interviews, the concept and content of the team briefing programme were explained, as well as how these were also changing as the research was progressing. The managers' opinions were sought to confirm and approve how the process was suggesting new directions for the research, and to gain opinions on general strategy, design, structure and objectives in the implementation process. These interviews also informed the content of the questionnaire which would follow this phase of the research process.

Survey-questionnaire

A questionnaire was sent out to the 46 most senior managers of the company. All 46 were returned, which showed an unusual interest and commitment to the programme. The information on the forms was coded and categorised to generate relevant points which related to the construction of a suitable team briefing proposal. A report was prepared and disseminated, and feedback from the report was triangulated between myself, a participant colleague, and respondents.

2 The launch

The programme was launched at a meeting in the boardroom by the chief executive with the senior management team. A letter from the chief executive was printed in the team briefing document which was circulated to all employees. The formal launch by the senior management team was of particular significance, showing a commitment to the project by taking time out of a hectic schedule. This kind of modelling is important for any company where commitment by senior management is taken to be confirmation of the importance of a particular initiative.

3 Programme implementation

The first set of briefing sessions were held in March 1996, with management and staff only, and feedback indicated that it was a success. The sessions were then held twice more with management and staff to resolve any outstanding difficulties. Confidence was building up around the programme. On the fourth occasion it was launched on the shopfloor and it was an outstanding success. Many of the fears previously expressed were never realised, and there was overall acceptance of the initiative. Employees welcomed it, and it is now an established core element in the official communications structure of the company.

4 Programme evaluation process

Evaluation of the programme was carried out using three separate approaches: evaluation interviews, feedback sheets from each team briefing session, and consultations between myself as researcher and a cross section of participants including briefers and briefees. Valuable insights were gained, and used in future sessions to help improve the effectiveness of the programme.

Conclusions

A number of learnings arose from the project, some of which are recorded here.

It would appear that action research is a valuable way to develop a communications system in a work environment such as a large industrial organisation which relies heavily on teamwork and the co-operation of many diverse interest groups. The cyclical nature of action research enables a sure and methodological introduction of any sensitive issues, as well as a calm reflective approach from a researcher who is aiming to gain an in-depth understanding of complex scenarios.

Involvement by all participants is essential for any such initiative to be successful. People have to be involved in their own work processes, as was evident from this project. The openness and transparency of the study was welcomed and became the foundation for the programme. Employees expressed pleasure at being consulted, and they responded positively and directly.

In the case of this project, using the Industrial Society format as a starting point was helpful in giving the initiative a tried and trusted framework on which opinions and suggestions could be constructed. My own organisational experience was a significant factor in navigating the complexities and power relationships within the organisation.

A final word on the power of action research: in action research it is engagement with rather than detachment from the things to be known which enables people to become change agents who are creating their own lives and circumstances. The validity of action research findings is in their working.

References

Elliott, J. (1991) *Action Research for Educational Change*. Milton Keynes, Open University Press.

Schön, D. (1983) *The Reflective Practitioner*. New York, Basic Books.

Schön, D. (1995) 'Knowing-in-Action: The New Scholarship Requires a New Epistemology' in *Change*, November/December, pp. 27–34.

Senge, P.M. (1990) *The Fifth Discipline: The Art and Practice of the Learning Organisation*. New York, Doubleday.

Chapter 11

Using action research as a means of exploring organisational culture

Miriam Judge

Background to the research

D-Ram[1] is a large high tech multinational company located in Ireland. Its Irish subsidiary operation had been operating in Ireland for a period of three years prior to the conduct of this study. Like many multinationals located throughout the world, D-Ram invests heavily in the training of its workforce, and spares no expense in this respect, even when training involves relocating large numbers of its subsidiary employees overseas, to the parent company's country of origin, for long periods of time. In D-Ram's case, several hundred of its new Irish recruits were relocated abroad, mainly to the United States, for training prior to the company commencing its manufacturing operation in Ireland. The training assignment abroad lasted for a period of 18 months on average. Recruited for D-Ram's training department, I was lucky enough to be among the start up team expatriated to the U.S. for such an extended period of time.

As a leading high tech organisation, D-Ram prides itself on its technical excellence and its innovative prowess. As a leader in its field, D-Ram, like many top class multinationals, is modelled on a corporate 'culture of excellence'. It is this combination of technical know-how and innovative flair combined with its strong corporate culture which has made it a leader in its field. As a result those employees sent overseas for training to understand and learn the technical intricacies of D-Ram's complex manufacturing process were equally learning as much about D-Ram's unique culture and value system. The overseas assignment was in many ways a cultural baptism of fire as the new recruits experienced at first hand the cultural norms and values that guided this successful multinational. This immersion into D-Ram's *modus operandi* and that of the wider American society in which the company originated, was comparable in many ways to the socialisation of a provincial governor or general in the Roman Empire as commented on by Anthony Jay in his book *Management and Machiavelli*:

> There was no question of appointing a man who was not fully trained... You knew that everything depended on his being the best man for the job before he set off. And so you took great care in selecting him. But more than that you made sure he knew all about Rome and Roman government and the Roman army before he went... (cited in Handy, 1993: 250).

And so it was that following prolonged and extensive training in the U.S. several hundred fully trained 'Irish provincial governors' enthusiastically returned home to bring D-Ram's Irish subsidiary into operation.

Identifying the research idea

It was against this background of cross-cultural transfer and based on my own experiences of living and working in the U.S. as part of D-Ram's start up team, that the idea for this study evolved. Since returning home to Ireland and because my role as a trainer involved significant interaction with many different departments throughout the organisation, I had begun to notice, within a period of 18 months of the organisation's start-up, that there was a sense of dissatisfaction with the company and how it operated. This manifested itself mainly in casual, off-the-cuff cynical comments about the company and the way it worked. To an outsider this would seem very strange because if one examined the company rationally, it would appear to be an excellent company to work for. The company was very professional, very secure and very profitable. Consequently employee pay and perks were very good. Yet there seemed to be a general sense of dissatisfaction. As a trainer, I was curious to investigate the reasons.

Intuitively, I sensed that the dissatisfaction lay not with the company's structures but ran deeper than that. It seemed to permeate the organisation's culture and value system and the effect which this was having on the Irish psyche. Was the organisation experiencing a clash of cultures – American versus Irish ? If so, it was, I believed, a problem which management needed to address to avoid organisation dysfunction in the long term. In identifying intuition as the basis for framing the problem, it is important to point out the important role that intuition is now acknowledged to play in the decision making processes of senior managers. According to management theorists like de Bono (1982) and Mintzberg (1987), intuition has its being in the ability instantly to access the mind's store of experience, knowledge and understanding. And as Cave and Wilkinson (1992) point out

> intuition may start as a gut feeling but it is tested against the bank of your own experience. The two key elements in intuition are (1) the part played by experience and (2) the part played by a thinking process (p.41).

In this context the intuitive insights used in defining the problem were primarily informed by my experiences as a participant in the organisation and by my willingness to explore and think laterally around the issue.

It was important at this stage to frame the research question and, as the concept of culture represented such a huge area for investigation, it was vital to narrow down the problem. Again at this early stage, while still using intuition for guidance, I had a hunch that the source of the problem might lie with the non U.S. trained employees who had been recruited by the company since the start up team had returned home. By now two thirds of D-Ram's workforce were comprised of employees who had not been trained in the U.S. Consequently I wondered if the organisation was now experiencing a clash of cultures – Irish versus American – because these employees who had not had the opportunity of working and living in the U.S. had not internalised D-Ram's culture and value system to the same extent as the U.S. trained employees. To find out if this in fact was the case I set out to explore this hypotheses using an action research methodology. Therefore the question which I set out to investigate was 'To what extent do non-U.S. trained employees commit to D-Ram's culture and value system?'

Organisational culture theory

The first phase of what Elliott (1991) calls the reconnaissance cycle of action research began with a literature review which involved extensive readings on the subject of organisational culture in management textbooks and more in-depth studies and analysis on the subject by Raelin, Peters and Waterman, Handy, Hofstede, Hampden-Turner, Trompenaars and Schein. The more I read the more my understanding of organisational culture deepened. As a result I came to realise that there were three strands to this issue which were relevant to my study. These were:

1   The 'structural' view of organisational culture which equates organisational excellence with strong cultures, and which views culture as a construct of organisational design, capable of being managed and changed by management. This view was popularised in the early eighties by Peters and Waterman in their book *In Search of Excellence* (1982)

2   The 'interpretive' view of culture which treats organisational culture as a process of reality enactment by the organisation's members through which systems of shared meanings evolve. The main proponent of this perspective is Edgar Schein in his classic study of this phenomenon in his book *Organisational Culture and Leadership* (1992).

3   The 'divergence' view of culture which maintains that national cultures can impact organisational structures and processes in different countries. This has implications for multinational corporations. The most well known and by far the largest organisationally based study carried out on these lines is Geert

Hofstede's investigation into the culture of IBM's world-wide subsidiaries (1980).

Of all the literature surveyed, Schein's (1992) *Organisational Culture and Leadership* provided the most stimulating and thought provoking analysis of the subject. By challenging my own narrow interpretation of organisational culture as a 'structural' construct, Schein greatly influenced my research approach, inquiry method and subsequent analysis of findings.

Schein (1992) argues that organisational culture can be analysed at three levels. Level One is the visible organisational structures and processes which he calls 'Artifacts'. Level Two is comprised of the organisation's strategies, goals and philosophies which he calls 'Espoused Values'. Level Three which is the deepest and most obscure level, is manifested in the members' unconscious taken-for-granted beliefs, which are the ultimate source of values and actions. This level he calls 'Basic Underlying Assumptions' (p. 16). Schein maintains that to understand an organisation's culture one has to be able to examine all three levels, for it is only by understanding levels One and Two that one can unlock the door to the most fundamental level, the Basic Assumptions level. Like management theorist Gareth Morgan (1986), Schein cautions against a superficial understanding of the organisational culture concept as manifested in the structural view of organisational culture which views culture as an entity which is largely created and controlled by management. In order to understand and to meaningfully effect a change in an organisation's culture one must, as Schein explains, be able to:

> Avoid the superficial models of culture and build on the deeper, more complex anthropological models. Culture will be most useful as a concept if it helps us to better understand the hidden and complex aspects of organisational life. This understanding cannot be obtained if we use superficial definitions (1992: 32).

As a result of my exposure to Schein's organisational culture theory model and my own reflective analysis on the subject, my thinking was transformed in the course of the literature review. Consequently, before ever conducting the first interview I found that I had moved from the more facile, structural interpretation of organisational culture to the 'deeper interpretive view of culture' (Wilson, 1992). Armed with Schein's model I was now ready to move to the next stage of the research cycle, the interview process.

The interview process – planning and conducting the interview

As it is for many action researchers, the interview process was central to my research methodology. My initial plan involved interviewing a number of non-U.S. trained and U.S. trained employees on D-Ram's culture and value system. This plan changed somewhat as a result of an unexpected event which I will deal with in greater detail in the next section. To introduce an element of triangulation into the process I also planned to interview one or two American members of the senior management team who had been relocated to Ireland for two years to assist D-Ram's start up operation. As things turned out I conducted in-depth interviews with four non-U.S. trained employees and one interview with the American chief executive of D-Ram's Irish subsidiary. He had been with the D-Ram Irish project since its inception and had also been living and working in Ireland for a period of approximately two years. He was also a corporate vice president of the D-Ram corporation world-wide, and consequently had great insights into D-Ram's corporate culture.

Each interview was conducted in the privacy of a D-Ram conference room and lasted for approximately 45 minutes. I had no problems securing an interview with anyone, not even a corporate vice president, which is in itself a commentary on the D-Ram culture and the expectation of total involvement and commitment at all levels. In many ways this was just another 'D-Ram project' in which one should participate if one had something to offer. In other ways, the participants were themselves interested in the project under discussion, perhaps because, as Helen Simons (1982) points out, 'People will treat the interview seriously if they think you can change something' (p.34).

The interview style

The interview style was the same for each interview. I did not adopt Tomlinson's (1989) hierarchical focusing as a research interview strategy, but opted instead for the open ended approach advocated by Simons. This I felt was the most effective way of creating an action research project of a collaborative nature. Through dialogue with my colleagues I was hoping that they would assist me in defining the problem and the issues to be addressed. As Simons points out

> Information people offer of their own initiative is more true, some argue, than what they say in answering questions. Whether or not this is so, interviewees' unsolicited responses frequently alert the interviewer to consider the subject under discussion in a new light (p. 34)

Elliott (1991) also maintains that the unstructured interview format is probably the best format to adopt at the early stages of action research and he goes on to suggest that even as a project matures and allows for a more structured questioning style, the 'interviewer should leave room for the interviewees to raise their own topics and issues' (p. 80).

To achieve an open ended participatory approach, I designed a straightforward 'values' form with three basic questions requesting participants to list

- four important Irish values
- four important D-Ram values and
- the differences between Irish and American values

At the beginning of each interview each participant was given ten minutes to answer the questions and I used their replies as the basis for our discussions. In keeping with the spirit of action research, I feel that the approach was participant centred rather than researcher centred, as together we explored what 'Irish values' and 'D-Ram values' meant for them and where the differences lay between the two.

The importance of probing

Conducting an interview in this manner is not easy. To do it well, one has to be familiar with the subject matter; be an effective listener and an expert prober. As Simons (1982) points out:

> Listening by itself, does not always lead to depth of understanding. Probing is necessary to get behind the expected response to test the significance of what you are being told (p.35).

I found this to be particularly good advice and I used probing in the course of the interviews to try to get to the essence of what people were saying. For example, when one interviewee mentioned that she thought the salaries at D-Ram were lower than those offered to contemporaries working for other companies, I probed further for clarification and asked her what that suggested to her about people at D-Ram. Initially her response was elusive but with constant probing and a rephrasing of the question I finally got to the essence of what she was trying to say – which was that 'People are undervalued at D-Ram.' Two and a half pages of probing later I was able to explore the question again, this time in a much more direct manner by asking, 'Do people matter at D-Ram?' The response was:

> *I think the job matters ... Generally the job matters and I think people will be swept away if ... That would be a general observation. That the job is first and that people would come an awful long way behind ...*

To put this in context, this response came from the most positive non-U.S. trained participant that I interviewed, someone who told me several times during the interview that D-Ram is a great place to work. If I had not probed to the extent I did, I would not have reached the level of 'basic assumptions' which Schein argues you have to reach in order to conduct a true and accurate culture analysis study. This example also illustrates very clearly the wisdom of Simons' insights on the common errors of open ended interviews:

A second related error is to seek closure too soon by accepting the initial response too readily ... or by asking questions which give the interviewee a plausible response without committing him to reveal what he really thinks or feels (1992: 35).

The importance of probing in the interview process should not be underestimated. Probing is a very useful device for asking respondents to provide further clarification or to expand upon an incomplete answer. It needs to be used wisely however and should never be used to intimidate or coerce respondents into revealing every piece of information which they possess.

Phenomenological analysis of interview data

In analysing the interviews I adopted Hycner's (1985) guidelines. This involved:

- Transcription in full of each interview tape
- Listening to the interviews over and over again to determine a sense of the whole
- Identifying clusters of meanings from the raw data and determining themes
- Identifying common themes for all the interviews

Based on this approach a number of key themes emerged as follows:

1 D-Ram's culture is a culture of long hours and constant pressure to meet deadlines. Most interviewees resented the long working hours, felt they were unnecessary but felt pressurised to continually work late. The long hours were viewed as anti-family and ran counter to the primacy of the family in mainstream Irish culture.

2 D-Ram is such a politically correct culture that there is no room for humour or fun in the organisation. The interviewees felt that this stifled a very important component of the Irish persona which thrives on humour and the freedom to 'slag' one's colleagues in a good humoured way without insulting them.

3   D-Ram's culture is one of every person for themselves. Time and time again the interviewees made the point that it was important to cover one's tracks all the time and to look out for number one or else you wouldn't survive.

4   It's a culture where results not people matter. At D-Ram you're just a number. As one interviewee pointed out while commenting on the physical environment, *'Everything here is the same. There are no distinguishing features about anything ... a room is a number. You are a number. The only personable thing about you is the fact that you have a name, that you are an employee and that's it.'*

5   D-Ram's culture is not as 'open' or as 'equal' a culture as its surface level implies or as the organisation would have us believe. The interviewees felt that there was a certain amount of pretence about the 'open' culture where everyone including senior managers were on first name terms and operated from bull pen cubicles like everyone else. Deep down they knew everyone had their place in the pecking order which the physical artefacts, no matter how well designed, could not conceal.

The U.S. trained employees' perspective

In the initial research plan I had intended to interview a number of U.S. trained employees. This plan changed as a result of a fortuitous event. Shortly after I had conducted the first two interviews with the non-U.S. trained employees, I was sent on a three-day consulting skills course by D-Ram along with eleven other colleagues. Eleven of the twelve participants on this course were part of D-Ram's start up team who had been trained in the U.S. Interestingly the consultants delivering the course encouraged us a group to spend a large amount of time analysing D-Ram's corporate culture. Initially there was a reluctance on the part of the group to engage in this exercise. However, when the engagement finally happened, there emerged a very negative critique about D-Ram's culture and value system. The communal confession ran as follows:

- We're all in very stressful jobs.
- D-Ram is shaping who we are.
- We work so hard at D-Ram we don't have time for a social life.
- The reward system creates discontent and mistrust.
- D-Ram shoots messengers. So you don't challenge.
- D-Ram pretends it's a great place to work. But it's not.
- D-Ram pretends that there's an open door policy. But there is a hidden agenda.
- There's an element of pretence by senior management that people matter. They don't. It's really the technology that counts.

This was raw stuff indeed and in many ways I was disconcerted by the revelations, mainly because they came from a group of people whom I would have regarded as very committed corporate citizens, excellent D-Ram role models; people whom I had known personally for a number of years and who seemed to thrive on the energy high that working in an organisation like D-Ram gave them.

In some respects the revelations from my peers at the consulting skills course really changed the essence of the study because they revealed that there was a serious problem with the D-Ram culture period. It didn't really matter whether you were U.S. trained or not – the only difference seemed to be that the U.S. trained employees were more brutally honest and openly critical when forced to examine their situation.

This conclusion is further reinforced when you compare the results from the Harrison culture survey completed by the two groups. As part of the cultural analysis exercise, the consultants delivering the consulting course requested the group to complete a culture survey entitled 'Understanding your organisation's culture' (Harrison, 1972). As part of this exercise the participants were required to rate the organisation's existing and preferred culture under the following four headings (1) power, (2) achievement, (3) role and (4) support. As it proved a very useful and effective cultural analysis tool I decided to use it as part of my research process with the non-U.S. trained employees also.

An analysis of the figures from the survey indicated that the non U.S. trained employees were not quite as burnt out as the U.S. trained employees. It was reasonable to deduce that this was because they had not been with the company as long. Nonetheless the Harrison survey shows that both groups rated D-Ram's culture as primarily an 'achievement culture' and secondly as 'power culture'. D-Ram as a support culture was given a very low rating by both groups. Under the preferred culture heading, both groups showed a dramatic swing towards a 'support culture' at the expense of the 'power culture'. Both groups were also looking for a reduction in the 'achievement culture' although this is most noticeable in the U.S. trained group. In sum then, the preferred culture mix for both groups was a balance between an achievement and support culture. So what did this all mean?

Table 1: Harrison Culture Survey Results

	Existing Culture		Preferred Culture	
	Non U.S. Trained	U.S. Trained	Non U.S. Trained	U.S. Trained
Power	2.0	2.1	0.75	0.6
Role	2.5	1.1	2.2	1.1
Achievement	4.5	6.0	4.0	4.6
Support	0.75	0.8	2.75	3.7

Conclusion

The results from the Harrison survey revealed that D-Ram is a high achievement culture but that the balance is wrong as it would appear to be a mix of an achievement and power culture. This points to an organisation dysfunction because as Harrison points out, the natural grouping tends to be a combination of (1) power and role culture or (2) achievement and support culture. The combination at D-Ram therefore is an unhealthy one, combining as it does the burnout and disillusionment of the high achievement culture with the control mentality of the power culture, where control lies with the dominant coalition.

This, coupled with the data revealed through interviews and the views of the consulting skills course participants, suggested that there was a compliance with rather than any real commitment to the D-Ram culture. At the surface level the U.S. culture and values would appear to have transferred successfully, but when you dug deep and got down to the level of basic assumptions, the reality was somewhat different. It was therefore my conclusion, based on this study, that beneath the smooth veneer of organisational life at D-Ram there lay a serious clash of two cultures, Irish versus American, which was causing organisational discontent and disillusionment. Clear, confident and effective leadership would be required to address this problem because as Schein points out 'leadership and culture are conceptually intertwined' (Schein, 1992: 5).

Finally I wish to comment on the applicability of the action research paradigm to this study. I found it to be an excellent vehicle for conducting a study of this nature. How else could I have reached the level of 'basic assumptions' except by exploring the members' thoughts, feelings and insights through in-depth interviews. A questionnaire, no matter how well designed, could not have revealed precisely what was going on in the organisation. As Schein argues, 'Questionnaires can be useful tools for getting at norms of behaviour and at organisational climate, but such data should not be confused with cultural assumptions. At best survey results are an artifact of the culture' (p. 186). The danger as he cautions in studying organisational culture using traditional research methods is that 'we end up sacrificing credibility and validity in order to satisfy canons of normal science' (p. 186). If one really wants to provide the organisation with a mirror onto itself, then the action research model is probably one of the best vehicles for so doing.

While I learned many lessons in the course of this study both about action research and organisational culture, by far the most important lesson was the change that occurred in my own reflective thought processes and my own understanding of the culture of the organisation in which I worked. As Schein eloquently phrased it (1992: 207:

> When we see the essence of a culture, the paradigm by which people operate, we are struck by how powerful our insight into that organisation now is, and we can see instantly why certain things work the way they do, why certain proposals are never bought into, why change is so difficult, why certain people leave… It is the search for and the occasional finding of this central insight that makes it all worthwhile. Suddenly we understand an organisation; suddenly we see what makes it tick. That level of insight is worth working for, even if in the end we can share it with only colleagues.

References

Cave, E. and Wilkinson, C. (1992) 'Developing Managerial Capabilities in Education' in *Managing Change in Education: Individual and Organisational Perspectives*. Milton Keynes, Open University Press.

de Bono, E. (1982) Lateral Thinking for Management: A Handbook. Harmondsworth, Penguin.

Elliott, J. (1991) *Action Research for Educational Change*. Milton Keynes, Open University Press.

Handy, C. (1993) (4th Edition) *Understanding Organisations*. London, Penguin.

Harrison, R. (1972) 'Understanding Your Organization's Culture' in *Harvard Business Review*, May/June.

Hampden-Turner, C. (1992) *Creating Corporate Cultures*. Reading, MA, Addison Wesley.

Hofstede, G. (1980) 'Motivation, Leadership and Organisations: Do American Theories Apply Abroad?' in D.S. Pugh (ed.) (3rd Edition) *Organisation Theory*. London, Penguin.

Hycner, J. (1985) 'Some guidelines for the phenomenological analysis of interview data' in *Human Studies*, 8, pp. 279–303.

Kotter, J.P. and Heskett, J.L. (1992) *Corporate Culture and Performance*. New York, The Free Press.

Mintzberg, H. (1987) *Power in and around Organizations.* New Jersey, Englewood Cliffs, Prentice-Hall.

Morgan, G. (1986) *Images of Organisation.* London, Sage.

Morgan, G. (1993) *Imaginisation.* London, Sage.

Peters, T. and Waterman, R. (1982) *In Search of Excellence.* New York, Harper and Row.

Raelin, J.A. (1985) *The Clash of Cultures.* Boston, Harvard Business School.

Simons, H. (1982) 'Conversation Piece: The Practice of Interviewing in Case Study Research' in McCormick, R. (ed.) *Calling Education to Account.* London, Heinemann Education.

Schein, E.H. (1992) (2nd Edition) *Organisation Culture and Leadership.* California, Jossey-Bass.

Schön, D. (1983) *The Reflective Practitioner.* New York, Basic Books.

Tomlinson, P. (1989) 'Having It Both Ways: Hierarchical focusing as research review method' in *British Educational Research Journal*, Vol. 15, No. 2.

Trompenaars, F. (1993) *Riding the Waves of Culture.* London, Nicholas Brealey.

Wilson, D. (1992) *A Strategy of Change.* London, Routledge.

Note

1 'D-Ram' is a fictitious name.

Chapter 12

Using Information and Communications Technology (ICT) to support action research and distance education

Margaret Farren and Edward Tweedy

Our session in the conference was entitled 'The potential of technology to support action research'. During the session, Margaret Farren of Dublin City University, Jack Whitehead of the University of Bath, and Fionnuala Howard of Sutton Park School, Dublin, used videoconferencing and Microsoft NetMeeting to link up with Ed Tweedy at Rockingham Community College (RCC) in the USA. Margaret introduced the session making use of several multimedia features of PowerPoint. Ed demonstrated the Introduction to Computing course which RCC offers via the Internet. Both Ed and Margaret showed the use of the NetMeeting program for collaborative work. Jack Whitehead also showed how he was making use of the Internet to create a World College of Teachers and Educators. Finally, Fionnuala Howard showed how she used the features of Microsoft Word for making presentations. This practical demonstration explored how technology can be used to support action research and distance education.

This chapter consists of four sections. Each section reports and reflects on different features and uses of ICT in support of action research and distance education.

We would first like to clarify our understanding of the terms 'action research' and 'distance education'. Action research, for us, is a form of enquiry in which practitioners reflect systematically on their practice, implementing informed action to bring about improvement in their practice. Distance education refers generally to a course where the learning supporter is at a different location from the learner. Teaching and learning is done over distance using appropriate technology and media in place of the traditional face to face contact between teacher and student.

Some of the technologies of distance education include Internet courses designed and used in-house, Internet courses marketed commercially, video courses, TV broadcasts, video streaming, and videoconferencing. Teaching methods range from presenting information to the student, in lecture note format, and then having the student submit assignments and/or sit an examination, to interaction between students, lecturers, and use of a variety of media such as visuals and audio. An example of an on-line course which makes use of audio and visual material is the Database module for the BSc in Computer Applications at Dublin City University (see http://www.compapp.dcu.ie/~asmeaton/pubs-list.html/ VIRTLECTCASE.html)

Videoconferencing

Videoconferencing is the process of using appropriate hardware and software to conduct a conference between groups of people not physically located in the same place. Videoconferencing technology allows two or more people, in different locations, to see and hear each other at the same time, sometimes even sharing computer applications for collaboration. This technology offers many possibilities for distance education, including communicating with speakers, collaborating on projects and sharing ideas. Placing a video call is similar to making a phone call, except that in addition to hearing the voice of the other person, you can see their image, share applications and documents, collaborate on document and project development, transfer files, and chat on a given topic. Most of these features can be shared among several people in various locations around the world who are participating in the videoconference or electronic meeting.

Connections between users can be direct connections using expensive ISDN lines for optimum quality or dial-up lines for lesser cost but with much poorer quality. For our videoconference session we tried to balance the cost and quality and chose to use transmission over the Internet from a PC connected to local area networks. There is minimum cost for such Internet transmissions and the quality of audio, video and shared applications is quite acceptable.

1 Features of Rockingham Community College Internet Course

Introducing the session, Margaret demonstrated the features of PowerPoint which could be used for presentations; hyperlinks to other resources, use of video and photographs to communicate our practice, and use of visuals to enhance text. Next, a PowerPoint presentation from Rockingham Community College was viewed at Trinity College. The participants in Dublin were able to hear the presenter at RCC and see his slides in the course of the presentation. The main features of the RCC Internet course were shown. These features include communication and collaboration via e-mail, communication via Web pages, use of chat rooms and forums, resources through Internet searches, communications via audio and video.

The following gives a more detailed account of each feature:

E-mail
E-mail provides the student with a resource they can use to communicate with other students and educators. Collaboration via e-mail is very important for team work and project work in the Internet-based class, and the same kind of collaboration is possible between students, teachers and peers. E-mail has been widely used to support teachers in their action enquiries, and makes it possible to communicate easily with other members of the class or project team.

For the RCC Internet course, each student is assigned an e-mail address. If they do not already have an address, one of the several free sources is used, as e-mail is a vital part of this course. The students are trained in the use of e-mail to communicate and transfer files as part of their orientation session.

Web pages

Web pages are another form of communication used in this Internet course. There are web pages for the course syllabus, schedule and outline. Web pages are used to publish assignments, lab projects, news and Internet links relevant to the classes. Students are encouraged to check these web pages daily just as they would check their e-mail. The web pages are maintained by the course tutor, and can be updated to reflect current information, schedules, assignments and course activities. It is recommended that any group working on a significant project set up web pages to communicate their findings and provide information for others.

Discussion forums

Discussion forums are used in the Internet courses for posting questions and ideas and getting responses from the group. In the Introduction to Computers class, for example, the questions are posted to the discussion forum each week by the tutor, and the students enter their responses at a second level. At lower levels there can then be responses to responses. The forum is a way to have discussion among participants in a class or project without the need for them all to be connected to the Internet at the same time. This technique is valuable, as students typically cannot get together at a common time, one of the reasons they are taking the courses in the Internet format. The forum allows anyone to post ideas and debate these ideas with other class members at a time convenient for each person, replacing classroom discussions. One important feature of this technique is that it allows one to get a printout of the entire threaded string of comments and responses for future reference and documentation. WebCT and Lotus Notes are other examples of collaborative learning tools, which have been used by the authors of this chapter for on-line professional development courses.

Chat rooms

Chat rooms are useful on Internet courses, as all students in a work group, or possibly an entire class, can get online at one time and have a discussion. In the chat room, a participant types in a contribution, and the other participants can identify the writer. Like the forum, the chat room provides for the printing out of the entire conversation, labelled by the speaker, for future study and reference. The difficulties of using a chat room can be getting everyone together at the same time, and managing a large group discussion. Various Search Engines are also useful in online courses, as they can provide links to useful material.

2   NetMeeting for Collaborative Learning

Margaret and Ed used the Microsoft NetMeeting program and videoconferencing to share applications during the presentation. They used the following features of videoconferencing:

- sharing of applications and files;
- collaboration on projects;
- presentations from remote sites;
- chat rooms and white boards;
- record of chats and discussions;
- audio and video capabilities.

We demonstrated how participants in different locations could work simultaneously on the same application. Through the use of the share feature of NetMeeting, Ed was able to share an Excel spreadsheet on his computer at RCC with the presenters at Trinity College. Changes could be made on the spreadsheet at Trinity and sent back to the host computer. The spreadsheet could be saved and printed where it was created. Finally, the file could be transferred electronically to the remote PC for printing and further use. The share facility of NetMeeting could be used for collaborating on action research projects.

We also showed the use of the chat room on NetMeeting. This feature allows participants to meet online at a planned time, and join in an ongoing typed discussion, with all comments labelled by speakers. The sessions can be saved and printed for documentation and further review.

We used the whiteboard feature of NetMeetings. These boards allow all users to draw on the same whiteboard simultaneously to produce a finished product. Pictures can be pasted to the whiteboard by anyone participating in the videoconference session, and can be moved, modified, and reviewed by any participant.

A participant with an inexpensive PC camera at their location can capture a picture, paste it to the whiteboard, and share it with the audience attending the videoconferencing session. To illustrate this feature, Ed pasted a copy of the picture of the Dublin audience that he saw to the whiteboard so that the Dublin audience could see themselves on the RCC screen. The white board is certainly a good tool for sharing graphic images with others in multiple locations! Chat sessions, graphic images and whiteboards can be saved for possible future use.

Audio and video capabilities wrap up the list of features of videoconferencing. Good quality video is important for a live presentation, but, in our link up, it was found that the communication via shared applications, whiteboards, chat sessions, along with voice, minimised the need for good on-line video in many cases. With Internet transmissions using NetMeeting, audio presents the greatest challenge. Sometimes it can be advantageous to communicate on the telephone line, using handsets or speaker-phones. However, in the RCC transmissions to Ireland, there was reasonably good audio, especially when the video was paused during the presentation. This can be credited to reasonably good equipment, and the fact that most live presentations were done at a time when Internet traffic was not at its highest volume.

Many of the features of videoconferencing used in this session could be useful in action research projects for collaborating and communication. In fact, when preparing for the Conference presentations, Ed and Margaret made extensive use of NetMeeting. The entire presentation was developed and reviewed, making as much use of these features as possible, thus saving time, costs and effort.

Features of NetMeeting

It is worthwhile summarising the specific features of NetMeeting such as have already been demonstrated. Some features apply to all participants in the videoconference and others apply between two participants only. The features include:

Audio and video sharing

When participants join a videoconference or meeting, any two participants can share video and audio.

Chat room sharing

This feature allows participants to chat with each other by typing their comments to everyone in the meeting or privately to one participant. Chat messages can be saved or printed for documentation of the discussions.

Shared whiteboard

All participants can contribute to drawings and text on the whiteboard at the same time. Images and text can be pasted on the whiteboard by any of the participants. The contents of the whiteboard can be saved or printed.

File transfer

Files can be easily transferred to other participants in the meeting.

Shared applications

Applications can be shared with participants in the meeting, under the control of the presenter. This enables the participants who join a meeting to view a PowerPoint presentation.

Collaboration on applications

All participants can contribute to the development or modification of an application. Each can gain control of the mouse in turn to add their own comments or take their turn. Collaboration requires some discipline among users, and is aided by a good meeting facilitator.

Ease of use and connection to other users
Meetings can be easily set up with one participant hosting a meeting at a predetermined time, and allowing others to join. Connection can be via servers using familiar addresses, or directly to another user's IP (Internet protocol) address.

User control and security
Participants can see what they are sending, whether it is video, chat text, or shared data, and can control who views the data.

Easy installation of software
Software can be downloaded easily from the Internet, or is available with Windows 98 or with many of the camera devices.

3   World College of Teachers and Educators

Jack Whitehead discussed how he was making use of the Internet to create a World College of Teachers and Educators. His Action Research Homepage at http://www.bath.ac.uk/~edsajw has links to Action Research Masters and PhD theses. There are links to action research web sites world-wide, including Ontario action research, Action Research Ireland, and Teaching Today for Tomorrow. He also showed links which he has created to relevant online journals. Jack showed the chat room he has set up on his homepage.

The purpose of this chat room is to enable practitioners to share and take their ideas forward. He showed sample conversations. These showed typical interactions within a chat room. For example, he showed how a PhD student who had a question about a particular article was able to make contact with the author of the article through the chat room. Jack is particularly focusing on the development of multimedia for communicating the nature of standards of practice of teachers around the world. We viewed a video clip of a teacher in her classroom in order to show how the visual medium can communicate the teacher's educational values in a way which would be difficult for text alone.

4 The potential of Microsoft Word for qualitative research

Fionnuala Howard showed the features of Microsoft Word which she had used in presenting her case study, which formed part of the Masters Degree with the School of Education, Dublin City University. She found that the program had all the features she needed to manage, analyse and present her study. Her diary entries and interviews were transcribed and then stored in Word. The *Find* command allowed her to retrieve chunks of data, which were copied and pasted into individual files under numerous headings. As Word allows paragraph and page numbering, it was possible to reference data selected to illustrate particular points. The use of multiple windows allowed reflection, as she was able to toggle back and forth between data, notes on literature, and the emerging research account. The features of *cut, copy, paste*, helped her to juxtapose her ideas and concepts. Once style sheets are appropriately assigned in Word, the task of compiling tables of contents and lists of exhibits takes only a few seconds. Through using style sheets she could experiment with visual presentations. This, she claims, assisted greatly in the cognitive process of reflection and synthesis.

Conclusion

The presenters in the conference had not met face to face to prepare the session. Technology allowed us to plan, organise and carry out our presentation effectively, despite the fact that we were continents apart.

We were able to show, in the presence of a live audience, how technology allowed us to introduce one another, and the session; how technology could be integrated into a particular course; how it could enable collaborative work; how it could assist practitioners to share ideas and thereby make improvements to their practice; and how technology could assist practitioners in their research, and in presenting their findings. From our reflection on this session, it is evident that ICT can be useful in action research and distance education.

For information on the Action Research Conference, see Conference Web Site at http://www.iol.ie-rayo

For reference to action research sites, see world-wide at http://www.bath.ac.uk/~edsajw

E-mail: RETweedy@aol.com
Ed Tweedy's RCC Web Site is at http://welcome,to/rcc

E-mail: MFARREN@compnpp.dcu.ie
For conference PowerPoint presentations, see Margaret Farren's Web Site at http://WWW.compapp.dcu.ie/~mfarren

References

Collis, B. (1996) *Tele-learning in a Digital World*. London, Thompson Computer Press.

Farren, M. (1998) 'Using the Internet for Professional Development' in *Conference Proceedings, Third European Conference on Integrating Information and Communication Technology in the Curriculum*, Dublin City University pp. 99–104.

Kaye, A. and Mason, R. (1989) *Mindweave: communication, computers and distance education*. Oxford, Pergamon Press.

Mircosoft Corporation (1998) Microsoft NetMeeting Web Pages [On-Line] Available: http://www.microsoft.com/netmeeting

McNiff, J., Lomax, P. and Whitehead, J. (1996) *You and Your Action Research Project*. London, Routledge.

Mills, R. and Tait, A. (1996) *Supporting the Learner in Open and Distance Education*. London, Pitman Publishing.

Pacific Bell (1998) *Videoconferencing for learning*. [On-Line] Available: http://www.kn.pacbell.com/wired/vidconf

Rockingham Community College, College Web Pages. [On-Line] Available: http://www.rcc.cc.nc./us

Smeaton, A.F. and Crimmons, F. (1997) 'Virtual Lectures for Undergraduate Teaching: Delivery Using RealAudio and the WWW', in *Proceedings of the ED-Media '97 Conference*, Calgary, June.

Summers, R. (1998) *Official Microsoft NetMeeting Book*. Washington, Microsoft Press.

Tweedy, E., Judge, M. and Sherry, L. (1998) 'Videoconferencing in the Classroom' in *Conference Proceedings, Third European Conference on Integrating Information and Communications Technology in the Curriculum*, pp. 235–243.

Chapter 13

Reclaiming school as a caring place

Carmel Lillis

Background to the research

I was in the third year of principalship of a nine teacher infant school when it was decided to amalgamate our school with another infant school on the same campus. I was appointed as Principal of the new school. My story is an account of how I worked to improve my practice as Principal in order better to serve the school community.

I am convinced that the role of the principal is an extremely important and influential one. I have had experience of working with six different principals during my career as a primary teacher and I have spent time reflecting on the unique contribution each one made to the school organisation and culture. I have also observed their impact on their colleagues. The legacy that principals leave has the potential for harm as well as benefit.

This reflection led to a quest on my part to discover as much as possible about what constitutes good leadership, and how I could ensure that my own leadership was such that it would encourage individual well-being and social benefit. I read widely around this subject and attended conferences and seminars in order to widen my knowledge base in the area. This theoretical foundation was a starting point on my journey, but I soon discovered that this alone would not bring about changes for good in the school or indeed in my own practice. I quickly realised that if I wanted to be a more effective principal then this would demand a conscious effort to act in a different way and then to act consistently in this new way. I was convinced that I could best change the social situation by first looking at my own practice.

The change in circumstances in school arising out of the amalgamation led me to think that I would benefit by undertaking a further course of studies. I felt I needed support in dealing with my new responsibilities in relation to colleagues, children and their parents.

I therefore enrolled to study for a Master in Education degree course. The research methodology used throughout the course of study would be action research. Action research is a practitioner-based form of enquiry, and the epistemological basis of our course was taken to be in the personal practical knowledge of teachers as they worked to investigate and improve their practice. We course members were encouraged to believe that we are the people best suited to research our own practice in a systematic and rigorous way. Jack Whitehead (1993) places the 'I' of the researcher at the centre of the research question; he suggests that professional education knowledge is generated through the descriptions and explanations of teachers as they aim to address the question, 'How do I improve my practice?'. This new knowledge may then be tested and critiqued against existing theories in the literature.

It seemed essential that whatever course of studies I chose to follow at that time had to have relevance to my work in school. So much the better if I could monitor my efforts to improve my practice in the company of a convivial and interested group of educators.

I wanted my practice as principal to support the excellent work of my colleagues, and encourage them to engage in on-going evaluation. I decided to monitor my general work as principal, and to identify specific areas of practice that might need special investigation. I used Whitehead's questions as an organising framework for my studies:

What is your concern?
Why are you concerned?
What do you think you could do about it?
What kind of 'evidence' could you collect to help you make some judgement about what is happening?
How would you collect such 'evidence'?

How would you check that your judgement about what has happened is reasonably fair and accurate?

(in McNiff, 1988).

When I analysed my reflection on these questions, I began slowly to unravel the history of my involvement in education and my experience of being student, teacher and latterly principal. My concern at the time was that some colleagues expected me to behave as a dictatorial principal. This was evident in the format of staff meetings where it was expected that I would preside, make decisions without consultation and have these decisions subsequently criticised. This way of living my professional life was in stark contrast to the values I hold as a human being. My educational values grew from experiences of family and community devotion to the ideals of democracy and freedom. I was also influenced by the experience of positive working relationships I have had with colleagues, including principals, where I was given the freedom to make my own professional decisions and had their permission and support to do this. This legacy of positive and democratic working relationships made my situation in school all the more painful, and constituted a dichotomy between my values base and the reality of my lived life (Whitehead, 1989; McNiff, 1988).

I therefore set about reviewing my practice in school in three specific areas:

1.   Communication throughout the school.
2.   Staff development.
3.   Nurturing a climate of care.

1   Communication

During my first year as principal of the amalgamated school, I made an effort to engage colleagues in a dialogue about our work. I asked for their opinions on various issues by means of questionnaires. Colleagues were asked to indicate any areas of concern by marking boxes. I had originally aimed to save time by disseminating questionnaires, but I became aware that the number of questionnaires returned, and the responses they contained, indicated that colleagues wanted to tell me their concerns in a more intensive, personalised way. I must admit that I was unsure how I could use the information I gathered. I collected and stored the responses, but at the time I did not communicate any analysis to my colleagues. I knew that I should be talking and exploring options but the ways and means of doing so eluded me.

I decided to experiment with the facilitation of staff meetings. These monthly meetings are our only formal opportunity for getting together to discuss school business. The meetings are based around an agreed agenda, but at the time they generally took the form of the principal having to answer questions on diverse topics. It was often an occasion for negative comment about the Department of Education and a time to tell the principal exactly what was wrong with the school. Determined to change this state of affairs, I asked for volunteers to take turns at chairing the meetings; the volunteers and I would meet to organise the meeting. Thankfully several colleagues were willing to form a rota for this.

Over time, this democratic form of facilitation became a characteristic of our staff meetings, and there were many visibly positive outcomes. For my part, I shared the burden of preparation with different members of staff. They were ideally placed to monitor the direct concerns of their colleagues and therefore our meetings were more focused. I found my discussions with groups of two or three helpful because they gave me a chance to communicate some of my values around different issues. These colleagues were also able to sense my vulnerability and, I hope, my courage and determination.

I sought staff opinion, again through a questionnaire, and in conversation with a group of experienced colleagues, about these changes, and there was majority support for our new way of working. Those who were part of this new process commented on the ease of shared facilitation. Younger staff members spoke about how they felt part of the decision-making process and more involved in the business of the meetings.

I asked members of staff for their opinions on this intervention.

E. wrote: 'With the re-organisation of our staff meetings the focus is taken off the principal and instead members of staff become the focus of the meeting. There is a greater feeling of solidarity and less pressure this way. Working in small groups also helps members of staff to voice their opinions.'

Some while later we again changed the organisation of staff meetings to allow a team of teachers to prepare and facilitate the meetings. I was gradually drawing more colleagues into serious debate about our work in school. I believe they were also learning the process of working together in small groups.

I was pleased to see colleagues taking charge of their own professional interests within the school. However, there were two or three colleagues who consistently wanted me as principal to chair meetings. There was also resistance from these same colleagues to discussing items in small groups within the meeting and reporting back to the larger group. On reflection, I felt that the expressed fears of some of the teachers were a symptom of lack of ease with new routines and new practices, and might be seen as anticipated reactions to unwelcome change.

I realised during that year how fortunate I was in having a highly motivated group of people in the school. I became increasingly aware of my responsibility to create an environment and discourse of considerate participation where people could explore their personal gifts and educative potentials.

With the help of the school secretary I arranged to print memos to staff on a weekly basis. The memos would remind colleagues of events during the week or keep them up to date with developments in already agreed plans. In the beginning I found that the memos were not being attended to and I had to remind colleagues, in a light-hearted way, that this was my effort to communicate with them. I wrote in my research diary:

> I wrote memoranda for them detailing the events of the day, which were handed out at break in the staff-room. When I visited the room later I found about one third of the typed pages left behind. I would like them to keep these notes but I must not become impatient' (research diary, January 10th).

I also placed a large flip-chart initially outside my office and later in the staff room, to record significant pieces of information. It appeared however that colleagues were too rushed in the mornings to see it!

Information was travelling from me to the staff at this point but I was not being responded to by my colleagues. I would have to find a way to get them to talk with me. Easier said than done – constraints of time and our duties to the children did not leave much space for talking with one another; this applied as much for teachers talking with each other as for teachers talking with me. How could I find space for teachers to talk together as professionals and still have the children in their care suitably supervised while learning?

I found the solution to this dilemma by creating an opportunity for me to be of service to my colleagues. I organised teachers into three groups. These groups would meet for one half-hour every Friday and discuss together matters of concern in the school. During the meeting, I would take the children in their classes for music in the assembly hall.

Teachers were very happy with this arrangement. Some observers, colleagues from other schools, saw this response as being typical of teachers who are getting time off class. Principals that I spoke to were sceptical of the outcomes. In some instances they spoke about giving 'too much' to staff. They asked if I did not have enough work to do already? Of course I do, but if I want my values to be realised, I must be prepared to put in strokes of daily effort.

The most senior teacher from the classes involved chaired each group meeting. They gave me a written resumé of the group's proceedings and decisions taken. Initially, these conversations centred on school organisation, such as Christmas concert arrangements. I later read through the combined reports and based organisational decisions on them. One colleague commented: 'We do not have to worry about staff meetings any more because all the difficulties have been discussed at the small group meetings' (research diary, January 21st). Now, some time on from these initial efforts, I am pleased to report that there is no longer a feeling of apprehension while colleagues assemble for staff meetings, and time during formal staff meetings can be more fruitfully spent considering our achievements and making plans for the future.

I asked colleagues, by means of a questionnaire, what they considered the most helpful aspect of current procedures in school. There was overwhelming support for the continuation of the Friday meetings.

B., M., and R. are three senior members of staff. B. expressed gratitude for the staff memos that are sent around. M. said that these were good but commented favourably also on the large notice board in the staff-room. R. said that this was a good way to keep colleagues informed about developments in other classrooms, for example, class tours to places of interest. B. asked if the reports from the Friday meetings could be circulated to all staff so that they would be aware of the decisions or attitudes of other groups. This was an obvious course of action and I immediately gave a commitment to it. As a follow-on from this, both B. and M. saw the Friday meetings as having eased the process of amalgamation of the two staffs. Priority had been given to staff discussion time and this had contributed to the excellent staff relations we have at present.

As an administrative principal there is a danger of retreat to the office if the atmosphere without is threatening or uneasy. I am reminded of what Humphreys says: 'The availability and approachability of the principal and the vice-principal are important factors in the creation of positive staff morale' (Humphreys, 1993: 70). During the period of my research I resolved to be available to my colleagues so that their concerns could be met as quickly as possible. Humphreys suggests that '[a]part from crisis situations it is good to specify times that are most convenient' (Humphreys, 1993:70). Bearing this advice in mind, I resolved to be near at hand, not in my office, in the morning. Unfortunately, this is when the phone always rings or I have to leave to speak to the caretaker or the supervisor of the Community Employment scheme, and such instances cut down on my availability. I decided to extend my availability and use every opportunity throughout the day to build closeness with my colleagues. 'Approachability is conveyed through good eye-contact, listening, concern, sensitivity to the stresses and strains teachers may be experiencing, personal time with each member of staff, requesting support and help, admitting one's own vulnerabilities and active response to teachers' requests for help and support' (Humphreys, 1993: 71).

I know that I was conscious of making an effort to be available to people during this time. I read the following in my research diary:

> I had occasion to speak at length to a colleague today (January 12th); ... Later in the day I deliberately spent time with another colleague (January 12th); ... I spoke to all my colleagues today. I regard this as an achievement of worth (January 18th); ... I had a chance to speak to the teachers and ask them how things were going for them (January 26th).

I was reminded of the advice given by the psychologist during my period of training as home/school/co-ordinator. He maintained that it is important to go to teachers and to ask them how things are for them. He said that if this is done it allows the teacher a chance to off-load the stress they are feeling. It might be the only chance for them to be heard.

I was delighted to receive a report on communications in our school from a student teacher who spent four weeks with us before Easter. She wrote:

> The communication relationships in this school are strong, friendly, caring, helpful and supportive. Even my supervisors have commented on the friendly attitude found here.

During the period of my research I had a sense of working in a highly charged, positive atmosphere. I was captivated by the sincerity of my colleagues. I believe that this sense of collegiality and genuine goodness led me to share the following quotation with colleagues at a staff-meeting. I read it because I wanted to communicate to them my belief in them, in their efforts to support one another and to revitalise our lives in school.

> Because power is energy, it needs to flow through organisations: it cannot be confined to functions or levels. We have seen the positive results of this flowing organisational energy in our experiences with participative management and self-managed teams. What gives power its charge, positive or negative, is the

quality of relationships. Those who relate through coercion, or from a disregard for the other person, create negative energy. Those who are open to others and who see others in their fullness create positive energy. Love in organisations, then, is the most potent source of power we have available (Wheatley, 1992: 39).

I believe that I have followed the cycle of action research in the actions I took to establish better communications through the school. I saw a problem and imagined a solution. I monitored the effectiveness of the new plan and made improvements as it progressed. I am convinced that I have highlighted an important area of concern to principals and staffs in school.

I also believe that my action has grown from the reflection I undertook on my practice as principal in school. McNiff (1995) reiterates the view that committed action is the hallmark of a professional: 'Action research is far from idle self-contemplation. It is a deep commitment undertaken by responsible practitioners to hold themselves accountable for their own ways of living and working. I as a practitioner acknowledge that I have to accept the responsibility of my own actions if I am to improve the world' (McNiff, 1995: 24).

2   Staff development

> Their potential to empower others is one of the strengths of manager action research (Lomax, 1996:16).

I determined to address the issue of staff development in my research. Sergiovanni offers the following as a guide for schools who wish to promote teacher growth and development. Schools, he says, need '...to create the kinds of management and supervisory systems, organisational patterns, and teacher growth strategies that:

- encourage teachers to reflect on their own practice;
- acknowledge that teachers develop at different rates, and that at any given time are more ready to learn some things than others;
- acknowledge that teachers have different talents and interests;

- give high priority to conversations and dialogue among teachers;
- provide for collaborative learning among teachers;
- emphasise caring relationships and felt interdependencies;
- call upon teachers to respond morally to their work;
- view teachers as supervisors of learning communities

(Sergiovanni, 1996:142)

Sergiovanni quotes Marilyn Evans (1994: 4): 'The premise is that if teachers are to build learning communities in their classrooms, they must first experience being part of a learning community' (in Sergiovanni, 1996: 142).

As principal I resolved to encourage individual and staff development. My first action was to identify staff members who were trying to develop their own practice. I noted that two colleagues took their classes to an art gallery and engaged with the materials there. Another colleague managed to combine excellent teaching with a constant display of the children's art and written work. A young teacher was interested in teaching the children about the environment through practical work.

I supported these colleagues by

• expressing interest in their work;
• providing them with the resources they needed;
• listening to them as they described the process involved;
• highlighting their achievements on the staff notice board.

As time passed staff members began to have faith in my commitment to support their positive ideas and contributions to school life. Responses from questionnaires about possible improvements to our situation in school included a request for a formal Discipline Plan. The staff member who suggested this surveyed her colleagues and we quickly realised that this was an initiative that we could work on as a group. I saw the process as being one that we could follow for subsequent staff development, and I invited Adrian Smith, a consultant in private practice in the UK, to lead a day's inservice for the staff. Following this, the debate about best practice went on for several weeks. I was alarmed at the slow rate of progress, but kept my counsel. The issue became a concern, however, when other members of staff shared their feelings of impatience. At a morning coffee break I handed out the following quotation about the process of adopting a new plan in an organisation:

> Even if the plan is excellent, it will be a long meeting in which the plan will be dissected, criticised, thrown out, brought back, and finally, almost always, approved in its initial form with only a few slight modifications. All of those participants, like the best scientists, need to observe the plan in detail, exploring its edges, searching out its interior, playing with its potentialities ... it is the participation process that generates the reality to which [people] make their commitment (Wheatley 1992: 67).

I believe that by supporting my colleagues in their desire actively to be involved in formulating a discipline plan for the school, I have begun a process of development for staff that would not have happened otherwise. I believe this is in line with the issue that it is not who or what position takes care of the problem, but what energy, skill, influence, and wisdom are available to contribute to the solution (Pacanowski, 1988, in Wheatley, 1992: 117).

We now have a very positive attitude to discipline in our school, with the full support of the parents. I say this with some certitude, based on the research data generated through my own observations; reports from staff, children and parents; and written reports from staff who are themselves now involved in their own professional development programmes through action research. My other principal colleague on campus reported several conversations she had had with members of our staff. She said that they were totally enthusiastic and determined to see the plan operate successfully in school.

I have received support from principals of other schools who have heard about our involvement in the Discipline for Learning plan. They have asked for information about the course and are in the process of arranging in-service in their schools.

I believe also that there is a new spirit of collaboration in the school. Hargreaves writes that collaborative cultures '...emerge primarily from the teachers themselves as a social group' (Hargreaves 1994: 192).

I value the comments of Adrian Smith who wrote to us following his course in our school. I quote two points from his letter that are relevant to this topic.

> Professional teachers who presented themselves well for a purposeful day. They are clearly used to working as a team and acknowledging each other's strengths.

> Principal clear about the need and outcomes for staff development day, realised that a 'ground up' approach is the best way forward. Allowed the staff to push the day as they saw fit and yet subtly interacted at suitable times for feedback. Relevant information fed back to course leader.

As I continue to monitor my practice as principal I will be aware of the needs of colleagues to find expression in their work for the values they hold strongly as educators.

3   Nurturing a climate of care

When I reflected on the quality of care in school, I realised that I needed to inject some energy into the quality of my own relationships with colleagues. I knew the potential value for them of my support and encouragement, as I had received such support in my own teaching career. I know that colleagues enjoy being commended on their work. All teachers need to feel that what they are doing is making a difference for social benefit.

When I was appointed principal I wanted to commit myself '...to building, to serving, to caring for, and to protecting the school and its purposes' (Sergiovanni, 1996:95). I was prepared to serve my colleagues by being an authentic leader, by supporting and encouraging them in their work and in their personal lives, and by working with them to make their professional lives as rich in experience and satisfaction as was possible. 'It begins with the natural feeling that one wants to serve, to serve first. Then conscious choice brings one to aspire to lead. The difference manifests itself in the care taken by the servant – first to make sure that other people's highest priority needs are being served. The best test is: Do those served grow as persons; do they, while being served, become healthier, wiser, freer, more autonomous, more likely themselves to become servants?' (Greenleaf, 1977: 44).

This commitment to professional service accounts for my decision to undertake extra study. I needed to know more about my work in order to serve the school more fully. Through my research I would look for ways in which I could demonstrate and nourish a culture of care in school.

My deepest held values are those of democracy, care and learning. As principal of the newly amalgamated school I was aware that these values were denied in some measure in organisational structures. Efforts made to democratise staff meetings were not enough to satisfy my commitment to democracy. I envisaged a scenario where individual staff members would take charge of aspects of school organisation and innovations so that ownership of these would devolve to the staff themselves. In this way their own thinking would develop and real educational conversations could take place. The results could be spectacular. My three prioritised educational values are clearly interlinked in theory and in practice. Sharing leadership with others, as in democracy, invites them to learn about the skills involved. The leadership roles assigned demand that colleagues learn about the various areas of responsibility entrusted to them. If I attend to the needs of colleagues, personal or professional, I free them to attend more purposefully to the tasks in hand. The fact that I wish to engage with them in a democratic way shows my respect for them as professionals and my care for them as individuals. If I encourage learning, I will have helped in their development. If I can engage them in learning it will possibly lead to more learning. I am conscious of my responsibility to lead an effective school. I claim that in living out my values I am achieving this.

I was concerned however that my actions of trying to show care for my colleagues might be seen as potentially manipulative or controlling. Course members on the MEd course, acting as a validation group for my research, also pointed this out. Would staff see my care as manipulative? I understand that perhaps it will take time for colleagues to understand that I am trying to work from motives that are informed by the value of the others' best interests. Sergiovanni recognises that in the end we must trust that '...any authentic act, no matter how small or seemingly insignificant, is upheld by the universe as worthy and honourable. Leadership is spiritually grounded. To lose this hope and this faith is to despair and to fall into cynicism' (Sergiovanni, 1996:96). Starratt also advises that we pay attention to the quality of our exchanges so that they '... move beyond a superficial ritual to a contractual obligation to a relationship of caring, when there is a deep attention to the unique human beings involved in the exchange' (Starratt, 1994:53). If I am constantly aware and understand the possibilities of trying to manipulate or to control, I hope I will be less likely to fall into this trap.

Starratt ends his discussion of the ethics of care by appealing for genuine compassion for others. I realise that the vision of care that I present to myself is possibly unattainable, and might lead me to feel that I have failed. If this is my predicament, then other colleagues might also have the same misgivings. The commitment to care is risky business: 'We have to extend our caring to forgiving. The forgiveness extended, then we go on with the business of making things right. And then forgive again' (Starratt, 1994:54). I take comfort from this advice: we need at least to try, even if our best efforts fall short of the mark.

I believe that the three strands of my research question are intrinsically linked. The quality of care I want to practise includes care for the professional well-being of teachers (staff-development) and for their inclusion in a collaborative network in school (communication).

Valuing teachers

Let me now briefly consider some other ways I undertook to show teachers that they were valued and cared for as individuals in school.

- I resolved to listen more attentively to colleagues as they expressed concern about pupils or aspects of school administration. This meant not interrupting, suspending my own thinking and judgement about issues and, more importantly, being available to colleagues in the evenings as they prepared to leave for home.
- I checked with colleagues about the resources they needed in their classrooms and bought extra materials when funds became available.
- I was conscious of the way I responded on the telephone to colleagues when they called to say they were unable to be at work. I tried to give a personal rather than a bureaucratic response.
- I took on the responsibility of leaving fresh hand towels for staff each morning and to make sure that the staff room was bright and welcoming. I cooked small treats for colleagues.
- I worked closely with the cleaning staff of the school to continue to present the building in as attractive a manner as possible for staff, parents and children.

I know my colleagues appreciate my efforts to make school as welcoming as possible for them. They constantly feed back to me the positive comments they receive about the clean and attractive building. Adrian Smith, the Discipline for Learning course leader, wrote in his report that: 'The building was so pleasant to be in. Clean, tidy and loved by the cleaning staff as well as the teachers. Things like plants are extras but make the difference.'

My attitude is one of trust. I trust that, if I do the right thing, in time people will realise that I am acting out of deeply held values and belief in the goodness of human nature.

I am attracted to the challenge of Koestenbaum (1991: 318): 'Present yourself to people. And be in contact with them, as you truly are. Do not manipulate. Do not pretend. You have nothing to fear, if you have a leadership mind ... In leadership, greatness matters.'

References

Evans, M. (1994), 'The Model in Ministry,' Dissertation in Progress, Dayton, Ohio: United Theological Seminary.

Greenleaf, R.K.(1977) *Servant Leadership.* New York, Paulist Press.

Hargreaves, A. (1994) *Changing Teachers, Changing Times: Teachers' Work and Culture in the Post-modern Age.* London, Cassell.

Koestenbaum, P. (1991) *Leadership: The Inner Side of Greatness – a Philosophy for Leaders.* San Francisco: Jossey Bass.

Humphreys, T. (1993) *A Different kind of Teacher.* Cork, Dr. Tony Humphreys.

Lomax, P. (ed.) (1996) *Quality Management in Education.* London, Routledge.

McNiff, J. (1988) *Action Research: Principles and Practice.* London, Routledge.

McNiff, J. (1995) *Action Research for Professional Development: Concise Advice for New Action Researchers.* Dorset, September Books.

Sergiovanni, T.J. (1996) *Leadership for the Schoolhouse: How is it Different? Why is it Important?* San Francisco, Jossey-Bass.

Starratt, R.J. (1994) *Building an Ethical School.* London, Falmer.

Wheatley, M.J. (1994) *Leadership and the New Science.* San Francisco, Berrett-Koehler.

Whitehead, J. (1989) 'Creating a Living Educational Theory from Questions of the Kind, "How do I Improve my Practice?"' in *Cambridge Journal of Education*, Vol.. 19, no. 1, pp. 41–52.

Whitehead, J. (1993) *The Growth of Educational Knowledge: Creating Your Own Living Educational Theories.* Bournemouth, Hyde.

Other Resources

Discipline for Learning Ltd., 90 Broadoak Road, Langford, North Somerset, BS40 5HB.

Chapter 14

Education for Mutual Understanding

Seamus Farrell

Education for Mutual Understanding (EMU) is an educational theme in the Northern Ireland curriculum. It is in many respects the predecessor of an increasing range of initiatives currently being pursued in the development of civic, social and political education in various parts of the world, including the Republic of Ireland. The conflictual circumstances which have prevailed in Northern Irish society gave particular momentum to the EMU initiative in the 1980s. The experience already gained in Northern Ireland provides valuable lessons for other initiatives elsewhere. These are relevant not just to regions of the world which share Northern Ireland's contexts of conflict. EMU has been described as Northern Ireland's response to a universal question: how best to equip young people with the necessary values, skills and attitudes for playing a full and active part in contemporary society, as citizens of nations and of an interdependent world.

Beyond issues of curriculum content, strategy, resources, teacher education timetabled space, there is a particular need in this area for what is being taught to be *modelled* in the practices and relationships of the school. In this paper I want to examine the opportunities and challenges presented by EMU to promote individual reflective practice and a culture of collaborative enquiry in schools. The values on which democracy is predicated coincide with those which underpin both good education practice and action research, and so EMU can potentially create a environment which encourages the development

of the skills and values of citizenship and also serve the wider needs
and purposes of education.

The EMU Promoting Schools Project

The EMU Promoting Schools Project (EMUpsp) supports, through
action research processes, the development and delivery of EMU in
schools. It has focused initially on the primary sector. We seek to be
'... a catalyst for change through education, assisting and fostering an
environment where mutual understanding can occur more effectively
and as part of the core of the school ethos' (EMUpsp Mission
Statement, 1995).

Our EMUpsp team comprises three researchers, working in a
university context, to support the school-based professional education
of teachers. We initially opted to work with the concept of Peer
Mediation – skilling 9–11 year old children to help each other find
solutions to their playground and street conflicts. We did so on the
basis that, as well as offering children training in conflict resolution
skills, it provided subsequent opportunity for them to practise and
further develop their skills in the context of issues of immediate
relevance in their lives. As such it seemed a particularly effective means
of offering EMU to that age group and as a good foundation for work
of a more explicitly socio-political nature in subsequent teenage years.
It effectively fulfilled the objectives of EMU for that age group (see
CCEA, 1997) – the enhancement of children's self esteem, which is of
course key to the development of social engagement skills; and the
development of their understanding of conflict and of ways to handle
disputes constructively. As such it seemed a useful exemplar programme
through which to research the prerequisites and the training
requirements for schools to be able to use programmes of this nature
– not just EMU but also programmes in the affective domain of
education in general, which of course require the use of experiential
methodologies.

I view teaching essentially as an emotional practice, requiring
emotional understanding and competence, and I suggest that teachers'

own emotional issues have everything to do with their practice. Evidence from the neurosciences is increasing that children's development is intensely rooted in and directed by emotion; emotional development is critical to cognitive development; emotion drives attention which drives learning. This suggests to me that self esteem, both of teachers and those whom they are teaching, is central to all teaching and learning. With that in mind our Project has always had an eye to the potential, within our particular engagement, to support delivery of the total curriculum, through looking at issues of the teaching and learning environments, school and classroom practice, the affective dimension of teaching and learning, teacher morale, adult and adult-child relationships within the school, ethos issues, and so on.

The development of the programme was undertaken in partnership with schools, and with teachers especially as practitioner researcher colleagues. Children, too, together with ancillary staff, parents and principals, were major players in the research process. While teaching and project staff, separately and together, explored the improvement of their practice, children raised challenging questions and comments to the process:

How do you [adults] deal with your conflicts?

I like peer mediation to help me if I have an argument because children understand children better and they listen to you and you feel that what you have to say about what happened is important. Teachers are too busy and don't listen like that. They just decide on the spot who was in the wrong and give them lines.

Despite all the good efforts of adults to adapt the basic mediation process for use by children, it was the feedback from children and how they used the process in practice that made it child-friendly, thus transcending the technical-functional mindset that adults are constrained to adopt in western intellectual cultures.

Similarly school ancillary staff, through being supported to appreciate their significance in the education process, were able to raise important issues with the teaching staff:

The playground is a more important place than the classroom as regards learning to relate to one another. It's where they fall out and make friends and are left out and included. There are as many things going on between children at playtime as there are children. We need support to make the best use of this time for the children.

We get to see a side to individual children in the playground and the canteen that teachers don't get to see. We need a chance to talk with teachers about what we see.

These comments are extracts from conversations with playground supervisors.

Some of our initial concerns included the problematic that parents would see the programme as tantamount to the school's shirking its responsibility for dealing with conflicts by handing this responsibility over to the children. Our concerns however were unfounded. Parents reported with pride and delight their child's growth in self esteem, often an improvement in academic progress and behaviour; and on occasion told stories of how their child offered their mediation skills to deal with disputes among siblings – and even between siblings and parents. It must be acknowledged, however, that the venture merely touched the surface of its potential (and the need) for training and team-building for ancillary staff, for promoting collaboration among the adults of the school community, and for enhancing relationships among the schools and the communities they serve.

Our learning

The entire action research process accumulated significant and substantial learnings around the requirements for teaching the skills and values of democracy. These learnings have to do with the importance of a supportive principal and school management team, and of the development of relationships within the school, among adults as well as among children, and also of course adult-child relationships, such as to provide an environment congruent for the work with children. Without minimising the importance of training provision for teachers in the use of interactive and experiential methodologies, and of adequate resources for the work such as curriculum materials and timetabled space, it seems to me that the field of civics education is one area where the issues pertaining to the so-called 'hidden curriculum' need to be uncovered. The values and attitudes on which democracy is predicated are caught before they are taught. Therefore the values, norms and beliefs which inform the practices of the school, such as management style, decision making processes, discipline policies, whether children experience being valued and respected (or not), whether teachers experience being valued and respected (or not), are of critical relevance to whether or not a school is capable of effectively teaching democratic values, attitudes and skills. Schools of course might settle for a cognitive approach to teaching civics and possibly by-pass the 'hidden curriculum' issues; and the opportunity of good marks in another subject might motivate students to engage with it. But on the principle that education is about what survives after what has been taught has been forgotten, I would seriously question the extent to which what is taught through a subject-based approach can be internalised by students and therefore survive into later life. The aim of civic, social and political education is the creation of an empathic society. It is not a cognitive exercise so much as primarily and pervasively an affective one. In these terms, process is paramount. Teaching a body of information will not necessarily contribute to people becoming better citizens or the development of a good society.

Values at the heart of democracy

From among the many attempts at a definition of what 'true' democracy would look like (given that actual models are scarce, and that there could be multiple interpretations of the idea), I have chosen one that I particularly like because it suggests that a democratic society is one which has achieved a balance between three core values or principles: equity, diversity and independence.

I should like to reflect on these from three perspectives:

- How can these principles be taught?
- How can they be reflected/modelled in the ethos and practices of schools?
- How appropriate are action research processes for exploring both these issues?

How the principles might be taught

Applying these to the values, attitudes and skills required to be taught in a civic, social and political education programme, the principles might be summarised as follows:

Equity
Care and respect for others as equals, located in the development of a child's own sense of her/his own worth.

Diversity
Tolerance and empathy: before trying to address the issue of tolerance and respect for people who are safely far away, in a travellers' camp or in the third world, I would suggest addressing diversity right here in classrooms and schools. Any classroom and school provides a rich context for learning about tolerance and respect for diversity as a lived experience. I am suggesting that the 'political' and 'citizenship' issues of the classroom, playground and school provide the most authentic and fruitful starting point for this work. I feel driven to this position from the experience of EMU being over-identified with programmes involving children from a Protestant and a Catholic school being together at a neutral venue for a day, in the care of resident staff so that their teachers don't have to interact. This is much safer than dealing with the relationship issues within schools of either tradition. It can however be a cosmetic approach to EMU, based on a contact hypothesis that presumes that there will, somehow, be some lasting value for the children from the experience of meeting each other.

Interdependence

Co-operation, including skills for handing conflict constructively.

How the principles might be reflected/modelled in the ethos and practices of schools

As indicated earlier, the findings from our work suggest that there are challenging implications for schools with regard to issues of ethos if they are to teach citizenship effectively. Democratic principles must be reflected in the policies and practices of the school. A democratic school would have these characteristics:

Equity	Care and respect for others as equals
Diversity	Tolerance and empathy
Interdependence	Co-operation

I suggest that these are the basis for good education and not just a civics component. Children learn best and teachers teach best in an environment where they feel valued and respected, are full participants in the teaching-learning tasks, have opportunities to work together, and are given the opportunity and skills to deal constructively with their conflicts – in short, an environment which lends itself to the practice of participative democracy. On the other hand, discipline policies and classroom practices based on control, privileged treatment of the brightest and the best-behaved in contrast to the rest, are inimical to the prerequisites for civics education, and education in general. So too is the culture of individualism among teachers, and the hierarchical culture in schools, which excludes collaboration with each other and with ancillary staff, parents and others. So too are the dynamics of unresolved inter-staff conflict affecting teacher morale and their capacity to teach.

The appropriateness of action research processes for exploring both visible and invisible curriculum issues in relation to citizenship education

The values and attitudes that underpin the practice of action research may be presented as follows:

Equity	Care and respect for others as equals
Diversity	Tolerance and empathy
Interdependence	Co-operation

The action research process is based on the core values of tolerance, care, and respect for others as equals. As with civics education it has an explicit social intent: it has an agenda of transformation and change. It seeks to promote movement from the rhetoric to the practice of collaboration. It is about participative democracy.

I have tried to point out the convergence between

- the democratic values, attitudes and skills needed to be taught in civics education;
- the fact that schools and teachers need to model these in their own practice in order to teach these effectively – and indeed to teach;
- the fact that the very same democratic values and attitudes are the basis of the action research process.

The potential of civic, social and political education, and its wider implications

There is consequently a potentially fruitful opportunity presented by the developing field of civic, social and political education. Some of the ways are as follows:

A process of educational change and school transformation needs to be developed, not just for the purposes of civics education, but also for the sake of all that schools represent.

As a means of doing this, the concept and practice of teachers as practitioner researchers needs to be promoted; teachers need to be encouraged to collaborate with each other, to practise democracy, to use the process to develop confidence in interactive learning experiences such as Circle Time. They need to use it to develop team practices and collaboration for their own relationships, and to enhance their own practice. It seems to me that the needs of civics education present an opportunity to develop, at a whole school level, a culture of enquiry, of self evaluation, of reflection informing practice, and of encouraging further reflection.

Quite apart from the needs of civics education, development of these principles makes good educational sense. Perhaps new worldwide initiatives in civics education present a catalyst opportunity for education itself. I believe that harnessing the concept of practitioner research could have a major impact on teacher morale, to liberate teachers from the utterly disempowering and demoralising effects of being the passive objects of external assessment, evaluation, inspection and visiting researchers, rather than participants and active agents in their own practice. Particularly when applied to the affective area of the curriculum, including civics education, engagement in research by teachers frees them from the objectives view of the curriculum and of themselves as deliverers of pre-packaged received knowledge.

As a school support agency, our Project can draw some satisfaction from the number of teachers who, as a result of our partnering them in developing their EMU practice, have remarked that they now like Monday mornings and find themselves looking forward to the beginning of a school term. One of them recently remarked, 'This involvement has transformed the total way I teach.'

Some dilemmas

But there are conditions to all this.

One of these has to do with the location of civics education, whether it is at the heart of the curriculum or on the periphery. While I endorse its central character to education, I would not advocate that it be located exclusively as a subject area within the curriculum. It belongs essentially to the affective curriculum, and is best located primarily as a cross-curricular, educational theme. A subject base, abundantly resourced, would offer excellent information about citizenship, but, in my view, this would not necessarily impact on a student's capacity to be a good citizen. Knowing about citizenship does not guarantee good citizenship.

Another priviso has to do with when civics education begins. There is not space here to argue for the importance of early years education, not least in terms of education of the emotions. It is worth making reference to recent research in Northern Ireland which suggests that children from the age of three onwards are capable of developing an awareness of 'categories of people' (in this case Catholic and Protestant) and of assigning negative traits to 'the other side' (Connolly, 1998). This early conditioning then provides the basis from which children later develop more elaborated and entrenched views about those who have different identities from themselves. The recognition in EMU from its beginning of the importance of work at primary school level is confirmed by the extreme difficulties that are experienced in EMU programmes in secondary schools, where inadequate foundations have been laid. It would be my view that beginning at a second level stage, as I believe is the case with Civic, Social and Political Education in the Republic, is not early enough.

My final and perhaps most central concern has to do with the research methodologies appropriate to civics education. Using technical functional criteria to assess any area of relationships education is a flawed and dangerous approach. When such approaches have been used in respect of EMU, it has invariably 'found against' teachers and schools: the failure of EMU to achieve its objectives is evidently because teachers lack skills and/or commitment. Training needs are held therefore as paramount in addressing the problem. These kinds of conclusions however overlook critical questions:

- about context, and the potential constraints of a school's hidden curriculum on teachers;
- about policy and definition: an objectives view of the curriculum is usually in radical conflict with the values underpinning EMU and ignores the deepest educational vision and values of teachers.

My response to the findings from research that EMU has 'failed' is to suggest rather that it hasn't been tried.

Even with regard to the conclusions of such research as regards training, there is a concern that traditional technical functional approaches would give shape to an inadequate training provision. The didactic approach of conventional inservice training provision is wholly inappropriate. It lacks the interactive methodologies needed to support the development of democratic values in children and the development of confidence as well as the competence of teachers to undertake this. All these aspects are embedded in the real life contexts and lived experience of teachers and pupils alike. Conventional inservice provision does not provide for the follow-up of the vital continuing personalised support of teachers that is a feature of professional education in areas of political and social sensitivity.

The value of conflict

I should like to add a note on the value of conflict. People at the chalk face who grapple daily with the constant drain on their energy presented by discipline and conflict issues inevitably view conflict in a negative light. Besides being a 'problem', however, it is a fact of social living which can never be eradicated. 'Where two or three are gathered there is conflict or at least the potential for it' (Darby, 1991). Conflict however it not a problem: what matters is how we deal with conflict. When used constructively it can be a unique source of personal growth and learning, challenging us to embrace other perspectives, liberating us from our imprisoning certainties, and opening us up to a truth residing not in a particular place or person but in our collaborative engagement in search of it.

From this perspective, conflict is 'good'. It is a potentially powerful teaching resource. It would be worth exploring how conflict can present a potentially positive and proactive whole school strategy, if only because, let's face it, reactive strategies such as authoritarian control and 'bullying the bully' simply haven't worked and, in my opinion, stand little chance of working. 'Fighting' it doesn't work either. But neither does 'flight' from it, consigning it to the carpet until the carpet is at the ceiling and the door won't open. It has become apparent from our Project that inter-staff conflict in many schools is the major factor in their being dysfunctional, while the schools themselves insist that the behaviour of students is the problem. However, quite apart from the destructive potential of conflict inadequately dealt with, I do feel that conflict, because of its potential for learning and growth, merits a positive characterisation to complement, or better still replace, its negative one, so that schools can begin to harness its potential to serve the purposes of schooling.

Trying new ways, at any level, to deal with conflict and promote peace is painful and risky. It has been said that peace is like a baby – enjoyable in its conception but painful in its delivery. Collaborative, reflective processes by practitioners, whether teachers or other practitioners engaged in the task of bringing peace from vision to reality, is a powerful model for promoting participatory democracy.

I like this definition of hope from Jim Wallis (1995): 'Hope is believing, in spite of the evidence, that things can be different, and in the strength of that belief, watching the evidence change.' When the hoping and believing are shared, the evidence can change.

References

Council for the Curriculum, Examinations and Assessment (1997) *Mutual Understanding and Cultural Heritage: Cross Curricular Guidance Materials.* Belfast, CCEA.

Connolly, P. (1998) *Consultancy Report to Channel 4 Education.* Northern Ireland Community Relations Council, Belfast.

Darby, J. (1991) *What's Wrong with Conflict?* University of Ulster, Centre for the Study of Conflict.

Wallis, J. (1995) *Sojourners Community Magazine,* September. Washington.

Chapter 15

An exploration of the education and training needs of educationally disadvantaged participants on a VTOS programme

Anne O'Keeffe

The announcement by the European Commission in June 1989 that there was a need for a Community-wide commitment to invest in people, their skills and their creativity through education and training identified adult education in general, and the Vocational Training Opportunities Scheme (VTOS) in particular, as a high educational priority. The primary objective of the VTOS as a labour market intervention is to enable long-term unemployed people to compete effectively in the workforce.

The Evaluation of the Vocational Training Opportunities Scheme (Duggan *et al.*, 1996), commissioned by the Department of Education and Science, stated that people entering the VTOS programme with little or no second level education are most likely to emerge from it without any formal qualifications. It is as a result of those findings and their relevance to one particular cohort which is not academically oriented, within the context of a particular VTOS, that this study was undertaken. The study was carried out over an academic year, using an action research methodology. As researcher and co-ordinator of a VTOS programme, I aimed to advance an understanding of the needs and wants of a specific group of unemployed adult participants on a second chance education programme.

Structural changes in unemployment

The explosion in information technology, the globalisation of economic activity and other structural forces are driving a dynamic transformation in employment, conditions of work, organisation of work and how work is performed within occupational labels. This requires diverse and continually evolving skills without which workers are less interchangeable, and adjustments to new situations are often difficult. Unemployment has become as much a qualitative issue as a quantitative one, as skills for the new and growing employment opportunities are often very different from those in the declining work areas. According to Clancy (1995: 482):

> the increased significance of the school as a determinant of future status is linked to changes in the occupational structures of our society. ... in 1926, 53 per cent of the work force were employed in agriculture; by 1991 this percentage had dropped to 14.

This change in occupational structure is reflected among the VTOS participants in our Centre in Abbeyleix, particularly those with an educational disadvantage. The Centre is in a rural area and many of the participants commented that the option of farm work as a job prospect was no longer a realistic one. The Report of the National Economic and Social Forum on rural renewal (NESF, 1997) notes that, in relation to educational disadvantage, contrary to the general perception, rural areas have the highest level of disadvantage (60.7%) with just under 40% in urban areas. A variety of studies in Ireland has found that the relative position of the least qualified groups has deteriorated over time (Breen, 1991; Hannan and Boyle, 1987; Hannan and Shorthall, 1991). Because educational qualifications are now almost universally used as 'tickets' to employment, many workers are over-qualified and their skills have not been utilised.

The County Laois scheme

The VTOS initiative was established in the Further Education Centre in Abbeyleix in October 1991, under the auspices of the County Laois Vocational Educational Committee (VEC). This Centre is located in a former Vocational school which had been vacated a number of years previously because of an amalgamation of four schools in the area. Abbeyleix is a small historic estate town with a population of 1,400. It is situated in the midlands, nine miles south of Portlaoise, the county town of Co. Laois. The catchment area is wide, covering all of Co. Laois, parts of Co. Kilkenny, Co. Offaly and Co. Tipperary. Because the majority of the students are from outside the Abbeyleix area, a service is provided to transport them from the larger urban areas.

The programme caters for a total of 80 long-term unemployed students. It is full time, and students have a choice of programme options. These include Leaving Certificate, Junior Certificate, Accounting Technician, Information Processing, Marketing, and a General Foundation Course. The participants on the Foundation programme were the focus of my study for a number of reasons, not least because of the increase in the number of participants enrolled with minimal formal education.

The Foundation Programme

This is one of five programmes on offer in the Centre, the other four programmes being academically driven with specific assessment and accreditation structures in place. Educationally, vocationally and probably socially, this student cohort was much more disadvantaged than students on other programmes. As literacy and numeracy difficulties were prevalent among the group, they were prevented from participating in the more academic subjects/courses in the Centre. A number of the group had been out of the educational system for a long time, had little or no work experience, and some had learning difficulties. Of the sixteen students who commenced the programme in mid-September, there was only one woman in the group.

The research question

The central question underpinning the study was: How can a full-time education and training programme such as VTOS meet the needs of long-term unemployed adults with considerable educational, social and vocational disadvantage? A significant number of students from our Centre returns to the live register on completion of the programme each year. This is mirrored by the findings of the VTOS Evaluation Report, which also stated that the participants who joined the programme with least (educationally and vocationally) were leaving with least. Could this be a factor in contributing to the formation of a disenfranchised 'underclass' of citizens? Is this phenomenon acceptable in a society which subscribes to the ethic of social justice? How can lifelong learning, which is increasingly recognised by investors in education, be encouraged and fostered, particularly among the more disadvantaged and unemployed?

The research design

Having taken the decision to carry out this study I needed to address a number of issues prior to commencement. The participants on the Foundation Programme, as the main focus of the study, would be the central and crucial source of data which would inform the research. This cohort for the most part had limited formal education; some experienced learning difficulties and all lacked self esteem and self confidence. A major challenge therefore would be self expression and articulation. In order to understand the nature and extent of their needs, wants, perceptions, experiences and difficulties, I believed that the participants on the programme would need additional support in the form of 'lifeskills' classes which would enable them to improve and develop their communication skills in a safe, non-threatening environment. My colleagues and I took the decision to integrate these areas as subjects into the timetable.

Data gathering techniques

Five data gathering techniques were used in the course of this research:

- students' brainstorming sessions
- participant observation
- standardised scheduled interviews with students
- semi-structured interviews with class tutors, employers, careers guidance teacher, a co-ordinator from a similar VTOS, and the national co-ordinator of the VTOS
- maintenance of a class journal and my own reflective diary for the duration of the year

The research findings

From the questionnaire/interviews with the students, it was evident that each individual had his or her own difficulties, all of which impinged on the individual's ability to participate fully in the learning process. In this respect, one might well ask: 'Are they any different from the rest of the students on other programmes in the Centre?' Obviously there are similarities in terms of lifestyle, poor self esteem, lack of confidence as well as the major characteristic which unites them and sets them apart – their experience of long-term unemployment. However, the findings show that these problems are exacerbated among the participants of the Foundation group.

1   Reasons for joining the VTOS
Multiple reasons were given for joining the programme. However, the most frequently identified reason, and the one most often voiced in the brainstorming sessions, was to 'get an education'. Their lack of formal education was perceived as the reason for their unemployment. While this may be a simplistic view, they supported their claim with comments such as:

*'If you don't have an education, employers have no way of knowing
what you are like or what you can do.'*
*'If you have a Junior Cert, it is a level of education that is known.
At least they know you can read and write.'*
*'If you have nothing in the line of a 'piece of paper', you are seen by
employers as nothing.'*
*'There are people working in ordinary jobs in supermarkets now
and they have a Leaving Cert.'*

Another reason forwarded for joining was the need for a structure to
one's day. Issues such as a sense of isolation, experienced by being
around the house all day without coming into contact with anyone
except those with whom they lived was also mentioned. The following
responses were typical:

'What is there to get up for if you have nowhere to go?'
'The day is very long if you don't meet anyone.'
*'Sometimes there is hassle when a few people from the same house
are at home all day.'*

Participants also spoke about the stigma attached to unemployment.
It was perceived by some students that returning to school eliminated
that stigma to some degree. All participants had aspirations of accessing
the workforce sometime in the future. Eight out of the twelve cited
'signing off [Social Welfare]' and 'getting a job' sooner rather than
later, among the main reasons for their enrolment on the VTOS.

2   The educational experiences of the participants

From the brainstorming sessions with the students it was clear that
for many their early educational experiences were disturbingly negative
and reflected badly on the education system. It is difficult for the
students to identify at what point, or how, they realised that they were
not going to succeed. Some had learning difficulties, had been members
of large classes and never got 'the basics'. Others indicated that their
socio-economic and/or family environment militated against their
coping with the demands of school.

'I was always at the back of the class in school.'
'I was not able to keep up and so nobody took an interest in me.'
'The teachers were only interested in the children who lived on the main street because they were big shots.'
'A couple of us in my class were always being told we were stupid and we would never do anything.'

3   The lack of literacy and numeracy skills

The literacy tutor commented on the range of abilities and the lack of skills within the group:

> *'Some of them are very weak, particularly their writing skills. Some of them have not written anything for a long time and are frightened and anxious about it … Another area in which some had huge difficulty was giving or following directions.'*

The maths tutor also noted the difficulties encountered by some students with regard to following simple instructions and directions. These findings are mirrored by the report, *International Adult Literacy Survey* (Morgan *et al.*, 1997), which claims that 25% of the Irish population between 16 and 65 has some degree of literacy difficulty. This is a very disturbing statistic with free post-primary education in place in Ireland for thirty years. The lack of adequate literacy skills was cited by most of the students as one of the factors contributing to their unemployment situation. Some participants, however, were unrealistic here. They believed that, with competence in reading and writing, their employment prospects would improve dramatically. This issue needs to be addressed in a sensitive but honest and realistic manner in order to prevent false expectations among some individuals.

4   The employment record of the participants

The fact that most of the group have never had a 'real' job since they left school was a source of great concern. Of even greater concern was the fact that some of them feared they may never access open employment. Only two out of the twelve participants had been employed for longer than a year and both were in their 40s. All the comments revealed a distinct lack of self confidence in their skills levels, together with poor self image and low self esteem. They tended to describe themselves in their situations as:

> 'When you go for a job, the first thing you have to do is fill in a form.'
> 'If I was asked to read something, I was finished.'
> 'Nobody listens to what you have to say when you are on the dole.'
> 'I'm never asked for my opinion on anything, not even by my own family.'

5   The lack of careers guidance

From the questionnaires and discussions with the students in their lifeskills classes, it became evident that they did not see the careers guidance teacher as having much relevance for them. It is unlikely that students with such minimal literacy and numeracy skills would be able to cope with the literacy demands of deciphering information and booklets on courses and careers. The Foundation students appear to see the role of the careers guidance teacher as being relevant if one is following a programme leading to the Leaving Certificate or courses accredited by the National Council for Vocational Awards. This perception is perfectly understandable in our Centre, because of, among other factors, the time constraint under which the careers guidance tutor operates.

6   The lack of self confidence and self esteem

Issues such as lack of self confidence, poor self image and self worth were pervasive throughout the data collected. The brainstorming sessions with the students at the beginning of the year painted a compelling picture of exclusion and a lack of focus and direction in many of their lives. Participants describe their experiences of interfacing with the various agencies as contributing to their low opinions of themselves. The following comments were typical:

'You are treated like someone who has a disease. You are left waiting for ages and frequently you are sent on to another office to face the same humiliation all over again.'
'I feel so small going in to get what I'm entitled to.'
'You have nobody's respect when you are on the dole. People think you are lazy or stupid and don't want to work.'

The careers guidance teacher maintained that these participants needed a lot more support than students on the other courses in the Centre. She noted that:

'... a particular feature of all the participants who start on the VTOS is that they tend to be very unsure as to where they are going or what they are doing, but I would certainly say that this particular group tends to be almost lost. ... they get support and encouragement from others to come rather than using their own initiative to join the programme. Then when they come in, they seem to need a lot more help, advice and support.'

7   The Foundation students' perceptions of other programmes in the Centre

As stated earlier in this study, the VTOS programme in Abbeyleix, similar to those in other centres throughout the country, is very much education led and academically driven. While this provision appears to be meeting the needs of the majority in the Centre, there are drawbacks for the minority which includes the Foundation group. Comments made by the students during the brainstorming sessions included:

'The students who are doing the Leaving Certificate here are more important than us.'
'Yes, they are the brainy ones.'
'I know some people who won't come here because of that. You have to be bright.'
'The VEC wants to have results in the {local} paper.'
'There is a lot to do with exams in this place.'

From such comments it became clear that the wrong messages were being transmitted both within and outside the Centre, a factor of central concern for all of us involved in the delivery of the VTOS. Is there a chance that we are replicating a system that has already failed this cohort? How representative are these students of the 'hard to reach' long-term unemployed who have been unemployed for more than a year and who constitute 40% of all unemployed people? It is noteworthy that only 4% of the national population in the VTOS are described as educationally and vocationally disadvantaged students.

The students on this programme commented during the course of the study that they knew 'others' who were also unemployed, who they believed would benefit from joining the VTOS but were deterred by the formal nature of the provision. Many are wary of school buildings, of formal enrolment procedures which involve interviews and form filling, of sitting in a classroom, of the teacher-student relationship, of being asked to read aloud in class, of the fear of failing. Notwithstanding, there were some students in the group who sought and expected a traditional didactic style of delivery. This mindset is testimony to the stubborn survival of conventional delivery methods of education which are entrenched in the psyche of some adult students.

8   Accreditation

Accreditation is one of the key issues on the agenda of adult education and this cohort was no exception. For some, the perception that in preparing for exams they are similar to the more academically minded participants appealed to them. The literacy tutor said:

> *'They have a longing to do an exam. An exam is a 'big thing' to them. I think they believe that there are jobs out there if they have an exam. ... They don't differentiate between Junior Cert and Leaving Cert, it's just an exam. However, ... when they get the exam ... they feel a real sense of achievement.'*

9 Constraints within the programme

There is little doubt that there are considerable operational and management constraints pertaining to the VTOS programme in general and the Foundation Programme in particular.

The fact that the programme is based in what was previously a Vocational school may well be a barrier for many adults with low educational attainment and unhappy memories of school. Some students spoke about this. In addition, the requirement that participants must attend full time is, according to some students, a real deterrent.

10 The benefits of computer assisted learning

The introduction of computer assisted learning into the timetable was perceived by all students in a positive light and as contributing significantly to the improvement in their literacy and numeracy skills as well as their computer applications. Students' comments included:

'I love computers. It is much easier than writing and all our work looks the same.'
'It is something I can do on my own.'
'My work looks very neat and there is no rubbing out.'

By the end of the school year all the students were comfortable with the basic functions of the computer and printer, and used it for writing up their projects.

11 Gains from the programme

When asked what they had gained since joining the programme, all participants spoke about the acquisition of self confidence and self esteem as the most significant gain from the programme. Eight attributed this directly to their improvement in reading and writing. The findings of the *International Adult Literacy Survey* (Morgan *et al.*, 1997) reiterated this point:

About four-fifths said that their skills had improved significantly since they began the literacy course. Furthermore, many students said that their confidence was greater as a result of literacy tuition. However, only a minority indicated that their job performance had improved, despite the fact that this was a crucial aspect of their motivation for taking the course (Morgan *et al.*, 1997: 10).

12   The benefits of the thinking skills programme

As part of the lifeskills programme, a specific module called 'Thinking Skills' was introduced. The methods used in this module appeared to improve motivation and reduce the fear of failure by creating a non-judgemental learning environment where ideas were explored and developed, rather than being pronounced right or wrong. The students' positive comments focused on the rules of participation, as well as the thinking skills activity. Some comments were:

> *'I have learnt to listen because I had to and now I make a better effort to listen no matter where I am.'*
> *'I think this is very good training because we all have to be polite to each other.'*
> *'I never knew I could think about so many things or that I had so many ideas. I am much better at getting involved in discussions now and I'm not afraid of what other people think of me.'*

13   The benefits of work experience

Most of the group were involved in a work experience programme from January until June for one day a week. The students who did not participate, with the exception of one, chose not to do so. There was much positive feedback from both the students and the employers. For some of the students, it was their first time in a work environment. The students' comments for the most part indicated that they derived enormous benefit from the experience:

'It was great to be going to work in the mornings with everyone else. It gave me a good feeling. … I would like to go for more than one day a week.'

'I liked going to work every day. I would love a real job like that where I could go every day.'

They also mentioned that the support from the Centre contributed to the apparent success with this module.

14 The benefits of group interaction and socialisation

There was evidence from the data that group interaction is very important to the participants on the Foundation course. This fits in with the view that one of the biggest difficulties associated with long-term unemployment is the isolation that many experience due to lack of contact with people outside their own immediate domestic environment. Activities such as trips to the theatre, table quizzes with other VTOSs and a two-day trip to an outdoor pursuits centre were all cited by staff and students as important opportunities for social activity. The programme in sports activities greatly facilitated the social and interpersonal relationships among the students. The PE tutor noted the benefits:

'The fact that we played several different sports and adventure sports gave a great sense of achievement to some people. Some are able to achieve better at sport than they are academically and it was a great confidence booster.'

It was also noticeable that the Foundation students involved themselves readily in a much wider spread of activities with students from within the Centre, demonstrating that a sports programme can be a potent equaliser.

Recommendations

The findings of my study demonstrated the strongly held views of the participants regarding the problems they encountered and the inadequacies they perceived to exist within the programme. As the students' perceptions were strongly reinforced by the various tutors within the Centre, and by other VTOS co-ordinators whom I interviewed, I decided that my findings would also become my recommendations to Management. My purpose in doing this was to ensure that a 'best practice' model would be put in place for these participants. In doing so, I realised fully that not all the recommendations could readily be put in place. By their nature, some were beyond the control of Management. Others, while theoretically within the control of Management, were such that they were not open to immediate realisation. However, some did not require either structural change or Management intervention, but required instead a proactive response from within our Centre. It was on these that I placed my immediate focus.

Conclusions

The challenge of the VTOS exists in a number of ways. There are, for all kinds of reasons, notable disparities between much practice on the programme and what, according to the literature, is appropriate adult education practice. However, the providers of this and other adult education and training programmes have a responsibility to explore and develop effective theories for their own practice, which would replace the theories that appear irrelevant in their situations. Within the context of the VTOS, the Foundation group is a sub group, whose members may be described as being more marginalised than the others. Members of this group bring to their situation a wide range of additional conditions which can further disadvantage them. Participants have been identified as being intellectually or cognitively challenged. Others have, or have had, a series of physical and/or mental health problems, resulting in poor school attendance during their early school years. Still others have been victims of substance abuse, and they and others may have had negative experiences with the police. Most of them have never had a job and in many cases are second generation unemployed.

Listening to the students' accounts of their experiences in primary school, one is struck by the determination that they now have to participate in an education and training programme. While there is an awareness of the obvious deficit present in some aspects of their educational and skill development, there is an anticipation and perhaps even an expectation that the VTOS would in some way rectify this and have a positive impact on their lives. The difficulty this creates for adult education providers is reflected in the dilemma: do we provide employment-related courses in areas where job opportunities are scarce, or do we, as some of us believe, more realistically provide a kind of education that aims to help people lead more satisfying and fulfilling lives while they are unemployed. The *Green Paper on Adult Education* argues:

> In the context of current growth, it is imperative that the needs of marginalised groups are kept to the fore. Such growth presents a unique opportunity to undertake innovative and well-resourced educational, training and other interventions so as to build the capacity of the marginalised sectors to secure a greater proportion of the national wealth and well-being than they have attained to date (Government of Ireland, 1998: 26).

The idea that personal skills should be developed as an explicit curriculum objective throughout education and training has received considerable attention over the recent past. Central to the discussion is the belief that there is a set of generic skills which is fundamental to the holistic development of the person and to his/her effective performance in the workforce. Harrison (1996) notes the benefits of such training:

> … to adult learners it offers the opportunity to acquire and gain credit for skills which are useful in, and transferable between, a range of learning programmes, work settings and life situations (p. 261).

The idea of a learning society points towards an all embracing view of education, which acknowledges learning in all its forms and settings and the many and varied ways in which people learn. The Director General for Education, Training and Youth in the EU outlines what the 'mission of education' is:

> ... to respond to the enduring needs of the human condition. Yes, education has a crucial role to play in the creation of knowledge and in its application to economic pursuits. But education must also respond to social conditions and cultural needs, to spiritual aspirations and personal requirements. Education is a multi-purpose, not a single-purpose tool. It is an investment – and a very wise one – in humanity and its future (Walshe, 1996).

How we, as a community of educators, work to engage or to alienate already disadvantaged adult learners, will determine whether the gap between the 'haves' and the 'have nots' will widen or narrow in the future.

References

Government of Ireland (1998) *Adult Education in an Era of Lifelong Learning: Green Paper on Adult Education*. Dublin, Stationery Office.

Breen, R. (1991) *Education, Employment and Training in the Youth Labour Market*. Dublin, The Economic and Social Research Institute.

Clancy, P. (1995) 'Education in the Republic of Ireland: the Project of Modernity?' in P. Clancy, S. Drudy, K. Lynch and L. O'Dowd (eds) *Sociological Perspectives*. Dublin, IPA.

Duggan, C., Ronayne, T., McCann, N. and Corrigan, C. (1996) *Developing Educational and Vocational Provision for Long-Term Unemployed*: Evaluation of the Vocational Training Opportunities Scheme. Dublin, WRC Social and Economic Consultants.

Hannan, D.F. and Boyle, M. (1987) Schooling Decisions: *The Origins and Consequences of Selection and Streaming in Irish Post-Primary Schools*. Dublin, The Social and Economic Research Institute.

Hannan, D.F. and Shorthall, S. (1991) *The Quality of their Education: School Leavers' Views of Educational Objectives and Outcomes*. General Research Series, Paper No. 153. Dublin, ERSI.

Harrison, R. (1996) 'Personal Skills and Transfer: Meanings, agendas and possibilities' in R. Edwards, A. Hanson and P. Raggatt (eds) *Boundaries of Adult Learning*. London, Routledge.

Morgan, M., Hickey, B. and Kelleghan, T. (1997) *Education 2000: International Adult Literacy Survey: Results for Ireland*. Dublin, the Stationery Office.

National Economic and Social Forum (1997) *Rural Renewal: Combating Social Exclusion*. Dublin, NESF.

Walshe, J. (1996) Special supplement in the *Irish Independent*, December 4th. Dublin, Independent Newspapers.

Chapter 16

The Mol an Óige Project
Developing and testing a model for applying action research at systems, institutional and classroom levels in order to promote a better educational experience, particularly for children at risk of failing in the system

Dan Condren

Introduction

I was a school principal for twelve years. During this time I introduced significant change and development in the school. As the years passed, however, I came to realise there were some aspects of the school and of my own practice as a teacher which I was unable to change. This was a source of frustration to me. It was also an unappealing thought that I would have to put up with this frustration for the remaining fifteen or twenty years of my career.

Three significant events which have had a profound influence on my career began in 1994. These were:

- I took secondment from my position as principal to work with VTOS and Youthreach;
- I began planning for the Mol an Óige project;
- I first made contact with action research.

In this paper, I will explore the ways in which my experience of action research has influenced my work with Mol an Óige and how that work in turn has allowed me to test the potential usefulness and limitations of action research as a process of school self-renewal.

My experience of action research

For most of my twenty years as a teacher, I had wished that my students would be more actively involved in my classroom. For my first action research project, I therefore studied my own practice in this regard and, to my surprise and relief, found some new methodologies to address this issue. I found this a very liberating experience. I found in action research a methodology for studying and changing my own practice in order to bring congruence between my values and my practice. I could look to the future with enthusiasm rather than trepidation.

Towards the end of the year, I presented my findings at a staff meeting, because I believed that many of my colleagues would have frustrations in their practice also and might welcome the opportunity of addressing them in an action research process. I was received with resounding indifference by all except one. This colleague and I have since completed a MEd in action research. Considering this experience, I realised that reflecting on one's own professional practice required a form of language which was not developed in the school.

The origins of Mol an Óige

North Tipperary Vocational Education Committee (VEC) had long been involved in innovative projects aimed at improving the educational experience of all students, including those at risk of failure in the system. The availability of European Union funding in 1995 was seen as an opportunity to further develop their ambitions in this regard. Consequently, a team of senior teachers and principals was assembled to devise a project which would address in a systemic way the causes of failure in the education system. Mol an Óige was the outcome.

It was initially planned as a two year project, 1996-1997. The particular question which animated the project was: 'Since failure in school and early school leaving are predictable in many instances from an early age, why are they not preventable?'. Criteria for selection of Youthstart projects were that they must be practitioner-generated, they must be innovative and they must create a multiplier effect, that is, their effect must extend beyond the project itself. For these reasons, it was decided that teachers participating in the process must have ownership of what they were attempting (it must be their project, not ours) and that it must equip them with new skills and understandings that would help them to continue to develop their practice after the project ended. We adopted the motto that 'it is not what we do, but what we leave behind that will determine the success of the project'. (In fact, the project received funding for two more years, 1998-1999, for what is referred to in this paper as the second round project).

The first round project, January 1996–December 1997

The project began in January 1996 and the project team consisted of Helen Byrne, Rose Tully, Sean English and myself. At the outset, we developed separate strategies for each of the identified objectives of the project. For the main objective of addressing the literacy and numeracy needs of the target group of students, we sought to encourage teachers to use an action research methodology. This involved identifying some needs of the target group/individual students which they wished to address, deciding what actions they might try, drawing up a written action plan, monitoring and evaluating progress and their own learning from the process. During the first round of the project, teachers in thirty primary schools developed action plans, and some very interesting ideas emerged. A full report exists on the first round project, *Mol an Óige, the Project and the Lessons* (Mol an Óige, 1997). A number of significant findings, however, led us to review our ideas and practice. Among these were:

- all participating schools were small (mostly four teachers or fewer), and no post-primary school developed an action plan;
- only one teacher took part in most schools, and the process did not spread out to influence the general practice in schools.

Reflecting on our experience during the first round project, a number of learning points emerged which we needed to address during the second round of the project. Among these were the following:

What we were offering was evidently not what schools wanted – in most cases they felt that all they required were additional resources and personnel. In addition, what we were asking was seen as an additional burden in an already heavy workload. We felt that if we could offer a small amount by way of planning time, teachers might respond wholeheartedly.

We came to realise that what we were attempting was nothing less than a change of culture within the school, and schools did not know how to go about doing this. In many cases, teachers saw change as an event rather than a process. We needed to develop a model that schools could use to begin a process of change. We would probably not see the process completed, given the limited duration of the project, but we could show them a way forward and help them get started.

We had focused on developing action plans to meet the needs of the target group; we had not stated explicitly that what we were trying to do was also designed to meet the needs of teachers, and we felt that the project was not as educational for them as we had hoped. We needed to be explicit about our intentions, and we needed to build in procedures to enable teachers to focus on their own learning.

We found that even where individual teachers were developing action plans, they found it difficult to interest their colleagues in joining in the process. We concluded that we needed to encourage teamwork in the process.

We were developing a practitioner-generated approach to school development. We realised that management needed to be involved in order to produce significant whole-school development. We also realised that individual teachers attempting to change their practice could end up even more frustrated in an unresponsive school structure. We needed to devise a process that would have the active support of the principal, but be not necessarily led by him/her – it needed to be both bottom up and top down.

Many schools saw our project as threatening, and as a reflection of some inadequacy on their part. They frequently asked questions such as 'What are we not doing that you wish us to improve on?'. We needed to find some way in which we could become involved in a learning relationship with schools, and we needed to say clearly to them that both they and we were learning from the relationship.

In short, we needed to devise a single strategy which would incorporate all the objectives of the project. Such a strategy must have a simultaneous focus on three of the key elements crucial to enabling schools to respond to the needs of the target group:

- identifying and responding to the individual learning needs of all students;
- ongoing teacher professional development;
- continuous school improvement.

We called the strategy Collaborative Action Planning, and it formed the basis for the second round project. It draws heavily on the principles of action research, and is educational both in its intent and in its methodology. The development of the model was also fine-tuned by researching the introduction of the process in six schools.

What is Collaborative Action Planning?

Collaborative Action Planning is a process that allows individual teachers or schools, in the context of the mission of the school, to:

- identify the needs of the school and the specific needs of the students in their care;
- plan, implement and document a course of action to meet these needs;
- evaluate and adapt their practice in the light of their experience.

Collaborative Action Planning is an ongoing process which allows individual teachers and schools simultaneously to:

- meet the needs of students;
- meet their own needs;
- influence whole school practice in relation to the target group.

Collaborative Action Planning is not a solution to immediate problems. Rather, it is a process which offers schools an opportunity and time to address these problems in new ways.

How Collaborative Action Planning operates in schools

A team of teachers, with a co-ordinator, manages the Collaborative Action Planning process in each school. The team typically consists of about five volunteers (fewer in smaller primary schools). This team, in consultation with the principal and with the rest of the staff, is responsible for drawing up the action plan. An important element of the process is establishing formal procedures for ongoing communication and feedback between the Collaborative Action Planning team, management, and the whole staff.

The team meets weekly (or fortnightly in some primary schools) to plan actions and monitor and evaluate progress. It is envisaged that the action plan itself will develop during the process, refining aims and proposed actions in the light of the lessons learned. The Collaborative Action Planning process also develops such skills as structuring meetings to be productive, developing collaborative approaches to responding to the needs of the target group, and ensuring that the process is a learning one for participating teachers and for the whole staff as well as for students in the target group. It is anticipated that these skills will enhance the capacity of the institution to respond more flexibly to meet the needs of the target group.

Mol an Óige provides clear guidelines for drawing up action plans. The plan identifies the target group, the needs to be addressed and the actions proposed in response. It also details the process – times for planning meetings, roles of different participants and so on. Important elements of the action plan are identifying how the support of parents, statutory and voluntary agencies, and the community in general can be harnessed to meet the needs of the target group. We found these areas were very challenging for most schools.

Mol an Óige provides planning time to schools to enable the planning meetings to take place. In addition, monthly meetings of the co-ordinators from different schools are held and have proven to be an important developmental aspect of the whole process. Mol an Óige also played a consultancy role with schools in developing the process and in meeting the professional development needs of staff arising from involvement in the process.

The development of Collaborative Action Planning during the second round project – our learning as a support team

The second round project began in January 1998. Team members this time around are Rose Tully, Mary Slattery, Philip Mudge and Norberta O Gorman, and myself, Dan Condren.

The process of Collaborative Action Planning was tested during the 1998–1999 school year in 35 primary schools, 13 post-primary schools and 4 training centres (see below for findings). We worked with them in a learning partnership in which they were learning from their experience and we were developing the model of Collaborative Action Planning and our own support role in the process. We came to realise that an important part of our work was to attempt to understand the realities of life as experienced by teachers in schools. They are the people who are involved in implementing change. Any intervention must engage with their realities if it is to be successful.

There is ample research evidence that many interventions in the education system have not produced significant change in the experiences of students failing in the system. This may be because these initiatives make unwarranted assumptions about schools. The result is that many interventions have been used by schools to compensate for inadequacies in current practice rather than as opportunities to change that practice. As we reflected on our experience during the year, a number of important learning points emerged which we have built into the process for the current school year (1999/2000). Among these are:

The nature of Irish schools is such that teachers have not had experience of collaborative planning. Thus, in devising interventions, it cannot be assumed that the provision of planning time will result in its being well used. We needed to draw up guidelines for teachers involved in Collaborative Action Planning in such areas as holding meetings, assigning roles, and leadership.

In this regard, one teacher stated that their school already had an allocation of time for planning from the Department of Education and Science in relation to the Leaving Certificate Applied programme, but they did not know how to use it effectively until they began Collaborative Action Planning.

A consequence of this is that many schools do not understand how to begin collaborative work or, indeed, in some cases, why they should do so. Any outside intervention must seek to provide schools with appropriate structures and supports which will facilitate collaboration and contexts for developmental professional dialogue.

Teachers initially focused on the learning for the students from the process but did not see themselves as learners also. We needed constantly to prompt the teachers to reflect on their own learning from the process so that there would be lasting benefit from the project. We needed to focus on schools as learning institutions. An important question is, 'Who is learning in this institution?'.

One of the most significant realities in the everyday life of teachers in many schools is a sense of isolation and lack of professional peer support, and there is an absence of structures for collaboration which would enable this issue to be addressed. This also limits the range of professional conversation that takes place in many staff-rooms, and has serious implications for the emergence of leadership among staffs. In focusing on the professional learning of teachers, we also needed to introduce a language for discussing professional practice and new forms of professional conversation among teachers.

We found that in the Collaborative Action Planning process, identifying how the support of parents, statutory and voluntary agencies, and the community in general could be availed of in meeting the needs of the target group was not a priority for schools. These areas were slower to develop than planning within schools. For this year, we needed to place a high priority on schools/centres addressing these areas in their action plans. We also needed to provide the necessary supports in terms of inservice.

In focusing on meeting the needs of the target group of students, teachers identified a range of areas where they themselves needed new professional skills and understandings. They also realised that the school needed to re-organise the way in which it delivered its services to the target group of students in order to meet their needs. We realised that Collaborative Action Planning needed to focus simultaneously on the needs of students, teachers and institutional organisation.

During the year we provided a range of in-service activities in response to requests by teachers/schools to enable them to carry out the actions in their action plans. This was an extremely important service. Indeed, Collaborative Action Planning offers an innovative model for in-career professional development.

We believed that decision-making authority should be devolved to institutions and teachers/tutors. We believed that this would be empowering for practitioners. Our experience indicates that while this is the case, it also requires substantial technical support. Without that, it will not be an empowering experience.

The learning partnership that we established with schools proved significant in enabling innovation. A clear contract based on an action plan and a commitment to the Collaborative Action Planning process was also very important. An unexpected outcome was that this enabled us to seek more information from schools than we could otherwise have done, and they were willing to co-operate because they knew we needed their help to develop our model, not to check up on them. This in turn enabled us to understand better what was happening at school level, to learn from it, and to respond more appropriately.

The idea of forming a learning partnership was significant in another way also. When schools are approached to participate in projects such as Mol an Óige, there is a tendency on their part to see what is in it for them, and to view participation in the project as a means of obtaining valuable extra resources and to compensate for inadequacies in current practice. The danger in such an arrangement is that there is no learning for either party and the initiative becomes an 'add-on' to current practice rather than an opportunity to offer a more holistic and integrated service. The fact that any supports we were offering to schools were available only to facilitate learning by both the school and the project helped to lessen the danger of the project being used in such a fashion. It is significant that at the end of the first year of Collaborative Action Planning, participating schools identified planning time and staff development as the areas where they would most like continued support.

Some schools found that the team of teachers involved in Collaborative Action Planning became isolated. They found that there was not a structure for communication with the rest of the staff and management. They found that other teachers could undermine the approaches they were developing. Sometimes, other teachers not involved in the process felt excluded. We modified the model so that for the coming year, teams should establish clear mechanisms for ongoing mutual feedback with school management and staff.

A further modification that we would recommend in the process at this stage is establishing procedures for the views of the students involved and their parents to be fed into the process.

Findings

We believe that Mol an Óige has facilitated significant learning and achievement at systems and institutional levels, and in the interactions between teachers and students. In this section, we outline some of the evidence for this belief.

Achievement and learning at a systems level
The range of activity and learning which has been initiated in schools

Schools report that the process of Collaborative Action Planning itself has been developmental for participants and, in some cases, for the whole school. In addition, it has generated a wide range of professional development activity. At post-primary level for instance, all thirteen schools have arranged inservice activity of some kind arising out of their involvement with Mol an Óige, as have more than half the participating primary schools. Other examples are detailed below under 'achievements at schools level'. The following comments are from primary school participants:

> *'The sharing of ideas has helped teachers. There is more awareness among staff of what is happening for other teachers and what is happening in the school as a whole'* (member of Collaborative Action Planning team).

> *'Collaborative Action Planning gave us the opportunity to discuss problems in a professional forum'* (co-ordinator)

Comments by participants and others associated with the project

Participants in the project have stated that their involvement in the Mol an Óige project has been liberating for them.

The following are some comments from those involved in the process:

> *'Collaborative Action Planning develops its own forward momentum. Each "little" achievement becomes a stepping stone to another achievement. Teachers become energised when they realise they can do things and are not just at the mercy of "the way things are"'* (principal).

> *'The impact on staff was very good – people are looking at how they teach – adapted practice to meet the needs of students'* (principal).

> *'Weekly meetings helped the reflective, evaluative and planning processes as well as promoting the idea that working in groups is a better way of dealing with issues than staff meetings'* (from summary by Collaborative Action Planning team, post-primary)

Schools and teachers see Mol an Óige as partners with them in their own development.

Teachers have said to us that they see Mol an Óige as supportive partners in their professional development, in improving their schools and in meeting the needs of their more needy students. They have found the co-ordinators' meetings very helpful in a number of ways:

- Sharing ideas, practices and difficulties;
- As a real form of professional peer support – developing, encouraging and supporting innovation and new forms of professional dialogue;
- As a model for structuring school planning meetings.

Schools have made a commitment to the Collaborative Action Planning process.

Many schools have identified ways in which they can support Collaborative Action Planning from their own resources in the current year. Each participating post-primary school has committed itself to matching the planning time provided by Mol an Óige with an equal amount from its own resources. A number of primary schools have approached their Boards of Management about supporting planning. Two have drawn up proposals for resources from their trustees and two others have obtained funding from their local Area Development Management projects to continue to develop their action plans.

Actually arranging planning time is a difficulty for some schools. At post-primary level, the difficulty is in timetabling the teachers for planning meetings. This results in many planning teams meeting at lunchtime which is not ideal nor, indeed, is it sustainable in the long term. A range of strategies has been used by primary schools to facilitate planning. One approach is to employ a specialist teacher (for example, speech and drama, or music) for a small number of hours each week. This releases teachers from class which makes planning possible. A difficulty for some primary schools is in finding trained substitutes.

A community of learners

The project team itself has, we believe, developed as a community of learners. The team meets regularly to reflect, not only on progress, but also on the development of our own thinking and understanding of what we are doing. The progress in our understanding of the process in which we are engaged is evident in the materials and the documents produced by the team.

Further evidence of the emancipatory nature of the project for those of us in the team is that four members have undertaken professional learning courses leading to MEd degrees in action research.

Achievements and learning at institutional level

Learning Support
Major developments in the structure of learning support have taken place in 11 schools. The main thrust of these changes has been a more holistic provision. Developments include re-defining the role of the learning support teacher, whole school approaches, active learning methodologies, and use of mentors.

> *'I can now work with students in senior cycle, whereas before learning support finished at junior cycle'* (learning support teacher).

In one school, an 'active retirement group' visits the target class every Friday evening for shared reading and social interaction, with significant benefits for both.

> *'More learning is taking place in the classroom – fewer discipline problems and the moral support of having another teacher in the classroom…'* (post-primary learning support teacher referring to the benefits of team teaching)

> *'Learning support is used more as a resource, and I am working as an "extra" in team teaching'* (primary school learning support teacher)

New teaching methodologies

Involvement in Collaborative Action Planning has encouraged teachers to explore participative person-centred practices. Team teaching has begun in 6 schools (in 5 cases this is linked to learning support). Three schools have introduced mentoring programmes linked to peer tutoring. Others are considering similar innovations for next year. Six schools have developed positive approaches to behaviour management. In many cases, the introduction of new methodologies has been supported by school based in-service activity.

> *'We discovered that we had shortcomings in our own skills'* (school Collaborative Action Planning team)

> *'Inservice arising out of Collaborative Action Planning is more relevant and this makes it more effective'* (classroom teacher)

> *'Relevant inservice enthuses people'* (principal)

> *'... there is a major change in thinking ... the school is moving towards a more student-centred approach ... the interaction between team members and the target group students highlighted the individuality of students' needs. Often what teachers perceived as the problem was not a problem. In one case the focus was on numeracy, but the child had very low self esteem ... and had become so passive and indifferent that the simplest of instructions had to be repeated several times. This issue had to be addressed before any thought could be given to the child's numeracy difficulties'* (team co-ordinator)

One difficulty we encountered in this regard, and which was mentioned by a number of teachers working with the project, was that exposure to the new ideas made them feel inadequate. We addressed this issue by trying to develop a learning partnership between Mol an Óige and teachers, and also by providing a type of small-scale inservice activities linked to issues identified by teachers themselves.

Parents as partners in their own children's education

Many schools had no tradition of including the parents of the target group as partners in their own children's education. Through Collaborative Action Planning, most schools now have plans to include parents in their own children's education. Thinking in this regard has developed significantly, but methodologies are at an early stage of development. All post-primary schools now have parental inclusion as part of their action plans for the coming year.

One primary school co-ordinator noted the time constraints they experienced:

> 'We could have benefited from having more contact with parents, but finding time for meetings was difficult. The benefits of parental inclusion have been seen by the planning group, and we will be recommending that it be part of our whole school policy.'

Maximising resources

We believe that participation in Collaborative Action Planning has enabled schools to maximise the benefits for the target group from current resources. This is particularly evident in the learning support area where students are now receiving support from more people and in a more integrated way. The emergence of leadership and assertiveness among staff on behalf of the target group is also significant in this regard.

> 'Staff are now badgering me to introduce the JCSP[1] and the LCA[2] next year' (principal)

Developing a framework for care

Students do not always perceive teachers as caring professionals. The Collaborative Action Planning process provided a framework that enabled the care of teachers to be experienced by students in the target group.

> 'The more academic teachers have become kinder towards the students in the target group' (principal)

Teacher professional development

We believe that the process itself was developmental professionally for teachers, and it has also has proven to be an effective catalyst for teachers engaging in further in-service activities. It has facilitated changes in awareness, attitudes and practice towards the students in the target group.

> *'Action Planning put the problems of early school leaving and the vulnerability of the target group on the agenda'* (principal)

> *'It provided the opportunity to learn from each other'* (from summary by Collaborative Action Planning team)

> *'Action Planning has encouraged more openness among the planning team. People are more inclined to offer and ask for help'* (primary school co-ordinator)

Achievements and learning in the classroom

We believe that significant learning and achievement occurred at classroom level. We cannot support our claim from evidence generated from our own involvement in classrooms, since we did not work directly with students. However, teachers indicate significant improvements in the areas of attendance, self-esteem, motivation, homework, participation in class and behaviour because of their own improved practice.

Twelve out of thirteen schools indicate an improvement in attendance by the target group.

A number of schools have indicated that target group students have remained in school as a result of the Collaborative Action Planning process in the school.

> *'The full cohort is still in school. In previous years, 30% of this group would not sit the Junior Certificate'* (principal)

> *'Teachers are kinder to me and I'm getting on better in school'* (student)

In one school, students from outside the target class tried to get a transfer into the class, whereas in previous years students would have been seeking to transfer out of that class.

One principal commented that this year the students in the target group 'sometimes smile at me', because they are no longer regularly in her office in trouble. In a number of schools the target group were no longer the focus of complaints at staff meetings ('they weren't even mentioned'), and in many schools, other members of staff have commented positively on them. In one school, two members of the target group received merit awards at the end of the year.

Mol an Óige as an action research project: some implications

Our project indicates that action research requires a nurturing context in order to be capable of fostering school self-renewal. In instances where an enthusiastic individual teacher begins a study of action research with a view to developing their own practice, it is possible that they may be able to enthuse others on the staff to develop school culture. Even in such situations, however, our experience in the first round project has been salutary. For action research by an individual teacher to have a ripple effect in the school requires as a minimum that it be supported by the school management.

However, in a situation where the impetus for change is initiated by an outside agency, then that agency must seek not only to promote an action research approach by teachers, but must also ensure, as a pre-condition, a nurturing environment within the school. If this does not happen, there is a danger of further isolation and frustration on the part of participating teachers. Hence, Collaborative Action Planning sets out as a pre-condition to create a collaborative environment within which action research can be used as a methodology for promoting school self-renewal.

Mol an Óige is work in progress. The provisional findings seem to indicate that an action research-based intervention has made a significant impact in terms of influencing the response by schools to the individual needs of potential early school leavers. However, it is only in a collaborative context that action research can influence whole school policy and practice.

The process has also led to continuous and exciting learning for the project team. For myself as project leader, Mol an Óige has been an amazing experience in terms of my own professional development. Perhaps the single most important element in the success of the project is the learning partnership which we established with schools. I can now see that the liberating effect of this partnership has all to do with the power relationship between us and schools.

Implications for professional development programmes suggest that managers have to commit to the idea of first focusing on their own self development, in order to communicate the growth of their own understanding to their fellow practitioners, so that they may learn from and follow their example; and this attitude has a significant bearing on the question of power relationships.

References

Government of Ireland (1995) *Charting Our Education Future: White Paper on Education.* Dublin, Stationery Office.

Government of Ireland (1997) *Education (No. 2) Bill.* Dublin, Stationery Office.

Hargreaves, A. (1994) *Changing Teachers, Changing Times: teachers' work and culture in the post-modern age.* London, Cassell.

Holland, M. (1999) *An Investigation OF The School Experiences Of Young People In North Tipperary Who Left School Early, And Of The Factors Which Led To Their Leaving.* Nenagh, Mol an Óige.

Houses of the Oireachtas (1999) *Report of the Joint Committee on Education and Science on Early School Leaving.*

Mol an Óige (1997) *Mol an Óige: The project and the Lessons.* Nenagh, Mol an Óige.

Swan, D. (1991) 'Recognising Inservice Education as the Key to Educational Reform and Teacher Renewal' in D. Swan (ed.) *Teachers as Learners: inservice education for the 1990s.* Dublin, The Standing Committee of the Teacher Unions and University Education Departments.

Notes

1 Junior Certificate Schools Programme
2 Leaving Certificate Applied Programme
These are programmes which promote student-centred approaches.

Chapter 17

Action Research in Initial Teacher Education

Diarmuid Leonard and Teresa O'Doherty

We work as supervisors of student teachers in a university context. This paper arises from our introduction of action research into a programme of initial teacher education. Our longer term aim is to demonstrate the relevance of action research and reflective practice as central aspects of teacher professional education with a view to influencing perceptions of what counts as the appropriate knowledge base of teacher practice. To help us evaluate our own practice as teacher educators, we used our research deliberately to raise problematics and confront dilemmas, including questions such as: What is the place of action research in initial teacher education? What do students gain from the experience of doing action research? What are the conditions that affect student action research? This paper seeks to share some of our own learnings about these issues, as we have worked through the introductory phases of our project.

The attraction of action research as a new element in our teaching practice experience is that it offers a rigour and methodology of inquiry and reflective decision making that is often, in our experience, conspicuously absent in student post-lesson appraisals and observations on their school experience. In introducing action research into our work, and into the work of our students, we hoped to show how the personal theories which student teachers generate from studying their practice can be a powerful force in their professional learning as beginning teachers.

Year Two: the context of initial action research

Action research is the paradigm offered in the second year of the programme to enable students to study their own practice. They are encouraged to identify an issue for study based on the real life situations they have encountered in schools, and to adopt an action reflection methodology to gain deeper understanding of the issue. For their assignment, students are asked to write up an account of what they have investigated and learnt through their action enquiries. It is expected that students generate their own theories of practice, and locate their emergent theories within the wider literature of relevant educational theory to inform their decisions and help them make sense of their experience.

Evaluation of Year Two action research: broad aims and values

We aimed to undertake an initial review of the effectiveness of action research as a methodology to support the professional learning of student teachers, and we did this by designing and issuing an open-ended feedback sheet for completion by students after their teaching practice. These sheets asked students for their comments on the college context, pre-teaching practice preparation, the school-based experience, their co-operating teacher, and their supervisor. We randomly chose forty-five feedback sheets for analysis, and the information they contained, combined with our own hunches and perceptions, led us to engage in our own action research to evaluate our effectiveness as supervisors. We decided to cross-check the issues raised in the open-ended feedback sheets. We suspected that the total context can strongly influence the quality of student action research and its potential benefits (or otherwise); so we decided to disseminate a questionnaire which explored several aspects of the context:

- the university context, lectures and tutorials pre-teaching practice; clarity of the assignments and the assistance given to students before leaving the campus;

- the school context during teaching practice; the familiarity of supervisors with and their support of student work on action research; the school environment; time and opportunity to reflect; and the co-operating teachers' attitudes towards reflection and teacher inquiry;
- students' data collecting processes during teaching practice;
- the relevance of students' identified concerns for reflection on their teaching practice grades.

Students were then requested to respond to almost twenty statements, both positive and negative, relating to the potential benefits of engaging in action research. These statements were designed to examine whether the project had helped them understand

- themselves as teachers
- the issues they investigated

The statements also examined students' ability to use their knowledge of existing educational theory in their planning before teaching practice, and in their reflections during and after teaching practice.

The data from the open-ended sheets were supported by evidence from 122 student questionnaires (122 completed questionnaires out of a possible 131 student population represents a 93% response rate). In addition, we analysed 56 reflective practice reports. Each of our sources provides, individually and collectively, a wealth of material relating to the quality of reflective practice engaged in by students, their attitudes to action research, and their overall first impressions of teaching practice.

In the analysis of findings which follows, we will initially consider the results of the student questionnaires and feedback sheets in tandem, as both these sources reflect students' perceptions of the processes and outcomes of action research. Students' reports on their work will then be examined in the light of such comments to consider the benefits of action research.

College context and preparation

As has frequently been found in research on students' sense of preparedness for teaching practice, students raised the issue of an inadequate knowledge base. In particular they asserted that they were concerned about what they perceived to be an inadequate foundation in classroom management. Typical comments were:

> *'We could do a lot more on actual teaching, more on classroom management, teaching methods.'*
> *'More classes on discipline and time management.'*

The assignment was to write a report on their action research, and students found this a difficult concept to understand. Their understanding of the rationale of action research appeared to be distorted by a number of factors:

- shortage of time: *'the first weeks before TP were rushed and stressful'*;
- multiplicity of distractions before teaching practice: *'TP should be for the whole semester instead of having to do exams and lectures {in various subjects}; it's really too much to handle; too much pressure'*.

School context

In the students' experience of the school context the issues investigated were the availability of time and space for reflection, and the role of classroom teachers. There was strong endorsement that the organisational and human support contexts provided by the school were positive. A large percentage of students (88%) acknowledged that they had time within the school day to write their post-lesson appraisals, but considerably fewer (68%) had access to a quiet place in which to work. Three quarters of the co-operating teachers within schools were both supportive of reflective practice and gave constructive feedback to the student teachers. The classroom teacher was an important resource for students while on teaching practice, and 86% of respondents felt that they had useful discussions with their co-operating teachers. While many students (57%) acted on their co-operating teacher's advice, a quarter of those surveyed rejected the notion that they 'did what their co-operating teacher told them to do'. This self-reported data suggests that a significant proportion of the students were developing independent modes of operation during teaching practice.

Data collection

Data collection is an integral part of the reflective practice of an action research methodology. This is the foundation upon which students examine their current practice and plan for future changes. Students' data collection methods were restricted, indicating their limited knowledge of this key area. Students could select as many sources of information as they wished: 82% of respondents cited the co-operating teachers as a source of information, while two-thirds of respondents also identified their teaching practice supervisor, student written work and student questionnaires as sources. Students drew heavily on three other data sources: 35% cited student teacher diaries; 37% identified field notes; and only 22% identified checklists, that is, observation schedules devised by the student teacher in consultation with the co-operating teacher for observation of classroom practice which is then used as a basis for further evaluation.

Knowledge base

The questionnaires tested the distinction between the adequacy of students' knowledge base and their ability to use this knowledge. In fact, these do not appear to be separate dimensions, on the evidence of students' self-perception. 68% of students felt that they were able to make use of their knowledge of educational theory in their planning before teaching practice, while 72% and 78% respectively stated that they made use of their educational theory in their reflection during and after teaching practice. Student responses appear to echo certain basic principles in action research, that conceptual knowledge is a valuable resource but what matters is the ability to make reflective use of that knowledge in generating personal theories of practice.

The perceived benefits of doing action research

Most students claimed they had experienced personal benefits as a result of reflecting on their experiences. The perceived benefits reflected the dual focus reported in much of the action research literature on (1) understanding the internal processes of self development and (2) understanding the external processes of the social situation.

Students' understanding of self as teacher

Improvement in student teachers' self understanding is a central goal of our programme. When asked about this, the majority of respondents replied positively: 68% stated that undertaking their action enquiries had helped them to understand themselves as teachers. Understanding of self extended to another unanticipated outcome. Students seemed to form a view of themselves as confident and autonomous practitioners: 88% felt that their self study enabled them to make decisions about planning and teaching, 82% having completed their teaching practice felt they could trust their own judgement now, while 79% felt they could rely on their own resources to make decisions about planning and teaching.

Students' understanding of the issues they investigated

In the questionnaire most students (88.5%) stated that the issue they investigated was important to them, and 90% felt they understood now better than before the issue they chose for investigation. 83% noted that their reflection affected the quality of their classroom teaching while a similar figure felt their performance improved during teaching practice.

We can infer from these findings that students were both capable of and positively disposed towards proceeding along a route of self-development through reflective enquiry. It can be argued that this experience has been extremely valuable in terms of their positive self-development and self-esteem, essential attributes of a successful teacher. They have acquired perhaps a limited experience of reflection but they have developed skills, laying the foundation for future enquiry. One could state, by contrast, that poor performers displayed little self-confidence and depth of understanding, and seemed content to draw upon common sense knowledge rather than research or in-depth probing.

Comments: Discussion of analysis of assignments

An interesting feature in student teacher work on action research is their choice of topics. We carried out an analysis of topics chosen for reflective practice reports on a random sample of 56. Results were as follows:

Motivating students	12	21%
Classroom management/ discipline	12	21%
Mixed ability teaching	10	19%
Questioning skills	5	9%
Planning lesson (pace and student activity, science process, active learning)	4	7%
Making a lesson interesting	3	5%
Classroom climate/rapport	3	5%
Improving student understanding (1 using stimulus variation)	2	4%
Others e.g. strategies for indirect teaching, assessing student progress, presentation skills	4	7%
No clearly identified issue	1	2%

Figure 1: Analysis of topics chosen

Marking procedures

To ensure objectivity and eliminate potential bias, the two of us in our role as markers cross-checked each other's work. We each selected a sample of approximately 20 scripts and reached a 90% agreement on grades awarded.

Quality of work

In general the work submitted ranged widely in quality. Of particular interest to our review are those students whose work was considered unsatisfactory. A few did not grasp the rationale of the exercise. Several omitted to undertake any data collection, and relied only on personal impressions. Some did collect data but did not draw on them as a basis for decision making. Several were unable to provide any theoretical basis for their planning, action, or evaluation.

Key concerns of student teachers

It seems clear that for most students, their main concern, as has been found before, seems to be their ability to control, motivate and manage a class. Such concerns, clearly linked to student teachers' major aim of doing a credible job in their new role in the classroom, are very important. Les Tickle (1993) found similar outcomes in his study of reflective practice among recently qualified teachers: teacher reflection was limited and constrained by preoccupation with control. It is notable that fewer projects are driven by concerns such as improving the quality of lessons. Qualitative concerns (making a lesson interesting, teacher-class rapport, improving student understanding) take second place in the list of topics chosen for students' action research.

An emphasis on procedure

A common observation regarding mediocre work was that, as Marian Dadds found (1993), accounts read as a mechanistic exercise rather than value-laden practice. Procedural steps conformed with models of action research as found in the literature, but these did not convey any sense that the process had engaged the researcher's sense of personal purpose nor any deep reappraisal of personal assumptions or values.

The knowledge base of decision making

A worrying aspect of the weaker assignments is the seemingly scant knowledge base which informs some decision making. Areas in which students felt their knowledge base was inadequate were classroom management, motivation, discipline and mixed ability teaching. These are all areas related to students' concerns about survival (getting through the lesson with some credibility, being able to adopt a teacher's role). One might suspect that some may rely upon common sense or craft knowledge rather than research-based knowledge as the basis of their decision making.

Reflections

At this point we now wish to address some major questions arising from our study. We begin by considering what we have learnt about the place of action research within an undergraduate teacher education programme. We can state with confidence that most students gained substantially from their experience of action research. Our confidence is based on what we have found in relation to student outcomes in terms of what they achieved and of how they felt about undertaking the enquiry. Most were able to tackle the task of engaging in personal enquiry with some success, particularly as indicated in terms of achieving enhanced understanding of practice and also some resolution of situational dilemmas. Two points should be noted:

The development of self esteem

Although the focus in our own self study of introducing action research into student work was upon cognitive outcomes, in terms of the development of self-understanding as becoming teachers, and understanding of issues, in fact a very large proportion of students felt they had benefited substantially in the growth of their own self-esteem, in relation to such qualities as self-reliance and independence. Such findings are, we feel, highly significant, for the development of self-reliance and self-confidence are key aspects of initial teacher education to help teachers become competent professionals.

Developing reflective practice

Doing the exercise has contributed towards the development of students' skills of undertaking personal enquiry. Learning such skills is an end in itself as much as a means; it helps assure the future capacity of teachers to investigate and think critically about their own practice.

Both the intended and unintended outcomes must be considered when offering justification for embedding action research within initial teacher education. However strong the student gains from action research, the problematics of school life need to be confronted within the total context, including both the college preparation and the teaching practice experience; and we now go on to discuss these aspects.

What are the conditions that affect students' experience of doing action research in their classrooms?

Our evaluative data show clearly that the total context in which student action research was carried out has the potential to affect student experience positively and also detrimentally. The main areas of this context we identified in our study are the teaching education programme preceding teaching practice and the teaching practice school context, and supervision during teaching practice. As Tickle (1993) found, student teachers were preoccupied with questions of control, and Munro (1993), investigating the learning experiences of student teachers in New Zealand, found that they were socialised into coping and survival strategies, not into doing reflection. Such findings seem to indicate that the realities of school life can militate against student learning and engagement with reflective practice, but this should not be interpreted to suggest that reflective practice is not central to teacher education. It does however mean that programmes need to prepare students in advance of their experience of school life. The need for a sound knowledge base within their subject and within education, especially in relation to areas of high concern, has long been recognised, but in addition the programme should aim to build up skills, habits and qualities associated with student capacity to conduct their own action research. Certainly students need time to assimilate and refine their own skills and abilities in doing action research. John Elliott (1993) suggests a gradual preparation for undertaking personal enquiry and reflection through training students' skills as critical and reflective observers of the realities of schooling. This has considerable implications for teacher education programmes during the period preceding the action research they will undertake within the school context.

We are pleased that our students reported that their schools supported them in their action enquiries. We believe, however, that the general context is so important that teacher education programmes should do whatever they can to relieve potential pressures that students are bound to encounter in the turbulence of school life. Critical support structures would include supervision, grading and teacher support. Supportive supervisors would see their role in terms of modelling the skills and qualities necessary to participate in reflective dialogue. A supportive grading system would encourage intelligent experimentation, and would not discourage risk taking. A supportive school staff would be capable of contributing to the students' action research as observers and critical friends.

Finally we believe that student action research should not on our evidence be regarded as a desirable element merely to be added to an existing programme; it is rather an holistic approach which is likely to integrate and enhance the quality of students' professional learning. Action research cannot be 'packaged' neatly; it is a methodology that respects and recognises the values base of teaching. The skills, habits and attitudes involved in action research cannot easily be learnt within the short space of time available in a single module. Such attributes are better regarded as professional practices that are developed over time, and should be, in our judgement, incorporated throughout the entire programme. Relevant skills and activities such as observation of good teaching, the collection and analysis of observational data, critical reflection on experience, appraisals of possible alternatives in decisions, discussion of teaching contexts and critical incidents are likely to enhance the gradual development of reflective skills but take time to develop and mature. Forms of disciplined enquiry are not isolated free-standing units of modules; they are aspects which should be firmly embedded within institutional practices as they reflect the values base of the entire programme.

Conclusion

This account offers an initial report on the first stage of our action research into introducing reflective practice and self study into programmes of teacher education. Our research continues. While encouraging the student teachers we support to undertake their action research, we also monitor our own practice and modify it in light of our evaluations, and we produce research-based evidence to show that we feel we are justified in making claims that we are improving our own understanding of our work with student teachers. Our wider educational aims are to develop communities of reflective practitioners who are committed to improving the quality of educational experience for pupils in classrooms first by improving the quality of their own educational experience as reflective practitioners.

References

Dadds, M. (1993) 'Thinking and Being in Teacher Action Research' in J. Elliott, *Reconstructing Teacher Education: Teacher Development*. London, Falmer.

Elliott, J. (1991) *Action Research for Educational Change*. Milton Keynes, Open University Press.

Elliott, J. (1993) *Reconstructing Teacher Education: Teacher Development*. London, Falmer.

Munro, R.G. (1993) 'A Case Study of School-based Training Systems in New Zealand Secondary Schools' in Elliott, J. (1993) *Reconstructing Teacher Education: Teacher Development*. London Falmer.

Stenhouse, L. (1975) *An Introduction to Curriculum Research and Development*. London, Heinemann.

Tickle, L. (1993) 'Capital T. Teaching' in J. Elliott, *Reconstructing Teacher Education: Teacher Development*. London, Falmer.

Part 3

POTENTIALS

Chapter 18

Action Research For Organisational Change

Gerry McNamara and Joe O'Hara

Introduction

This paper sets out to tackle some of the key issues which arise when attempting to move an action research approach to change and improvement from the individual to the collective and the level of the whole organisation. The papers in this collection show clearly how effective action research strategies can be in the context of individual professional development and how such individuals can act as change agents when an organisation adopts and implements the fruits of their endeavours. However the general debate which concluded the conference at which these papers were presented made clear that the move from the individual or group to the organisational was in practice very difficult. In fact it often did not take place thus frustrating forward thinking individuals or at best took place in the form of the adoption of ideas of individuals 'taken up' by management. The debate was firmly characterised by the general feeling that action research was therefore very much in the realm of the personal and the individual and perhaps had little to say in the context of changing, leading and managing organisations.

This paper will suggest that on the contrary action research may in fact be capable of contributing to the process of managing change in organisations. However in order to do so it begins by acknowledging, in the context of the analysis of a research project involving the authors, that this process is very problematic for a number of reasons. For example, a great deal of action research theory in placing emphasis on the emancipation of the individual professional, often implies a false assumption about the level of freedom and possibility for action enjoyed by practitioners. Perhaps more importantly it also assumes an identity of interest between those at different levels or with differing roles in an organisation, which seldom exists. Also much action research theory, while emphasising the significance of dialogue and collaboration in the achievement of organisational change, does not make explicit how this process might be expected to occur given the difference in roles, expectations and interests mentioned above.

In this paper it is suggested that systematic strategies need to be employed if the benefits of personal growth and development associated with action research are to become a tool for organisational management. The following account of the outcomes of a research project on collaborative decision making through action research illustrates some of these points.

Collaborative decision making through action research: the project

The project reported here was initiated and developed in a well-established post-primary school on the north side of Dublin. By the early 1990s, extensive social and economic change in the school's catchment area had begun to alter the profile of students enrolling in the school. As a result of this, the school community began a process of organisational exploration and evaluation. A first stage in this process of re-appraisal was the decision to draw up a draft school development plan in 1994. As part of the consultation process engaged in during the drafting stage, a strengths, weaknesses, opportunities and threats (SWOT) analysis was carried out. This analysis identified indiscipline as one of the major problem areas in the school.

A widespread alteration in discipline patterns, seen by many as being a key aspect of the school's culture, seemed to augur badly for the continuance of the open and friendly climate which many teachers and pupils saw as being at the core of the community. As a result of these investigations, the Principal invited eight interested staff members to form a study group committed to examining the issue of discipline as it affected the school. This group began exploring alternative approaches to discipline currently employed both within Irish schools and abroad. Eventually the group decided that a policy containing some elements of the 'positive discipline' approach of Smith (1994) and Wheldall and Merritt (1989) would be the most appropriate for their particular situation.

Although the process of developing and implementing this new school policy was of an iterative and inductive nature, using a whole school collaborative approach, the funding requirement as laid down by the major sponsor demanded the specification of research objectives and the evaluation of the process. This requirement of setting terminal objectives for a developing process was to a certain extent contradictory yet essential for funding purposes. In order to satisfy the requirement, the Principal, in consultation with representatives of the working group, involved Dublin City University in drawing up a set of specific research objectives for the project which were to be achieved by its end. In the view of this group, the attainment of these four characteristics would ensure the development of a positive ethos within the school.

The key objectives identified were:

1 To address disciplinary problems in a positive way.
2 To provide teachers with a coherent strategy for engaging students in effective learning.
3 To produce a coherent strategy which could be used as an exemplar for implementation in other schools.
4 To provide an opportunity for teachers to formally engage in professional reflection and dialogue.

It is important to note that from the outset there was a strong formal link between the group engaged in the initial stages of the research and the staff as a whole. As the objectives suggest, they saw the ultimate effects of the project in a whole school context. The focus of their research was to find ways to realise the stated objectives in the school as a whole, not just in their own practice. In consultation with the University advisors, the working group of eight chose an action research approach to the collaborative planning process for the following reasons. Action research claims to support the change management process in organisations such as schools. Never an easy task, effecting change in the school context is particularly challenging. Factors such as school culture, teacher tenure and centralised management can obscure the many expectations of change which occur as a result of the increased participation by vociferous stakeholders such as curriculum groups, economic interests and the parent community in education. Practitioners concede the complexity of managing change in this educational context aptly described by Fullan (1992) 'where the insurmountable basic problem is the juxtaposition of a continuous change theme with a continuous conservative system' (p.3). In what way is action research effective in such contexts?

> Action research is intended to support teachers and groups of teachers in coping with the challenges and problems of practice and carrying through innovations in a reflective way (Altrichter *et al.*, 1993: 4).

Action research has a breadth of application that enables it to be taken into the 'swampy lowland where situations are confusing "messes" incapable of technical solutions' (Schön, 1983: 42). It is a form of research which is designed to involve the researcher as participant, the 'human-as-instrument' (Maykutt and Morehouse, 1994: 26), in defining the problems and posing and implementing solutions. By encouraging these participatory collaborative practices and acknowledging the context specificity of all research, it aims to optimise the role of tacit knowledge gained through experiential learning (Polanyi, 1973). In this way, it attempts to bridge the theory-practice gap that has undermined the utility of more traditional research in educational contexts. Effectively action research can contribute to a re-framing of the notion of knowledge.

This key feature of action research, the importance of participant knowledge, is seen by McKernan (1996) as a professionalisation strategy which is both empowering to teachers and a means of establishing teacher autonomy in the area of school development. However, as this project demonstrates, the 'how to' of action research can pose significant practical difficulties for teachers such as:

• the absence of systemic support for the teacher researchers, e.g. time off, school-based management support and funding if required;
• substantial skills acquisition not necessarily closely aligned to teaching skills is required on the part of the teacher practitioner if the research is to be academically validated;
• the absence of a critical mass of understanding or even awareness of the concept requires significant advocacy work on the teacher practitioners' part in their own communities.

Academic writers on action research underestimate these problems. For example McKernan (1996), in stressing that the reflective practitioner must not fear failure – 'the reflective practitioner does not advance a hypothesis as being correct, rather as being worth testing empirically. He or she claims to be intelligent; not correct' (p. 40) – overlooks the duality of the role of the teacher researcher. In advocating a new methodology in what may be a sceptical community, while simultaneously attempting to resolve problematic issues, and with only a tenuous link with the academy, credibility can certainly be an issue for the teacher researcher. There is also some naiveté in McKernan's (1996) claims that 'curriculum inquiry belongs to the practitioner' (p. 38). Curriculum writers have demonstrated clearly that the area of curriculum inquiry is a highly politicised arena, long considered too influential in social engineering to be left to practitioners to determine. Kelly (1989) states that:

> many groups in society seek to steer the work of schools in certain directions in which they have some vested interest and the school curriculum has been described as a battleground of competing ideologies (p. 12).

In some respects both of these issues, credibility and constraints on the process were significant factors in the outcomes of this project.

The model for the research work chosen by the teacher researchers was based on the Deakin Action Research Model (Carr and Kemmis,

1986). Described by McKernan (1996) as 'critical emancipatory educational action research' (p. 24), this model contends that 'critical inquiry enables practitioners not only to search out the interpretive meanings that educational actions have for them but to organise action to overcome constraints' (p. 24). Critical emancipatory action research perceives curriculum problems as value-laden and moral concerns rather than as purely technical and representative of what Habermas (1972) refers to as the two knowledge-constitutive interests: 'practical' and 'emancipatory'.

Figure 1 is an adaptation of the Deakin Model (Carr and Kemmis, 1986) designed by researchers at Dublin City University (Dunne, 1999). It is provided here to describe the central issues in the project.

Issues of collaborative planning arising from the project

The previous section offers a necessarily brief outline of what was a long and complex process. This section moves to the heart of the matter by analysing the key issues which emerged from the project in relation to collaborative planning through action research. The evaluation process undertaken identified three broad areas of contention which remained at issue throughout the process.

Programme Leadership

The issue of leadership was a central one in the development of this project. Traditionally leadership in schools was seen as the sole preserve of the Principal. He or she decided what was to be done and then told others when and how to do it. This model of leadership has come under sustained attack in recent decades. Writers such as Fullan (1992), Hargreaves (1994), Hopkins *et al.* (1994) and Senge (1993) have developed an alternative view of school leadership. This view emphasises the importance of collaborative decision-making and collective decision implementation. Leaders are now

designers, stewards and teachers. They are responsible for building organisations where people continually expand their

	Reconstructive	Constructive
Discourse (among participants)	4 Reflect: Interview teachers to get an overall picture in the wider context of the school as a learning community. This creates the reconnaissance for future planning.	1 Plan: To provide a new discipline policy as per voluntary wishes of staff
Practice (in the social context)	3 Observe: As participants document issues arising, reflect on the value of the process and provide other participants with the opportunity to do the same.	2 Act: Design, and evaluate a new approach to discipline. Support the course design and facilitation as much as possible, being aware of the diversity of participants' needs and schools' objectives.

Figure 1:
The central issues of the project (adapted from Carr and Kemmis, 1986)

capabilities to understand complexity, clarify vision and improve shared mental models - that is they are responsible for learning (Senge, 1993: 340).

Laudable though this view may be, some individuals dismiss the whole dynamic as nothing more than a way of avoiding work on the part of those in management. The particular approach adopted by this school community emphasised the importance of flexibility in the establishment of adequate leadership structures. A key issue to emerge was the concept of fitting the appropriate leadership style to the particular stage of organisational development. There was concern regarding the roles adopted by key individuals in the organisational structure, particularly the roles of the Principal and the de facto change co-ordinator. Implicit throughout the project is a concern regarding the distribution of authority and responsibility within the leadership structure adopted.

The locus of leadership within this project changed a number of times over the lifetime of the research intervention. In the first phase, the position of leader was held by the Principal. He was responsible for the creation of a sense of need among the school community to re-evaluate the structures and culture of the school in the general area of discipline. This re-evaluation came as a result of an institutional analysis programme instituted at his behest. In the preparatory phase of the project, he took a visible leadership position establishing a

- mentoring group,
- positive discipline working group, and
- applying for a Departmental research grant.

He consciously chose the individuals who made up the personnel of these groups and facilitated their work by altering the timetable structure. He broadly guided the direction taken by the group to ensure that its work would be of value to the organisation. At the end of the preparatory phase, he withdrew from a formal leadership role and allowed an alternative leadership structure to emerge. This could be seen as providing evidence of the style of empowerment leadership that some of the informants attribute to him.

The alternative leadership structure was a group-based one. Individuals involved in the positive discipline working group took it upon themselves to develop an implementation structure for the project. This allowed them to broaden the ownership basis of the research goals and began the process of operationalising them. The authority focus of this group was a collective one and no one guiding figure emerged.

The implementation structure was to be a collaborative one seeking to involve the whole staff in the development of a new positive teaching programme. To do this, an outside expert was brought in to act as a catalyst for dissemination of these ideas to the staff. Despite the apparent success of the project, significant problems emerged resulting in a new shift in the leadership focus at the beginning of the second year of the project. By default, responsibility for the programme fell to an individual group member. This member was committed to using a collaborative process for introducing a school-wide discipline plan. As a result of her commitment to the collaborative methodology, she chose to adopt a role as communicator as opposed to authority figure. This worked well for the consultation phase of the project's development. In the second phase of the programme, that of project implementation, some individuals felt that there was a lack of focus due to the absence of an authority figure. However most staff felt comfortable with the style adopted as they felt it allowed them interact with the person most immediately associated with the project's implementation (O'Hara, 1998).

Project Ownership

Ownership, as it emerged in this project, was connected to the ability to influence the design, development and implementation of the innovation. The evaluation findings suggested that although the majority of staff acknowledged that they were consulted about the above, there was a degree of uncertainty regarding the actions that resulted from this consultation. For this reason, no finding on the overall staff's perception of their sense of ownership could be produced. Rather the ambiguity that lay at the heart of the issue had to be acknowledged.

Two reasons were put forward for this ambiguity over the ownership issue. They revolved around the selection procedures used in the initial group formation process and the dual role played by the research co-ordinators. Some staff suggested that the mechanism used to select the initial consultation group was flawed. By choosing its members directly, giving them the sole remit to research the future role to be played by discipline in the school and providing them with free periods to conduct these discussions, the Principal alienated other individuals who had a genuine interest in the discipline issue. As a result, when the initial programme was announced there was a perception that it belonged to the research group and not the staff as a whole.

The dual role played by the programme co-ordinators was also considered a problem by some. Suggestions were made that some staff apparently resented being used as a path to career advancement by the teacher researchers. While there is no evidence to suggest that this was a widely-held view, survey data did indicate that the majority of staff felt that the prime beneficiaries of the project were the teacher researchers (O'Hara, 1998: 43).

There was some contrary evidence to the overall thrust of this finding provided by one of the teacher researchers. She felt that the collaborative culture that had been fostered during the second year of the programme had substantially increased the sense of programme ownership among the staff. The survey evidence on this point was again ambiguous. Several solutions were put forward to broaden the sense of ownership:

- co-ordinating groups should be self-selecting rather than chosen by the Principal;
- more information should be provided about all stages of the research programme and the benefits accruing to the whole organisation resulting from the formal link with an outside institution should be stressed.

The Collaborative Process

From the outset of this process there was a commitment on the part of the teacher researchers to the development of a genuine collaborative approach to the implementation of the new programme of discipline (Mulcahy, 1997).

The commitment seems to have its roots in a combination of conceptual as well as practical issues. On a conceptual level, the project team showed a considerable awareness of the role played by collaboration in the institutionalisation of any innovation. Citing the work of writers such as Hopkins *et al.* (1994) and Hargreaves (1994), it charts the development of an understanding of change and institutionalisation processes in schools, and argues very strongly that if innovatory programmes are going to survive, not only must they change certain structures within the organisation, they must also change the basic orientation of the organisation. In other words, they must change the cultural presuppositions of the organisation (Mulcahy, 1997).

Referring to the work of Hopkins *et al.* (1994), the teacher researchers suggest that it is a combination of an ability to change and the presence of a genuine culture of collegiality that allows organisations to initiate innovatory programmes. Perhaps of greater importance is the insight that 'changes that do not directly affect the culture of the school will be short lived' (Mulcahy, 1997: 12).

The culture that the project was trying to promote throughout the process was one of teacher collaboration based on the understanding of collaborative cultures developed by Hargreaves (1994). Hargreaves suggests that there are four basic cultures to be found in schools, those of the collaborative, the individual, the contrived collegiality model and the balkanised. He argues that

> the confidence that comes from collegial sharing and support leads to greater readiness to experiment and take risks, and with it a commitment to continuous improvement among teachers as a recognised part of their professional obligation (p. 186).

This then seems to provide the conceptual backdrop against which the intensive series of meetings held in the first six months of the project's implementation phase must be viewed. Put simply, the commitment to collaboration demonstrated by those meetings had a practical purpose. The teacher researchers were aware that a collaborative staff was more likely to be an innovative staff and an innovative staff was more likely to take risks. The change of something so central to a teacher's self definition as a discipline system demands that teachers be prepared to take risks.

It must be acknowledged, however, that the evaluation finding in relation to programme ownership would tend to question the presence of a real collegial culture. While the staff felt they were allowed to contribute and were listened to, the evaluation research indicates that only 23.8% agreed and 4.8% tended to agree that their input was acted upon. Also, a majority of respondents disagreed that they had sufficient input into the programme design (with 28.2% disagreeing and 27.3% tending to disagree).

Thus it is clear that the key issues of ownership and collaborative dialogue continued to be problematic throughout the process and the evaluation team have attempted to identify why this should be so. First, while collaboration and participation are intrinsic to school-based planning, Gibson (1985) acknowledges the difficulties for would-be action researchers engaging at three levels: 'interpersonal ... institutional ... structural' (Gibson cited in Webb, 1996: 68). This concern, particularly at school level where norms of isolation and self sufficiency are pervasive, continues to be central and therefore teacher researchers, while aspiring to a collaborative working culture may find it difficult to achieve in practice. Second, collaborative planning resonates with the ideal speech situation referred to by critical theorists. While engaging in the research process, teachers act as critical friends to each other – who mediate the shifting function of dialogue. However this view underplays the power relations not only between group members during this process but also between the group members and their roles as researcher, facilitator/observer/participant and critical friend. A number of steps were taken at various stages to equalise such relations: (1) while gaining access, (2) presenting guidelines for giving feedback, (3) advancing reflection and interview guidelines prior to interviews taking place, and (4) member checking throughout. However a degree of alienation between researcher and the researched, even where the former were practitioners within the same organisation, continued to hamper the process throughout.

The third dimension common to both collaborative planning and critical social sciences relates to values. Action research requires practitioners to interrogate their espoused theories and their corresponding theories in action. Webb (1996) asks if this dialectic, theory and practice can ever be resolved. This issue emerged in the project in the form of a perception that those most in need of engaging in critical self-reflection were the least likely to be willing to do so. In short, there was little sense that the internal collaboratively-based nature of the project eliminated or reduced the defensiveness often caused by external modes of appraisal and inspection.

Finally, both critical theory and action research espouse the emancipatory interest, that is, they both encourage the practitioner to develop a critical reflection, a critique of the social milieu within which the group operates. Action research thus seeks to lead participants in a reflexive and dialectical process of critique. Clearly this element of the process may have implications in terms of the issues of leadership and ultimate control discussed earlier and can potentially lead to what Webb (1996) defines as the danger of rational conformity where distortions are eliminated by group consensus. Webb, after Kemmis and McTaggart, states that 'the approach is only action research when it is collaborative'. However this insistence on the group consensus may well produce that which action research seeks to avoid, 'false consciousness' and 'self delusion' (Webb, 1996: 69).

The persistence of the problems outlined above cannot be said to have damaged the project in one sense – the achievement and implementation of a whole school approach based on positive discipline. On the other hand it must be acknowledged that the failure to overcome these constraints may have longer term effects not only with regard to the sustainability of the discipline reforms but also in the sense of the limited extent of cultural change which appears to have taken place.

Action research and the principles of learning organisations

The above experience shows that action research, even in a form designed to enable organisational development through collaborative planning is by no means straightforward. Despite this, various 'manuals' of action research, action learning and action planning tend to treat the relationship of the individual or group of practitioner researchers to the improvement of the organisation as almost an automatic process (for example, McKernan, 1996; Frost, 1997; McMahon, 1993). Recently however, a number of authors in the field have begun to recognise that the relationship is not automatic and cannot be left to hopes that general goodwill, critical mass or a kind of domino effect will move organisations forward (for example, Zuber-Skerritt, 1996;

Preskill and Torres, 1999). These authors stress that individual practitioner research and reflection represent only one 'loop' of the learning strand and that a second 'loop' is required to move beyond 'linear change' to more lateral and all embracing forms of change.

The solution being proposed essentially includes a marriage of action research and learning organisation theory drawn from contemporary writers in the field of organisational development, human resource management and contemporary evaluation. The argument here is, in essence, that an action research approach to organisational development can only work in the context of organisations that are trying to develop and inculcate the principles of the learning organisation; only such organisations are wholly susceptible to tools such as action research, action planning and action learning.

A good example of this type of approach is to be found in the work of Ortrun Zuber Skerritt (1996). Her model of 'Emancipatory Action Research' is a combination of more traditional cyclical action research design merged with organisational change theory. This approach, which also promotes management development, is heavily influenced by Lewin's (1952) and Beer *et al.*'s (1990) organisational change models. According to Zuber-Skerritt (1996) this form of practitioner inquiry into a problem or issue is collaborative, critical and self critical and follows the cyclical process of strategic planning, implementation, observation/evaluation and critical reflection. This action research is emancipatory when it aims not only to promote

> participants' transformed consciousness and change within their organisation's existing boundaries and conditions, but when it also aims at changing the system itself or those conditions which impede desired improvement in the organisation (Zuber-Skerritt, 1996: 88)

Zuber-Skerritt argues that practitioners have historically been involved intermittently in planning organisational change but it has been part of what she refers to as single looped learning instead of double looped leaning. The difference being that the former is '... technical, functional and short term oriented ... is any detection and correction of error that does not require change in the governing values ...' (Zuber-

Skerritt, 1996: 93-94) whereas the latter does require change in those values. Senge (1993) suggests that the organisations who will perform in the future will be those which can harness their employees' commitment and ability to learn at various levels within it. Zuber-Skerritt (1996: 94) refers to Senge's definition of a learning organisation as 'a place where people are continually discovering how they can create and change their reality'. This reflects a learned attitude where learning is viewed as a lifelong and co-operative process which emerges from discussion and dialogue. According to Zuber-Skerritt (1996: 94) there is evidence that quality improvement programmes using action learning and research is an effective way of developing a learning organisation. Discussion and dialogue are central to the process of developing a change culture.

Zuber-Skerritt (1996) recognises the importance of organisational culture and how it impacts on nurturing change. According to Kotter (1995: 166) organisational culture is an '...embodiment of group norms or traditional ways of behaving that a set of people have developed over time'. In addition there is a suggestion that the role of management is to promote an integrationist culture. Zuber-Skerritt (1996) has identified the following common features which encourage innovation and change in an organisation:

- more receptivity to new ideas
- faster approval, less red tape
- more collaboration between departments
- abundant praise and recognition
- advance warning of changes
- open circulation of information
- extra resources available
- the attitude that we are always learning
                    (Zuber-Skerritt, 1996: 93)

Beer *et al.*'s (1990) six step model has been adapted by Zuber-Skerritt and integrated into the classical action research spiral(s) methodology of plan, action, observation and reflection. In tandem she integrates an adaptation of Lewin's (1952) model of organisational change, which now consists of four stages: Unfreezing, Moving, Refreezing and Revise.

According to Zuber-Skerritt (1996) what underpins this theoretical framework is the recognition that change is cyclical rather than a 'linear' process fostering ongoing learning (rather than a series of single interventions) based on collaboration and teamwork.

This model and similar efforts by other theorists represent an attempt to explore the ways in which action research can move forward from the individual to the collaborative at the level of the entire organisation. Such models clearly will need considerable further research and testing in practice but the underpinning theory that action research and organisational development are interrelated and move in tandem rather than in a linear way appears to make sense. Whatever its merits or demerits (and Zuber-Skerritt herself remarks that

> more research and development work is needed to resolve the problem of dealing with people and organisations having persistent mindsets and being resistant to notions of action research, change and empowerment of people: 1996: 96)

this approach at least acknowledges and tries to respond to the perceived shortcomings of action research as an organisational change agent.

Conclusion

This paper has attempted to analyse the obstacles which can limit the effectiveness of action research as a way of managing organisational improvement. It has been argued that action research as a model of practitioner led, professional improvement has demonstrated great capacity and indeed this is illustrated in the papers in this collection. The next step however, the move from the individual or group to the organisation as a whole is more problematic. The issues arising in attempting to make this transition are illustrated in the context of an action research project on whole school collaborative planning. It is argued that these problems have to a large extent been overlooked or underestimated in much of the action research literature. However recently a number of theorists have begun to acknowledge this dilemma and suggest approaches to a solution. The work of Zuber-Skerritt

(1996) seems particularly progressive in that in common with a number of others it identifies the integration of organisational learning and development theory with action research as the way forward.

Zuber-Skerritt (1996) takes this argument further by elaborating a complex model of 'emancipatory action research for organisational change' involving the integration of classical approaches to the management of change with the typical, cyclical action research model. The paper concludes by suggesting that while this type of model may require further work it takes the argument to a new level by recognising the interrelationship between the state of 'change readiness' of the organisation and the potential of action research in enabling change. It suggests that organisations need to be deliberately prepared in terms of adopting the principles of the learning organisation and that only in this context can an action research methodology become an appropriate and effective element in the management of change.

References

Altrichter, H., Posch, P. and Somekh, B. (1993) *Teachers Investigate their Work: an introduction to the methods of action research.* London, Routledge.

Beer, M., Eisenstat, R.A. and Spector, B. (1990) 'Why change programmes don't produce change' in *Harvard Business Review*, November/December, pp. 158–166.

Carr, W. and Kemmis, S. (1986) *Becoming Critical: Education, Knowledge and Action Research.* London, Falmer.

Dunne, F. (1999) 'An Exploration of Whole School Training in Information and Communication Technology Interaction in a Primary School.' Unpublished thesis presented as part of MSc in Education and Training Management, Dublin City University.

Frost, D. (1997) *Reflective Action Planning for Teachers.* London, David Fulton.

Fullan, M. (1992) *The New Meaning of Educational Change.* London, Cassell.

Gibson, (1985) 'Critical Times for action research' in *Cambridge Journal of Education*, Vol. 15, No. 1, pp. 59–64.

Habermas, J. (1972) *Knowledge and Human Interests.* London, Heinemann.

Hargreaves, A. (1994) *Changing Teachers, Changing Times: Teachers' Work and Culture in the Postmodern Age.* London, Cassell.

Hargreaves, D. and Hopkins, D. (1991) *The Empowered School.* London, Cassell.

Hopkins, D., Ainscow, M. and West, M. (1994) 'School Improvement in an Era of Change' in P. Ribbins and E. Burridge (eds) *Improving Education: Promoting Quality in Schools.* London, Cassell.

Huberman, M.A. and Miles, M.B. (1994) 'Data Management and Analysis Methods' in N.K. Denzin and Y.S. Lincoln (eds) *Handbook of Qualitative Research.* Californian, Sage.

Kelly, A.V. (1989) (3rd Edition) *The Curriculum Theory and Practice.* London, Paul Chapman.

Kotter, J.P. (1995) 'Leading Change: Why Transformation Efforts Fail' in *Harvard Business Review,* March–April, pp. 59–67.

Lewin, K. (1952) 'Field Theory in Social Science' in D. Cartwright (ed.) *Selected Theoretical Papers.* London, Tavistock.

Maykutt, P. and Morehouse, R. (1994) *Beginning Qualitative Research: A Philosophical and Practical Guide.* London, Falmer.

McKernan, J. (1996) (2nd Edition) *Curriculum Action Research.* London, Kogan Page.

McMahon, A. (1993) *Action Research for School Managers.* Bristol, University of Bristol.

Mulcahy, C. (1997) 'The Theatre of Daylight.' Unpublished action research report submitted as part of MSc in Education and Training Management, Dublin City University.

O'Hara, J. (1998) *Towards a Positive School.* Unpublished Evaluation Report for the Department of Education and Science. Dublin.

O'Hara, J. and McNamara, G. (1999) 'Evaluation: Business or Vocation?' in *Evaluation,* Vol. 5, No. 4, pp. 73–76.

Polanyi, M. (1973) *Personal Knowledge.* London, Routledge.

Preskill, H. and Torres, R.T. (1999) *Evaluative Inquiry for Learning in Organisations.* London, Sage.

Schön, D. (1983) *The Reflective Practitioner: How Professionals Think in Action.* New York, Basic Books.

Senge, P. (1993) *The Fifth Discipline: The Art and Practice of Organizational Learning.* London, Random House.

Smith, A. (1994) *Discipline for Learning.* Bristol, Teaching and Learning Associates.

Webb, G. (1996) *Understanding Staff Development.* Milton Keynes, Open University Press.

Wheldall, K. and Merrett, F. (1989) *Positive Teaching in the Secondary School.* London, Paul Chapman.

Zuber-Skerritt, O. (1996) (ed.) *New Directions in Action Research.* London, Falmer.